Religion, Empire, and Torture

RELIGION,

The Case of Achaemenian Persia

EMPIRE,

With a Postscript on Abu Ghraib

AND TORTURE

Bruce Lincoln

The University of Chicago Press
Chicago & London

Title page illustration: Bas-relief from the Apadana (audience hall), Persepolis (fifth century BCE). (Photo: Stierlin.)

The University of Chicago Press, Chicago 60637
The University of Chicago Press, Ltd., London
© 2007 by The University of Chicago
All rights reserved. Published 2007.
Paperback edition 2014
Printed in the United States of America

21 20 19 18 17 16 15 14   2 3 4 5 6

ISBN-13: 978-0-226-48196-8 (cloth)
ISBN-13: 978-0-226-25187-5 (paper)
ISBN-13: 978-0-226-48191-3 (e-book)
10.7208 / chicago / 9780226481913.001.0001

Library of Congress Cataloging-in-Publication Data

Lincoln, Bruce.
    Religion, empire, and torture : the case of Achaemenian Persia, with a postscript on Abu Ghraib / Bruce Lincoln.
        p. cm.
    Includes bibliographical references and index.
    ISBN-13: 978-0-226-48196-8 (cloth : alk. paper)
    ISBN-10: 0-226-48196-4 (cloth : alk. paper)
    1. Religion and politics. 2. Religion and politics—Iran—Case studies. 3. Achaemenid dynasty, 559–330 B.C. 4. Iran—History—To 640. I. Title.
    BL65.P7L56 2007
    935'.05—dc22
                                                                                        2006037841

♾ This paper meets the requirements of ANSI / NISO Z39.48-1992 (Permanence of Paper).

For Clarisse Herrenschmidt
in admiration and gratitude

Contents

Illustrations

TABLES

Preface

This book is concerned with two timely topics: religion and empire. More precisely, it explores the contribution of religious discourse, practice, imagination, and desire to emergent imperial ambitions. In exploring this theme, I hope to get past the familiar debate on whether ideals and beliefs or material interests constitute the *real* motive force in history. As most serious observers have long since realized, productive discussion begins with the recognition that consciousness and material circumstances are dialectically related and mutually sustaining. The problem to be addressed in any concrete study is not the chicken-egg dilemma—"Which comes first?"—but how a given group reshapes its consciousness (of self, other, morality, and purpose) through select acts of discourse such that its members feel licensed—or, alternatively, inhibited—in pursuing their material advantage in increasingly aggressive ways. Further, how the practices they develop in that pursuit and the success (or failure) they experience reshape their consciousness, discourse, and practice over the empire's later history.

Creating an empire is no easy matter, nor is maintaining one. Whether new or old, any empire involves massive projects of military conquest, political domination, cultural encompassment, and economic extraction that are necessary for its survival. When would-be imperialists come to regard these practices—and the violence that goes with them—as religiously wrong or morally repugnant, the likelihood that they will realize their ambitions is, thereby, greatly diminished. Conversely, when the frontline troops, administrators, strategists, tax collectors, lackeys, toadies, and lords of empire succeed in persuading themselves that their tasks are somehow just, holy, and sacred, the project is, thereby, enormously facilitated.

Although these issues have acquired new urgency and cachet since the cold war gave way to America's War on Terror, attempts to engage them on contemporary terrain encounter real difficulties. To do so successfully, one would have to resolve the following questions: (1) Has the American Republic effectively become an empire, or is it in the course of such a transformation? If so, over what period of time did this happen? Alternatively, what further steps are necessary for the completion of the process? (Here, one obviously needs to provide a clear, cogent model of what constitutes "the imperial"). (2) Has American religion and/or the role it plays in American politics—domestic and international—changed as well? If so, over what period of time, in what ways, and with what consequences? (And, here, a cogent model of what constitutes "the religious" is equally requisite). (3) Are there ways in which the observed changes in the religious have produced or facilitated changes in the political that incline the United States toward empire? Have changes in the political produced similar changes in the religious? And how do these interact with other factors (e.g., the economic, the technological, and the demographic)?

These questions have been much discussed, occasioning sharp disputes among academics, journalists, activists, officeholders, and ordinary citizens. In all these circles, passions run high, perspectives differ markedly, and debate serves largely to reinforce well-entrenched opinions. None of this is surprising, for the stakes are enormous, and there is no agreement on basic terms, or on what data might have relevance, let alone on the proper means for their interpretation.

In the face of such difficulties, an obvious gambit is to engage the problem obliquely by considering examples sufficiently removed from our own as to afford some critical distance. To this end, the religious politics and political religions of the British, Roman, Ottoman, Chinese, and Japanese empires have been studied in recent years, as have those of the Hapsburgs, Romanovs, Aztecs, Incas, and occasional others.

The present volume is meant to extend this discussion by taking up a case that has received surprisingly little attention, given that it is of foundational importance, reasonably familiar, and extraordinarily revealing. Founded by Cyrus the Great ca. 550 BCE, and overthrown by Alexander of Macedon some 220 years later, Achaemenian Persia was by far the largest, wealthiest, most powerful empire of the ancient world prior to the emergence of Rome, controlling territory that stretched from Thrace and Egypt in the west to India and Sogdiana in the east. Over the past twenty-five years, our knowledge of the political, cultural, and social history of this empire has improved dramatically, but work on Achaemenian religion has neither kept pace with nor benefited from these other studies. Thus, of the 14,295 items listed in the comprehensive bibliography of the Achaemenian Empire compiled by Ursula Weber and Josef Wiesehöfer in 1996, only 33 are devoted to the religion of the dynasty and 28 to its religious policies. Nor has the situation changed much since that bibliography was completed.

Since the Achaemenian royal inscriptions were first deciphered in the middle of the nineteenth century, virtually all who have studied their religious content have felt obliged to concentrate their attention on the vexed question of whether the Persian kings and their people were Zoroastrians or not. That the debate should have continued so long is understandable, the evidence being maddeningly ambiguous, but the energy that this issue has consumed is quite disproportionate to its importance. For our purposes, it is relatively inconsequential whether we regard the imperial religion as Zoroastrian in a strict and narrow sense (i.e., consciously adhering to religious reforms effected by Zarathustra) or more broadly as Mazdaean (i.e., marked by worship of "the Wise Lord," Ahura Mazdā, who is understood as a pan-Iranian, and not a strictly Zoroastrian, deity). Far more important than the question of labels and classification is identifying the core principles of the Achaemenians' cosmology, ethics, and soteriology—their sense of space, time, history, and purpose—and understanding how this interacted with their will to empire.

Fortunately, there are a few works that suggest ways in which such an inquiry might be pursued. The first of these is Clarisse Herrenschmidt's "Désignation de l'empire et concepts politiques de Darius Ier d'après ses inscriptions en Vieux Perse" (1977), which showed the overwhelming importance a myth of creation had in Achaemenian discourse. Thus, of the twenty-nine longer royal inscriptions (i.e., those having three or more paragraphs), eighteen (62 percent) open with this myth, thereby investing all that follows with a cosmogonic consciousness: a concern for how the Creator conceived his world and what he intended for it. Notwithstanding the brevity and formulaic nature of this account, Herrenschmidt showed how intricate is its diction and conceptualization, how crucial it was for the empire's self-understanding. Pursuing her pioneer study, there is more that can be said regarding the project the Achaemenians set for themselves: that of restoring perfection on earth, as it was originally created.

Whereas Herrenschmidt's article identified a cosmogonic consciousness as a central part of Persian imperial religion, Marijan Molé's *Culte, mythe, et cosmologie dans l'Iran ancien* (1963) called similar attention to the Achaemenians' soteriology and eschatology, including their active sense of responsibility for accomplishing the world's salvation. A key part of Molé's argument was his consideration of the word *fraša*, which occurs in several different Iranian dialects. In Avestan and Pahlavi (the languages of the Zoroastrian scriptures), it is a technical term, denoting the cosmic renovation expected at the end of history, when all evil will be swept away and the pristine perfection of the cosmos restored, consistent with the Wise Lord's original intentions. Further, as Molé skillfully showed, every performance of certain Zoroastrian rituals—above all, the daily sacrifice—anticipates the Renovation and helps lead the world toward its fulfillment. In Old Persian (the language of the Achaemenian inscriptions), however, *fraša* occurs in two different contexts. First, in some variants of the creation account, this word encompasses God's first two (or three) creations and designates them a "wonder" or a "marvel" (the word's most literal meaning). Elsewhere, the same term is used for the most sumptuous palace built by the king, which is, thereby, described as, not just a wonder of comparable status, but an act of quasi-divine creation, a microcosm patterned after the world itself, and—like the Zoroastrian rituals—an undertaking through which a privileged actor (here the king, there the priests) helps accomplish the world's eschatological renovation.

Strikingly original, Molé's book was decades ahead of its time, and many of the initial reactions were hostile. Most devastating of all was the response of Émile Benveniste, who refused to accept it as Molé's *thèse de doctorat,* prompting Molé's suicide. While some of his views remain controversial, Molé's understanding of the ways in which cosmogony and eschatology, as well as priestly ritual and royal action, were related in pre-Islamic Iranian religions is now widely accepted and has important implications for our understanding of Achaemenian religion.

Although Herrenschmidt's article points us toward speculation about creation and Molé's book toward that on time's end, there remains the space of history in between. In Achaemenian discourse, cosmogony and eschatology converge, moreover, on the same historical figure, for the myth of creation ends when the Wise Lord made Darius king, just as the Renovation begins with the wonder that Darius produced in his palace at Susa.

We are, thus, led to reflect on Persian kings and kingship, for which there is a fairly large and thorough literature. Best of the lot is Gregor Ahn's *Religiöse Herrscherlegitimation im Achaemenidischen Iran* (1992), which focuses on the question of how Achaemenian rulers sought to legitimate their power. Toward that end, Ahn explores numerous items of discourse through which they represented themselves as God's chosen agents, continuous beneficiaries of his support, and defenders of the cardinal virtues—"truth" (*arta*) above all—against their adversaries. Chief among these was "the Lie" (*Drauga*), a demonic force that corrupted all those it inspired: rebels, foreigners, and enemies of the king being regularly perceived, defined, and, thereafter, assaulted as such.

Such operations were crucial for the formation of empire, and it is easy to understand them as instances of false consciousness or, simply, bad conscience, to use a different theoretical vocabulary. Such judgments rest on the perception that the relation of discourse and practice was distorted, self-serving, and cynical. Legitimation, however, is not just an argument of convenience that the powerful advance after the fact to justify their privileged position and aggressive actions. Admittedly, that is so in some extreme cases, but cynicism is not the only possibility, for it is often the case that those who would persuade others are themselves most persuaded of all. They do not invent theories of legitimacy to serve their purposes but, instead, inherit, embrace, and, occasionally, in finite measure, adapt these to their use. Such theories shape the consciousness of the theorists and help determine their actions while simultaneously helping determine how others will perceive and judge them. Rather than simply providing an apologia ex post facto, they constitute an indigenous metaphysic of power and an ideological precondition for the confident, relatively guilt-free use of same.

Taking up the lines of inquiry suggested by Herrenschmidt, Molé, and Ahn, the chapters that follow pursue a set of interrelated questions. How did the Achaemenians understand their place in the cosmos (chapters 1 and 2) and their moral status in relation to others (chapter 3)? What was their view of cosmos, creation, and the struggle of good and evil (chapter 4)? What consequences did this have for their sense of historical mission, including their desire to regain paradise lost (chapter 5)? How did this lead them to deal with enemies and critics as imperial power ran its course (chapter 6)?

In the chapters that follow, I hope to show how Achaemenian Persia perceived itself as God's chosen instrument for the project of world salvation and, as such, supreme benefactor of the peoples it conquered. Beyond this, I am led to argue that such a perspective led the Achaemenians into severe contradictions, which they attempted to suppress and deny, using some rather desperate measures toward that impossible end. This analysis suggests comparison to certain contemporary data, which I consider in the postscript. For some readers, this discussion will seem the payoff for wading through the ancient materials; for others, it will seem dispensable and gratuitous. I can understand and respect both reactions.

Acknowledgments

Thanks are due to many friends and colleagues, from whose expertise and generosity I have benefited. First, to Jean Kellens, whose invitation to deliver a series of four lectures at the Collège de France in May 2003 was the immediate stimulus for the research that led to this book. Second, to Clarisse Herrenschmidt, with whom I cotaught a seminar on Achaemenian religion in fall 2002, where some of these themes were first developed. Third, to those who provided opportunities to present one piece or another of this work or who offered suggestions and feedback on those occasions: Università degli Studi di Siena, Scuola di Studi Umanistici, Pier Giorgio Solinas and Maurizio Bettini; University of Oklahoma, Department of Religious Studies and the Renaissance Project, Jill Irvine; European Association for the Study of Religion, Bjorn Dähla and Nils Holm; University of St. Thomas, School of Education, Don LaMagdelaine; University of Washington, Henry Jackson School of International Studies, Kyoko Tokuno and James Wellman; Deutsche Verein für Religionsgeschichte, Vasilios Makrides and Jörg Rüpke; University of Arizona, Center for the Study of Religion and Violence, Linell Cady; Bucknell University, Program in Comparative Humanities, John Hunter; University of Chicago Workshop in Ancient Studies, Chris Faraone and Matthew Stolper; Colgate University, Departments of History and Political Science, Faye Dudden and Joseph Wagner; Emory University, Department of Religion, Paul Courtright; University of North Florida, Department of Philosophy and Religion, Julie Ingersoll and David Fenner; Ohio State University, Departments of Comparative Studies and Classics, Fritz Graf, Sarah Iles Johnson, and Hugh Urban; Scuola Normale Superiore, Salvatore Settis and Maria Michaela Sassi; the Silk Road Foundation, Roger Olesen, Guitty Azarpay, and David Stronach; Johns Hopkins University, Department of Classics, Marcel Detienne; Colby College, Goldfarb Center for Public Affairs and Civic Engagement, Carleen Mandolfo; and University of Chicago Divinity School, Rick Rosengarten. In these and other contexts, I benefited from exchanges with Carmine Ampolo, Jes Asmussen, Françoise Bader, John Collins, Mauro Corsaro, Ricardo DiDonato, Gérard Fussman, Fritz Graf, Cristiano Grottanelli, Jonathan Hall, Jens Kreinath, Charles de Lamberterie, Saba Mahmood, Nanno Marinatos, Bernard McGinn, Jay Munsch, Michael Murrin, Eric Pirart, James Redfield, Martin Riesebrodt, Martha Roth, Erik Sand, Martin Schwartz, Jørgen Podemann Sørensen, Guy Stroumsa, Brendan Swagerty, Philippe Swennen, Alexs Thompson, Barbara Turk, Tove Tybjerg, Angeliki Tzatzanetou, Sunthar Visuvalingam, Margit Warberg, Morten Warmind, and Steven Wasserstrom, to all of whom I am deeply grateful. Fourth, to my teachers, who gave me the tools and inspiration to pursue this project: Carsten Colpe, Mircea Eliade, Paul Friedrich, Daniel Gillis, Charles Long, William Malandra, James Redfield, Peter Slater, and Jonathan Z. Smith. Last, as ever, to my family—Louise, Martha, and Rebecca—for love, understanding, patience, forbearance, and support.

Note on the Text

Translations of the Hebrew Bible are taken from the Revised Standard Version. All other translations are my own unless indicated otherwise. Editions for the original-language texts are listed in the bibliography.

The abbreviations with which one conventionally cites the Achaemenian inscriptions were established by Roland G. Kent in his *Old Persian* (1953). Briefly, the first (capital) letter denotes the king responsible for a given text, with regnal number where appropriate C = Cyrus; As = Arsames; D = Darius, D^2 = Darius II; X = Xerxes, A = Artaxerxes; A^2 = Artaxerxes II, A^3 = Artaxerxes III); the second (capital) letter denotes the site (B = Bisitun, E = Elvend, H = Hamadan, M = Murghab, N = Naqš-i Rustam, P = Persepolis, S = Susa, V = Van, Z = Suez); the third (lowercase) letter differentiates among texts discovered at the same location. For example, DPd = Darius, fourth inscription published from Persepolis. Most of the inscriptions are trilingual, including Old Persian, Elamite, and Babylonian (i.e., Akkadian) versions. Unless otherwise noted, all citations and translations refer to the Old Persian. When other versions enter the discussion, this is indicated by a parenthetical reference to "Bab." (Babylonian) or "Elam." (Elamite). Readers interested in a fuller explanation should consult Kent 1953: 4.

Introduction   **1**

I

Wherever the Achaemenian Empire spread, servants of the Great King built walled gardens, inside of which they exercised every possible care to create an atmosphere of peace, tranquillity, relaxation, and well-being. Irrigation canals were constructed to carry cool water and keep everything moist. Dense collections of shade trees were planted to keep temperatures pleasant. Plantings were arranged in geometric patterns to create a sense of perfect order and exquisite beauty. Plants of every conceivable species were imported from all corners of the empire, transplanted, and made to flourish. The same was done with animals, some of which served as game for royal hunts, while others were left to wander. At their leisure, the king and his nobles frequented such sites, understanding them, not only as ideal spaces of repose, but also as models of the empire they were more actively laboring to create and prefigurations of what the world would be when their work was fully accomplished. To these exquisite gardens they gave the name "paradise" (Old Persian *pari-daida*), and the word, with all its nuances, resonances, fantasies, desires, and connotations, spread from them throughout the world.

This charming image of what the Persian Empire was like and what it took itself to be stands in stark contrast with another. Offended by the conduct of a Persian soldier, King Artaxerxes II (r. 404–359 BCE) had him subjected to the torture of "the hollowed-out troughs." This involved two troughs designed to fit tightly with one another and crafted in such a fashion that a man's head, hands, and feet could project outward while the rest of his body was encased within. Once the man was locked in this device, the king's henchmen fed him lovely foods and let the resultant excrement accumulate inside. Not only did the latter stink; it also spawned worms, maggots, and insects, which swarmed over the victim's flesh and slowly ate through it, fighting their way to his vital organs. After seventeen days, the poor man was dead, and the troughs were opened for all to see. And, however much this gruesome spectacle may repulse us, it was meant to instruct, for it had a profoundly religious significance and motivation.

The contrast between these two vignettes—the elevated pleasures of the paradise and the degrading agony of the troughs—frames the problematic of this book, which makes use of these and other Achaemenian data to concentrate on two issues. First, what is the relation between religion and empire? Or, to put it more concretely, how is it that the highest religious ideals—the desire to perfect creation, to act as God's instrument of salvation, and to establish a realm of ideal morality in which all living beings can flourish—come to animate and legitimate the project of imperial conquest, domination, and exploitation? Second, at what point do the contradictions between the grandeur of such a religious vision and the brute facts attending the exercise of power become so extreme and pernicious as to become uncontainable, even obscene? When—and how—does the pursuit of paradise find itself inside the troughs? And what does empire tell itself on that unfortunate day?

This book is written for a general audience in a world where the realities of Guantanamo and Abu Ghraib make these issues far from academic. Rather than adding one more cri de coeur against the contemporary outrages, however, I have found it more useful to explore an example quite removed in time, space, and cultural particularities, but where similar issues arise in a form that is particularly dramatic and particularly revealing. This is why Achaemenian Persia holds considerable interest.

The picture of Achaemenian religion, politics, and culture that I present is based on painstaking examination of virtually all the relevant primary texts in a variety of languages, together with a few choice pieces of iconographic evidence (albeit regrettably less than art historians might think ideal). For the most part, in the interest of providing a clear and accessible account, I have chosen not to burden nonspecialist readers with philological details and technical discussions. Those are available in articles that have been published elsewhere, reference to which is provided in the notes, where those so inclined will also find suggestions for further reading. Since my discussion presumes no more than a passing familiarity with the Achaemenians and their world, it seems useful to provide in this introductory chapter a historical overview, a sketch of the sources, and a few words on method, before engaging the issues and primary source materials. Those for whom such background is unnecessary can skip directly to chapter 2.

II

The older Persian Empire is commonly referred to as "Achaemenian," and I will continue this practice, for all that it is something of a misnomer. But the fact is that the empire was founded on two different occasions by audacious usurpers, both of whom history has rewarded with the epithet "the Great." The first of these, Cyrus (r. 558–530 BCE), began as a local ruler who seized power from his Median overlords. While Darius (r. 522–486 BCE) might have been equally justified in depicting himself as having started a new line and a new era, he chose, instead, to stress continuity, and, toward that end, he employed several different strategies to connect himself and his descendants to the royal line of Cyrus. Shortly after ascending the throne, for instance, he took Cyrus's daughters and the wives of Cyrus's sons as his own. By the foremost of these women, he fathered Xerxes (r. 486–465 BCE), whom he made his heir, in place of a son born earlier to a wife who could claim no relation to Cyrus. As a result, all subsequent Achaemenian kings descended from both royal families.

If these royal marriages provided a biological means to suture one family line to another, the manipulation of genealogies gave Darius a discursive instrument with which to advance the same project. Thus, in the longest and most revealing text written by Cyrus and his scribes, a text commonly referred to as the Cyrus Cylinder and dated to 539 BCE, the first Persian dynasty-founder identified himself as follows:

> I am Cyrus, King of the World, Great King, Mighty King, King of Babylon, King of Sumer and Akkad, King of the Four Quarters, *son of Cambyses, Great King, King of Anšan, grandson of Cyrus, Great King, King of Anšan, descendant of Teispes, Great King, King of Anšan.*

(Cyrus Cylinder, lines 20–22)

Several things are noteworthy about this genealogy. First, Cyrus assumes much greater titles for himself than he accords his ancestors, signaling a move from local kingship to imperial status. Second, none of the names that enter this list—his own included—have an identifiable etymology, least of all one that would place them in the Iranian language family. Third, there is no mention of Achaemenes, whose name is Iranian, but who enters history some twenty years later in the first text authored by Darius, a trilingual inscription cut into a rock face at Bisitun and dated around 519. There, the second dynasty-founder introduced himself in this fashion:

> Proclaims Darius the King: I am Darius, Great King, King of Kings, King in Persia, King of lands/peoples, *the son of Hystaspes, grandson of Arsames, an Achaemenian. My father is Hystaspes. Hystaspes' father is Arsames. Arsames' father was Ariaramnes. Ariaramnes' father was Teispes. Teispes' father was Achaemenes.* Therefore we are proclaimed Achaemenians. From long ago we are noble. From long ago our lineage has been royal. There are eight of my lineage who were kings before. I am the ninth. Nine, now as before [*or:* in two lines], we are kings.
>
> (DB §§1–4)

Again, there are several points to be made. With regard to the royal titles, these have been changed, reflecting changes in circumstance and Darius's different concept of the empire. With regard to the family line, two of those named—Darius's father and grandfather—were still alive when the inscription was written, as indicated by the use of the present tense ("is," rather than "was"). With regard to the names, all save one have a clear Iranian etymology. The way this lineage is connected to that of Cyrus also holds interest, for it is done by implication, not directly. Thus, the only ancestor whose name is not Iranian—Teispes—happens to recur in the genealogy Cyrus gave for himself. Whereas Teispes held the paramount position in the Cyrus Cylinder, however, at Bisitun Darius puts Achaemenes in the spot of highest privilege, with Teispes set just below him.

The impression that Teispes has been appropriated and made to serve Darius's purpose (i.e., connecting his lineage to Cyrus's while subordinating the latter to the former) is reinforced by an extraordinary word that appears in the last line quoted above. This is Old Persian *duvitāparanam,* a word that is deliberately ambiguous. On the one hand, it most properly means "now as before," which stresses the continuity of this royal lineage while also faintly suggesting its restoration to power after some disruption. The word's phonology is such, however, that it invites a second, alternative interpretation: "in two lines [*or:* wings]." The effect is to conjure up a family with Achaemenes—Darius's ancestor—as its founder, from whom it is named "Achaemenian." Teispes then appears as Achaemenes' heir and successor, after which the family splits into an elder and a cadet lineage. The former leads to Cyrus, but—as readers of the Bisitun text would know—that line ended with the death of Cyrus's sons in the turbulent year 522. The cadet line then leads to Darius, who assumed the kingship and provided continuity in that same year of crisis (see figure 1).

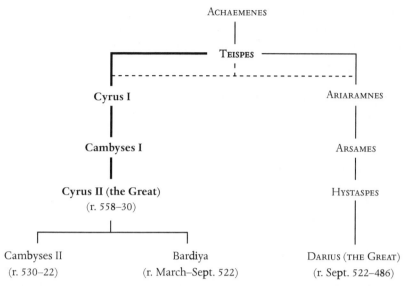

Figure 1: (Con)fusion of two lineages, as accomplished by Darius in DB §§1–4. Names appearing in boldface type are mentioned in the Cyrus Cylinder; those in caps and small caps are in DB §§1–4; those in regular roman type are mentioned elsewhere in DB. The thicker lines indicate relations mentioned in the Cyrus Cylinder, the thinner lines those in DB, and dotted lines the relation implied by the use of the (intentionally) ambiguous term *duvitāparanam,* which invites readers to imagine the structure indicated here: a royal family split in two lineages.

It thus appears that a properly "Achaemenian" dynasty was founded by Darius and dates from 522 but that its foundational discourse was crafted with consummate skill to encompass the earlier "Teispid" dynasty (i.e., one with Teispes as its eponymous ancestor) founded by Cyrus, which was, thus, redefined as "Achaemenian" *avant la lettre.* To clinch the deal, Darius engraved new inscriptions at Pasargadae, Cyrus's capital, details of whose epigraphy and placement reveal that they must have been written ca. 510. All are quite short and have the same point: "I am Cyrus the King, *an Achaemenian*" (CMa).

III

Virtually all the titles assumed by Cyrus echo those claimed by Nabonidus, the last king of Babylon (r. 556–539), whom he overthrew in 539. The text we now know as the Cyrus Cylinder was written shortly after the Persian king's conquest of the great city, with the assistance of Babylonian priests and scribes who, for reasons of their own, preferred him to Nabonidus and helped him secure the loyalty of the Babylonian population. More will be said about these events in chapter 3, but of interest for the moment is the royal title that Cyrus accorded his ancestors, and used for himself on an earlier occasion, but dispensed with when his status became imperial. This is the older—and decidedly lesser—title "king of Anšan," which was not based on any Babylonian (or Assyrian) precedent but had its origins in a different locale.

The site in question lies to the east of Babylon, more precisely, in what was once the kingdom of Elam but was divided into two fragments perhaps as early as the eighth century: a western piece, centered on the great city of Susa, and an eastern piece, centered on Anšan. The former of these fell to the Assyrians under Assurbanipal in 646, while the latter—more distant from Assyrian power—saw the gradual influx of a new population. This was an Iranian-speaking group whose members called themselves the Parsa, Parsua, and/or Parsuma that migrated from the central Zagros Mountains under circumstances that are still very badly understood. It is these people and their descendants whom history designates as the Persians. And, as the land formerly known as Anšan came under their control, it was renamed by and for them.

Cyrus's ancestors were, thus, petty kings, located in the southwest corner of modern Iran (ancient Parsa or Persis [as the Greeks called it], the modern Iranian province of Fars). Cyrus himself began his career with similar status, a vassal of the Medes, another Iranian people who, in combination with the Babylonians under Nabopolassar, had overthrown Assyrian domination and destroyed the Assyrians' capital at Nineveh in 612. These two powers jockeyed with one another during Cyrus's youth, a situation that ended when Persian troops under his command vanquished the Medes in 550. Persian power continued to rise with his conquest of the Lydians under Croesus in 547, and in subsequent years Cyrus gained control over Elam, Armenia, Parthia, Central Asia, eastern Iran, and the Mediterranean littoral, Babylon itself finally falling in 539. With these victories he obtained mastery over Syria, Palestine, Anatolia, and parts of Arabia.

Cyrus thus established the largest, most powerful empire the world had seen to that time. As his adoption of older titles suggests, he—or, more properly, the scribes who worked at his direction—appropriated certain pieces of royal ideology from those he overthrew, as is clear from table 1.

In addition, the scribes responsible for Cyrus's propaganda churned out a steady stream of fabulous narratives (dream omens, childhood exploits, etc.) designed to establish his extraordinary gifts and divine charisma. Many of these, including the theme of the royal child abandoned at birth for fear of its powers but miraculously saved and raised by animals, had their origin in legends associated with Sargon I (r. ca. 2334–2279 BCE), the founder of the dynasty of Akkad. Other patterns of discourse and royal practice were adopted from Elam, Babylon, and the Medes, with whom the Persians shared certain

TABLE 1: Royal Titles Inherited and Adopted by Cyrus the Great as He Moved from Local to Imperial Kingship

Titles of the Teispid Line[a]	Early Titles of Cyrus the Great[b]	Titles of Nabonidus[c]	Later Titles of Cyrus the Great[d]
	King of the World		King of the World
Great King		Great King	Great King
King of Anšan	King of Anšan		
		Mighty King	Mighty King
		King of the World	(King of the World)
		King of Babylon	King of Babylon
			King of Sumer and Akkad
		King of the Four Quarters	King of the Four Quarters
		Caretaker of Esagila and Ezida	

[a] From the Cyrus Cylinder.
[b] From the seal found at Ur.
[c] Text found on a brick at Ur, available in Schaudig 2001: 549.
[d] From the Cyrus Cylinder.

pan-Iranian aspects of language and culture. Unfortunately, the Medes left no written records, and there has not been serious archaeological investigation of Ecbatana (modern Hamadan), their capital city. Most of our knowledge about them comes via Herodotus, whose accounts have received critical scrutiny in recent years. As a result of the doubts that have been raised, one can no longer have full confidence in the Herodotean *Medikos logos* as a precise record of historical events, but it retains considerable value as an ethnographic sketch of cultural tendencies and orientation.

Cyrus established his capital at Pasargadae, close to where he won victory over the Medes, marking the site with a palace and a garden. Ultimately, it also housed his tomb, after he died fighting the Massagetae in 530 while attempting to expand his empire to the far northeast. On his death, the kingship passed smoothly to his son, Cambyses, who had earlier served as his coregent.

Almost equally ambitious as his father, Cambyses conquered Egypt in 525 and kept marching west until checked in Libya. Surviving Egyptian records suggest that Cambyses tried to style himself a proper pharaoh, adopting indigenous titles, and performing the requisite rituals in traditional fashion. Herodotus gives a very different picture, however, drawing on stories cir-

culated by Cambyses' enemies—whether Egyptian, Persian, or Greek is un-
clear—that depicted him as mad, impious, and arrogant. Whatever the real-
ity may have been, his long stay in Egypt created problems back in Persia and
Media, where his brother Bardiya seized the throne in March 522. In July,
Bardiya had himself crowned king and proclaimed a three-year suspension of
taxes and military service as a means to cement his popularity.

Confronted with this, Cambyses headed home to meet the challenge
but died en route under mysterious circumstances. Bardiya's rule, however,
was brief, for, in September 522, he was assassinated by a conspiratorial
group of seven Persian nobles, one of whom—Darius—subsequently assumed the throne.

IV

Darius's accession was not well received. Almost immediately, rebellions
broke out across the empire, and his armies had to suppress uprisings both at
the core (Persia, Elam, Media, Babylon) and the periphery (Assyria, Egypt,
Parthia, Margiana, Sattagydia, Hyrcania, Sagartia, Armenia, and Arachosia).
The monumental inscription at Bisitun was erected to celebrate his victories
in these struggles. There, Darius claimed that, within one year of taking the
throne, he had vanquished nine rebels, winning nineteen battles in the process. The battles, moreover, were bloody. Casualties in excess of 120,000 dead
are reported, and all the rebels were executed, often by impaling, and accompanied by scores of their noble supporters. Special treatment was accorded
two rebels (Fravarti and Tritantaxma) who claimed to be descendants of the
Median royal line. These unfortunates were tortured, mutilated, and placed
on public display, lest anyone think it was possible to roll back the clock and
restore the situation that preceded Persian supremacy.

The cases made by each of the rebels were similar, to judge from the brief,
formulaic, and highly prejudicial descriptions provided by the Bisitun text.
Each one claimed to be the rightful heir to an old royal lineage in a kingdom
that had been encompassed by the expanding Persian Empire. In this way,
they offered themselves as the rallying point for nationalist sentiments, em-
bodying their people's desire to extricate themselves from Persian rule. In response, Darius passed the harshest judgment available on these men and
their aspirations, a judgment simultaneously political, legal, moral, and religious. Stating of each one in turn, "He lied," he dismissed their claims and
pretensions, thereby construing them—and all they represented—as illegitimate, deceitful, and corrupting. Not kings, but imposters; not the heroes of
independence, but instruments of "the Lie" (*Drauga*), an entity that Achaemen-

ian ideology construes as the incarnation and source of all evil. More will be said on this topic in subsequent chapters.

Once having vanquished those whom he associated with the Lie, Darius availed himself of the opportunity to assert the "truth" (*arta*), that is, to control the historical record. The first four columns of the Bisitun text were inscribed on a dramatic cliff overlooking the main north-south highway between Susa and Babylon, shortly after 521. The final paragraph of this text (DB §70) suggests that the Old Persian (cuneiform) script was invented for this occasion, and it also says that copies were made on clay and parchment for distribution throughout the empire. Some of these have turned up, including a version in Aramaic, and it is clear that the new king meant to disseminate as widely as possible his version of how the relevant characters and events ought to be understood. His discourse advanced his cause no less than did his armies, perhaps showing even greater strategic acumen.

At Bisitun, Darius consistently represented himself as God's chosen (a theme to which I return in chapter 3), the savior, not just of his family, his people, and the Persian Empire, but of law, order, all that is good and true. In properly dualistic fashion, he depicted his enemies as liars and malefactors.

Worst of them all was the man Darius replaced on the throne: Bardiya, son of Cyrus, who—as certain Babylonian documents make clear—had been accepted as king through much of the empire. However one might have felt about his usurpation, in September 522 Bardiya was dead, and Darius was the only surviving claimant to the Teispid kingship since Cambyses had left no progeny. Bardiya's murder thus constituted nothing less than regicide and the extinction of Cyrus's lineage. To exculpate himself from such charges, Darius invented an audacious fiction. In DB §§10–14, he announced that it was actually Cambyses who had killed Bardiya, this having supposedly been done in 525, just before Cambyses left Persia for Egypt. What is more, Cambyses kept the deed secret until 522, when a wily magus (i.e., a Median priest) named Gaumata took advantage of the situation by assuming the dead prince's identity and proclaimed himself king. The man Darius and his fellow conspirators slew was, thus, represented as having been no legitimate monarch in any sense but the first instantiation of the Lie, the one that gave rise to all others.

V

In the second year of his reign (521–520), Darius had another Elamite rebellion to suppress, and he also waged his first campaign of aggressive war, adding a group of Asiatic Scythians to the empire. To celebrate these accomplishments, he added a fifth column to the Bisitun text, and, in that context, he sought to justify his war against the Scythians. Being unable to portray the Scythians as rebels, since they had never been under Persian rule, and equally unable to depict their king as a liar, since he was exactly what and who he claimed to be, Darius's scribes were forced to produce a new category to account for their military initiatives. The Scythians were "vulnerable to the Lie" (Old Persian *arika*), they charged, which is to say that, although the Lie was not yet manifest in their words and deeds, it had begun penetrating their thoughts and worse was sure to follow. Darius's invasion thus acquired the character of a preemptive strike launched in prudent self-defense against the gathering forces of evil.

Darius remained on the throne for another thirty-four years, during which time he added conquests in India (ca. 517) and Thrace and Macedonia (516–512); suppressed serious rebellions by the Ionian Greeks (499–493) and the Carians (496); introduced sweeping administrative, legal, and fiscal reforms; and mounted unsuccessful campaigns against Scythian populations north of the Black Sea (ca. 512) and mainland Greece (490). None of these events, however, leave the slightest trace in the epigraphic record. After Bisitun, the last phase of which was completed by 518, none of Darius's inscriptions show much concern with history, save to register the Great King's pride in his vast construction projects (palaces at Susa and Persepolis, the canal at Suez), about which more will be said in chapter 6. Typical, in this regard, is the earliest inscription that Darius placed in his new capital of Persepolis:

> Proclaims Darius the King: This land/people Persia, which the Wise Lord bestowed on me, which is good, whose horses are good, whose people are good, by the will of the Wise Lord and of me, Darius the King, it does not feel fear of any other. Proclaims Darius the King: May the Wise Lord bear me aid, together with all the gods, and may the Wise Lord protect this land/people from the enemy army, from famine, from the Lie. Against this land/people may the enemy army not come, nor famine, nor the Lie. This boon I ask the Wise Lord, together with all the gods. May the Wise Lord, together with all the gods, grant this boon to me.
>
> (DPd §§2–3)

Surely the diction is formulaic, so much so that it lulls most modern readers into a state of torpor. Yet, as Clarisse Herrenschmidt, the most astute interpreter of these texts, has consistently stressed, formulaic discourse is exceptionally dense, efficient, and economical. As such, it requires the most meticulous attention. To make sense of a given passage, it must be read against others to which it is related, and even the smallest variations in form can contain nuances of great importance. Read with such care, this inscription discloses a great deal, and it can be regarded as an early programmatic statement that touches on the most important themes of the whole Achaemenian corpus.

To begin, we should note the privileged position that it accords to Persia, an issue considered more fully in chapter 2. This passage is, in fact, the only place where any territory or population is described as "good," and the term the text uses—Old Persian *naiba*—holds deep religious significance. It denotes an existential perfection that derives from the Wise Lord, being harmonious with his intentions for the creation and ideally suited to make all life flourish, as the specification "whose horses are good, whose people are good" indicates. *Naiba* is, moreover, a term that stands in implicit contrast with the term for "evil" (Old Persian *duš*-), evil having its source in the Lie. This opposition of good and evil, God and the Lie, Persia and others, is regularly associated with other binary oppositions, for example, light and dark, center and periphery, moist/warm and cold/dry, life and death, above and below, and fragrant and foul, to name some of the most important. Of particular interest, however, is the opposition of "happiness" (Old Persian *šiyāti*) and its loss or absence, a theme taken up in chapters 4 and 6.

Beyond characterizing Persia and the Persians as uniquely good, this passage also depicts them as without fear, something that is, once more, said of no other land and people. This freedom from fear is attributed to the cooperative relation between the Wise Lord and King Darius. In all his other inscriptions, Darius was careful to depict himself as the grateful beneficiary and subordinate instrument of this omniscient, absolutely benevolent (but not omnipotent) deity. Here, however, in the phrase "by the will of the Wise Lord *and of me, Darius the King*," he claims greater status than he does at any other moment in his proclamations, representing himself as God's near-equal partner in the project of keeping Persia fearless.

Fear, as he goes on to specify, is a reaction to the presence—or even the proximity—of three entities filled with menace: the enemy army that threatens invasion; famine born of crop failure (most literally, "a bad year"); and, worst of all, the Lie. Fearlessness is the state of confidence that results when these threats are held so firmly in check that one ceases to worry about them: when peace is guaranteed by the strength of one's army; when food is abundant and the means for its production sure; when truth is guaranteed by the righteousness and integrity of the king. Darius prays to the Wise Lord for assurance that he will keep these threefold menaces at bay, and he shows confidence that this prayer will be granted. But he also implicitly claims to have

TABLE 2: Darius's Implicit Claim to Have Overcome the Three Great Menaces, Thereby Establishing the Conditions for Fearlessness and Well-Being

Menaces[a]	Instantiation of the Threats[b]	Darius's Response[c]
The enemy army	Now, that [rebel] came with an army to make battle against me. (DB §19 etc.)	Then we made battle. The Wise Lord bore me aid. By the Wise Lord's will, I defeated that army utterly. (DB §19 etc.)
Famine	The pastures and livestock and servants and houses of the people, which Gaumata the Magus had taken from them. (DB §14)	I restored the pastures and livestock and servants and houses of the people. (DB §14)
The Lie	When Cambyses went to Egypt, then the people became vulnerable to the Lie, and the Lie grew greatly. (DB §10)	For this reason the Wise Lord bore me aid, he and the other gods that are: Because I was not vulnerable to the Lie, I was not a liar, I was not a deceit-doer. (DB §63)

[a] DPd §3.
[b] DB.
[c] DB.

secured the conditions for fearlessness by his own actions since, in the earlier Bisitun text, he showed himself victorious over instantiations of these same three threats, as table 2 makes clear.

VI

Having mastered these threats during the crisis year of 522–521, Darius implicitly claimed to have established the conditions for an enduring—perhaps even eternal—state of well-being in Persia and its domains, and this is reflected in the tenor of all his subsequent inscriptions. Thus, of the fifty-three texts that postdate Bisitun, not one acknowledges turbulence, difficulty, or struggle, except in the most indirect fashion. Rather, they are resolutely ahistorical, depicting a stable political, moral, and cosmic order, established by the actions that the Great King undertook as God's chosen, and maintained by his ongoing relation with the divine.

What is more, the inscriptions of Darius's successors all adopt these later texts of his as their model. They too project a timeless calm and a profound disinterest in the vicissitudes of mundane existence. The most one gets is an occasional hint, as when Xerxes replaced one of his father's more expansive royal titles, "King of lands/peoples of *all* races," with a more modest substitute, "King of lands/peoples of *many* races," to acknowledge that the global nature of Achaemenian ambition had been checked when the Greeks defeated his forces at Salamis (480) and Plataea (479). Even here, however, change coexists with continuity, for this title stands third in a set of four, which otherwise is identical over multiple generations of Achaemenian kings. Starting with the smallest, most modest of their claims—"I am *X*, Great King"—these expand in their scope, asserting that the Persian monarch rules over other kings, other lands and peoples, and, ultimately, over the entire world. The term used to denote the world, moreover, Old Persian *būmi,* originally meant "earth" (like its cognates in Avestan and Sanskrit) but was adopted by the Achaemenians to denote the political formation they introduced, that which we call "empire." Through this terminology, it was, thus, implicitly conveyed that, in its ideal form, the empire is coterminous with the earth. Although it may fall short of that ideal in the present moment, this situation reflects the flawed and fragmented nature of historical existence. The Wise Lord intended for all humanity to be united, just as he intended for all living beings to thrive. The extent to which actuality falls short of this ideal results from the corrupting activity of the Lie, and, as the Lie is overcome, humanity will be united under the Persian king. In that moment, the actual empire achieves its proper global scope. And, for all that Xerxes may have backed away from his father's claims regarding lands and peoples, he maintained those regarding empire and earth, claims that will still be advanced by Darius II (r. 423–404), Artaxerxes II, and Artaxerxes III (r. 359–338) (see table 3).

TABLE 3: Set of Four Titles Employed from Darius the Great through Artaxerxes III, Showing Levels of Ambition That Expand to the Global

Darius[a]	Xerxes[b]	Later Kings[c]
I am Darius, Great King,	I am Xerxes, Great King,	[I am *X*], Great King,
King of Kings,	King of Kings,	King of Kings,
King of lands/peoples of *all* races,	King of lands/peoples of *many* races,	King of lands/peoples,
King in this great, far-reaching earth/empire.	King in this great, far-reaching earth/empire.	King in this earth/empire.

[a] DNa §2, DSe §2, DZc §2.
[b] XPa §2, XPb §2, XPc §2, XPd §2, XPf §2, XPh §2, XE §2, XV §2.
[c] D²Sb §1, A²Sa, A²Sc §2, A²Sd §1, A²Ha §1, A²Hc §2, A³Pa §2.

VII

For information about any historical events after Xerxes' accession, we are dependent on foreign sources: mostly Greek, but occasionally Babylonian, Egyptian, Latin, and biblical. Were we to rely on the inscriptions alone, we would be ignorant of the invasions of Greece by the Persians and the defeats they suffered (480–479; also the earlier war of 490); the rebellions they put down in Egypt (486–484, 460–454, 405), Babylon (484, 482–481), Syria (ca. 454), Media (410–408), and Phoenecia (349–344), not to mention the period when Egypt reestablished its independence (393–342); or such events as the murder of Xerxes II (424), the revolt of Cyrus the Younger against his brother, Artaxerxes II (401), the great satrapal revolt (367–359), the murder of Artaxerxes III (338), and the final conquest by Alexander (334–330).

Obviously enough, foreign authors do not report things from a Persian perspective, and one must guard against naturalizing and reproducing their Orientalist tropes as regards Persian luxury, decadence, despotism, and palace intrigue, to cite some of the most common examples. But, if one exercises reasonable caution, there is a wealth of information to be gathered from Herodotus, Aeschylus, Xenophon, Aelian, or Polyaenus, as Pierre Briant has amply demonstrated in his numerous writings, and the reporting of even so biased an author as Ctesias can prove useful, particularly if one dispenses with his interpretive additions. What Ctesias and others describe with disdain as "luxury" (Greek *tryphē*, a term that has connotations of wantonness, self-indulgence, softness, and effeminacy), for instance, can provide a useful picture, not only of Persian wealth, but also of the extent to which it was deployed in ritual practice and symbolic displays, the significance of which was utterly lost on outsiders. This is true, for instance, in the case of the Great King's banquet table, which was simultaneously a means of redistribution, a display of royal generosity, and a microcosmic image of the empire at large. A similar mix of reasonable accuracy in the details and very partial understanding as regards evaluation and interpretation is also evident in Greek reports of many practices through which the Persians instantiated royal virtues, including those that the Greeks (mis)construed as arrogance, cruelty, and the like.

One is able to guard against such misunderstandings by extricating these data from the distortions of a Hellenocentric perspective and restoring them to a Persian, or at least an Iranian, context. Sometimes it is sufficient to compare the Greek texts to the Achaemenian inscriptions, iconography, and archaeological remains. Thus, for instance, Herodotus's contention that the Persians pray, not for benefit to themselves, but only for the king's welfare and that of the Persian people (1.132) preserves—but also distorts—the much more complex ideology of the inscriptions, where the Wise Lord bestows kingship on the ruler, who thereafter mediates all significant dealings between the human and the divine.

Other cases are somewhat more difficult since the language of the inscriptions is brief and allusive, assuming familiarity with religious and cultural constructs of considerable complexity. While the authors and initial readers of those texts may have possessed the requisite knowledge, we can recover it only through some painstaking operations. Of greatest value in this regard is the evidence from Zoroastrian texts, written in other Iranian languages that are separated from Old Persian by space (as in the case of Avestan, an east Iranian dialect) or time (as in the case of Pahlavi, a middle Iranian dialect of western Iran).

Comparisons of this sort have frequently been entangled with the question of whether the Achaemenians were Zoroastrians, a question that has been much debated, with very inconclusive results. Those who wish to make the case tend to stress the similarities, including the fact that the supreme deity named in the inscriptions, like that of the Zoroastrian scriptures, was called "the Wise Lord" (Avestan and Old Persian *Ahura Mazdā,* Pahlavi *Ohrmazd*). Conversely, those on the other side of the question stress those places where the two corpora differ, for example, the Wise Lord's great adversary, whom Zoroastrians call "the Evil Spirit" (Avestan *Angra Mainyu,* Pahlavi *Ahriman*), "the Adversary," and "the Lie," while Achaemenians speak only of "the Lie" (Old Persian *Drauga,* cognate to Avestan *drug* and Pahlavi *druz*). Complicating things further are a host of terms that are cognate and concepts that are similar in their broad outlines but show significant differences in their particulars. As an example, one might note the Old Persian *paridaida,* a pan-Iranian term that denotes a walled enclosure but that the Achaemenians (as we have seen) used to describe their pleasure gardens and the Avesta used to denote a space in which those most tainted by death could receive purification (Avestan *pairidaēza*).

These relations can be understood in one of two ways. Conceivably, the Achaemenians (from Darius, at least) were Zoroastrians whose views were inflected by political—and, perhaps, also other—considerations such that they differed from the ones priestly authors spelled out in more strictly religious texts. Alternatively, the Zoroastrian texts and the Achaemenian inscriptions can be understood as two variants within a broad, pan-Iranian tradition that one might label "Mazdaean." Both thus inherited common linguistic, cultural, and religious features that they developed in their own fashions and for their own reasons. These two hypotheses are not mutually exclusive, and to affirm the second—as I do—does not necessarily falsify the first.

In truth, I find the question of whether Cyrus, Darius, Artaxerxes, or any of the others was Zoroastrian in any meaningful sense to be of relatively little interest. Ultimately, I suspect that it is either unresolvable or simply a matter of semantics. In either case, the question has received more attention than its importance merits, and I would far rather turn to matters of broader significance.

Although this book will focus exclusively on the Achaemenians, I treat them as a spectacularly instructive example that lets us consider more general issues, not as an object of inherent fascination. The issue of prime interest is, as I suggested initially, how religion, empire, and torture can be interrelated. More specifically, I hope to explore how certain Achaemenian religious constructs that resemble those found elsewhere—reverence for a benevolent creator, a theology of election and vocation, a dualistic ethics, eschatological expectations, and a sense of soteriological mission—helped inspire the project of empire and informed even its most brutally violent aspects.

As part of this study, I am led to consider certain aspects of Achaemenian cosmology, a cosmology that I have come to understand as self-consciously moral and acutely political. Among the most important aspects are religiously valorized constructions of time and space, self and other, ruler and ruled, unity and fragmentation, happiness and its corruption, all of which found expression in Achaemenian discourse and practice. The chapters that follow thus take up a set of interrelated questions. How did the Persians orient themselves in space, and how did this affect their dealings with other peoples (chapter 2)? What relation to deity and virtue did political power claim for itself (chapter 3)? What pattern and purpose did the Persians perceive in history, and how did this inform their sense of sacred mission (chapter 4)? What ideals did the empire mean to pursue, and how did it work to realize them (chapter 5)? What gaps opened up between ideals and performance, or, more pointedly, how did its ideals lead the empire into contradiction (chapter 6)?

Center and Periphery   2

I

Before placing his text on the rock face at Bisitun, Darius graced that site with a stunning piece of relief sculpture that told his story in pictorial terms (see figure 2).

Toward the top of this composition, which draws freely on Assyrian prototypes, is a divine figure in a winged lozenge and wearing a type of crown conventionally reserved for deities (see figure 3). This is the Wise Lord, Ahura Mazdā, greatest of deities and creator of all things good, a god who was understood to be entirely benevolent but, unfortunately, not all-powerful. With his left hand the god makes a gesture well attested in older Mesopotamian art, proffering a ring that signifies kingship. With his right hand he salutes Darius, who stands at the center of the composition, wearing a royal diadem and an elegant squared beard, and who returns the gesture of greeting (see figure 4).

At the bottom, a third figure also has his hands outstretched, although his gesture is one of supplication, not greeting or blessing. This is the woeful supine figure who has Darius's left foot firmly planted on his chest (see, again, figure 4). A short inscription beneath this figure serves as a caption: "This is Gaumata the Magus. He lied. He proclaimed thus: 'I am Bardiya, son of Cyrus. I am King'" (DBb).

The vertical plane thus organizes a radical contrast between God above and an archrepresentative of the Lie below, with the righteous King Darius between them. The intermediate space that Darius dominates, that of the earth's surface, is, thus, understood as an arena of struggle between good and evil. There, forces of the Lie can—and do—mount serious challenges to the Wise Lord, but they

Figure 2: Rock relief with inscriptions at Bisitun in western Iran representing Darius the Great after his victory over Gaumata and other rebel kings. (Photo: Leo Trümpelmann/German Archaeological Institute, Berlin.)

are—and will be—defeated by the men he supports and chooses to defend him. The opposition of God and Adversary, above and below, carries with it many other associations in Iranian thought. For example, the spatial contrast is reminiscent of those drawn in the opening passages of two important Zoroastrian texts:

> The Wise Lord is highest in omniscience and goodness. He exists for infinite time, always in the light. That light is the place of the Wise Lord. It is called "Endless Light." Omniscience and goodness exist in infinite time, as do the Wise Lord, goodness, and religion. The Evil Spirit exists in darkness, in ignorance and love of destruction, in the lowest depths. His crude love of destruction and that place of darkness are called "Endless Darkness." Between the two spirits was a space called "Air," in which the two mingle with each other.
>
> (*Greater Bundahišn* 1.1–5 [TD² MS 2.8–3.6])

> Now, in the Religion, it is revealed thus: "Light was above and darkness below, and openness was between the two." The Wise Lord was in the light and the Evil Spirit in the darkness, and the Wise Lord was aware of the existence of the Evil Spirit, also that he was coming to battle. The Evil Spirit was not aware of

the existence of the light and of the Wise Lord. The Evil Spirit always went down in the direction of darkness and shadows. Then by chance he went up. He saw a ray of light, and, for the sake of its difference from his nature, he strove to arrive at it and to exercise power over it as he did over the dark realms. When he came to the border [between them], in order to repel the Evil Spirit from his own realm, the Wise Lord went forth to give battle. And, with the pure speech of a deity, he made him stupefied and threw him back into the

Figure 3: Detail from the Bisitun relief: the Wise Lord gestures to Darius.
(Photo: Leo Trümpelmann/German Archaeological Institute, Berlin.)

Figure 4: Detail from the Bisitun relief: Darius plants his
foot on the fallen Gaumata. (Photo: H. Luschey.)

shadows. For the sake of protection from the Lie, in the highest realm, he spir-
itually created the spirit of heaven, water, earth, plant, cattle, man, and fire.

(Selections of Zad Spram 1.1–4)

Returning to the Bisitun relief, if the vertical plane organizes an overdetermined contrast of good versus evil, truth versus lie, light versus darkness,
omniscience versus ignorance, creativity versus destruction, the horizontal
plane organizes a weaker form of the same oppositions. Thus, on the left-
hand side of the relief stand two men armed with spear and bow who face in
the same direction as Darius. Their clothing, shoes, hair, and facial features
closely resemble those of the king, although they lack the diadem, stature,
and long beard that mark his royal status. Although they stand a bit shorter
than the Great King (1.47 meters, as opposed to his 1.72 meters), they are still
considerably taller than the nine figures who occupy the right-hand quadrant

and face in the opposite direction (1.27 meters each). Further, the erect bearing of the Persians contrasts with the stooped posture of these others, who have a rope tied round their necks, in token of their subjugation. Unlike the Persians, these men bear no weapons, and, indeed, it is impossible for them to do so, their hands being tied tightly behind their backs. Not simply unarmed, they have been defeated and disarmed by Darius's Persian armies: the accompanying inscriptions (DBc–DBk) identify them as rebels who, on the accession of Darius, rose up and whom he vanquished in sequence.

Each of the rebels is identified with a caption like that given to Gaumata. "This is Açina," it says under the first in line. "He lied. He proclaimed thus: 'I am King in Elam'" (DBc). Behind him stand the other defeated rebels, all condemned as liars. The captions connect each one to a specific national uprising, and the relief also establishes the rebels' national identity through details of physiognomy, coiffure, and clothing. Their other individual differences notwithstanding, all the non-Persians are more or less the same height and significantly smaller than the Persians. The Persian king is always the largest of all, physical size serving as an index of the power the Persians possessed and their subject peoples all equally lacked.

As figure 5 shows, the composition of the Bisitun relief has five broad areas that relate to one another in structurally elegant and ideologically significant fashion such that the opposition of above versus below is echoed in that of left versus right, which contrasts powerful, victorious, and righteous Persians with disarmed, defeated, and lying others. That the others outnumber

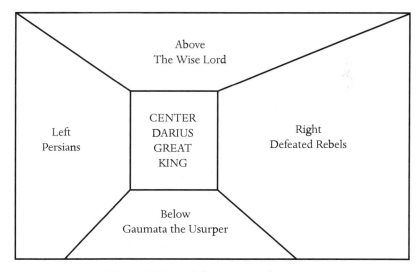

Figure 5: Bisitun relief, compositional structure.

the Persians helps make an important point, for, within Iranian ideology more broadly, the triumph of a smaller over a larger force is possible only when the former receives divine assistance and constitutes proof after the fact that such was the case.

Both the vertical and the horizontal axes center on the figure of Darius, who triumphs over Gaumata with the Wise Lord's aid and leads the Persians to triumph over other peoples, as represented by the lying rebels. Darius also mediates between the two positively valorized quadrants, for kingship descends to him from the Wise Lord above, to let him lead the Persians who stand behind him. Kingship is, thus, construed as a divine charisma, which includes the capacity for truthful speech (he alone does not lie when he says "I am King") and military success.

The relief thus associates its top, left, and central fields to form a bloc that outweighs and overpowers those figures it denigrates by locating them in the lesser fields to the right and the bottom. The empire consists of this whole field of forces, where (1) ethnic self is privileged above ethnic other, (2) the divine sanctions suppression of that which is defined as false, (3) the Persian king mediates all relations, and (4) loyal Persians are connected by their king to a divine, transcendent above while disloyal others are similarly consigned to a devalued below. Characterized in negative terms by the absence of weapons, stature, dignity, and truth, as well as by distance from the divine, that space might also be considered infernal or demonic.

II

Whereas Cyrus adopted the Babylonian title "King of the Four Quarters" to voice the spatial extent of his status and ambitions, in the Bisitun inscription Darius abandoned this claim and produced a formulation that used nuances of grammar to specify his differing relations to various pieces of his realm: "King in Persia, King of lands/peoples" (DB §1), where the noun *Pārsa* occurs in the locative case, indicating the geographic space in which the king situates himself, the province that defines his proper place and identity. As Darius says in a later inscription at Suez, using the same grammatical form: "I am Persian, I am from Persia" (DZc §3). The locative of this form stands in marked contrast to the plural genitive *dahyūnām*, which designates all the other lands and peoples—Old Persian *dahyu* denotes both a population and its territory— *over* whom he ruled *from* his locus in Persia. Later, Darius will adopt other titles, but here, in his earliest inscription, he locates himself in Persia, the central space from which he and the Persian "dominant class-ethnicity" (to use Pierre Briant's phrase) exercised power over a large (and growing) number of other peoples, who retained their ethnic identity but were politically and economically subordinated to him. This is the very model of empire.

The same Persocentric model also finds expression in the lists where Achaemenian kings enumerated the lands and peoples under their dominion. As might be expected, these show some variation from one king, inscription, or historical situation to another, but five organizing principles are consistent:

1. If Persia appears in the list, it is always mentioned first.
2. If the list is defined in a way that makes explicit reference either to conquest or to the payment of tribute, the Persian people are not included, for Persians were exempt from such payments, as Herodotus (3.97) also records. Rather, in such cases they are always mentioned separately, before the conquered, tribute-paying peoples are enumerated, as when Darius begins a list in this fashion: "These are the lands/peoples that I seized far from Persia. I ruled over them. They bore me tribute" (DNa §3, DSe §3; cf. DPe §2, XPh §3). Here, Persia figures as the point of departure from which conquest of other lands and peoples originated, a land that was not itself subject to conquest, domination, or extraction. And, as noted in chapter 1, Persia is the only land/people ever described as "good" (Old Persian *naiba*) in the religious sense.
3. Although the sequential order of peoples and lands varies considerably, only three of the thirty-six peoples named in the seven surviving lists ever occupy one of the top positions (see table 4). These are the Medes, the Elamites, and the Babylonians, all of whom were in close geographic proximity, had close cultural relations with the Persians, and provided historical models for the Persians of what proper kingship should be. As a further token of the special status of these three peoples, moreover, the Persians took over their foremost cities— Ecbatana, Susa, and Babylon—and made them capital cities of their own.

TABLE 4: First Three Lands/Peoples Mentioned in Imperial Lists

	1	2	3
DB §6	Persians	Elamites	Babylonians
DNa §3	(Persians)	Medes	Elamites
DPe §2	(Persians)	Elamites	Medes
DSe §3	(Persians)	Medes	Elamites
DSm §2	Persians	Elamites	Babylonians
XPh §3	(Persians)	Medes	Elamites
A³Pb	Persians	Medes	Elamites

Note: The Persians are omitted from lists that record tribute obligations, where their primacy—here registered by parentheses—is marked by absence.

4. If Persians define the empire's absolute center, with Medes, Elamites, and (less often) Babylonians constituting a set that lies just beyond, a third concentric sphere is filled by other lands/peoples, these being organized in groups oriented to the four cardinal directions.

5. When the time comes to list these lands/peoples, the text will begin in one of the cardinal points and work its way outward from those who are geographically closest to the center, step by step, until it reaches those who are most distant. That being accomplished, it will rotate ninety degrees and repeat the operation. Once all four quadrants have been covered, the list is complete, although there are certain peoples (Nubians, Carians, and Makans) who tend to be reserved for last, even if this means breaking with other principles that govern the sequence. As an example, consider the earliest of all the lists, that of Darius at Bisitun, which reflects Achaemenian holdings in December 521 (DB §6; see figure 6).

Differential values do not seem to have been attached to the cardinal directions, and the lists vary in terms of whether they begin with lands to the north or lands to the south. Similar alternation is evident between east and

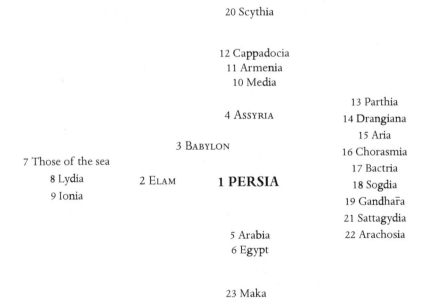

20 Scythia

12 Cappadocia
11 Armenia
10 Media

                                                                       13 Parthia

4 ASSYRIA   14 Drangiana

                15 Aria

3 BABYLON   16 Chorasmia

7 Those of the sea   17 Bactria

8 Lydia   2 ELAM   **1 PERSIA**   18 Sogdia

9 Ionia   19 Gandhāra

21 Sattagydia

5 Arabia   22 Arachosia

6 Egypt

23 Maka

Figure 6: Lands and peoples listed as part of the Achaemenian Empire by Darius at DB §6. The number preceding each national/ethnic category reflects the sequence in which the passage enumerates these peoples. Placement in the diagram reflects the geographic and cosmographic logic organizing the text.

west, although the north-south axis is regularly treated before east-west. With regard to relations of center and periphery, however, there is no ambiguity. The center has absolute primacy, and peoples closer to the center take relative precedence over those further out. The logic of this arrangement is as Herodotus (1.134) described:

> After themselves, they give honor above all to those who dwell closest to themselves and second to those who are second closest. And, proceeding thus, they distribute honor proportionately. They treat with least honor those who dwell farthest away from themselves, considering themselves to be in all ways the best of people by far, while the others partake of excellence proportionately, such that those dwelling farthest from themselves are the worst. When the Medes were ruling, peoples ruled over each other, and the Medes ruled over all together, especially those dwelling nearest to them. The latter ruled their neighbors, and they in turn ruled those who came next. The Persians distribute honor following the same principle.

III

At Bisitun, Darius introduced the list of his imperial holdings with a simple statement: "These lands/peoples that came to me by the Wise Lord's will, I was King of them" (DB §6). Slightly more elaborate is the version he used at Persepolis, written sometime after 515: "By the Wise Lord's will, these are the lands/peoples that I took hold of with this Persian army. They feared me and brought me tribute" (DPe §2). With remarkable brevity and precision, this statement describes the reciprocal processes that constitute and maintain any imperial system. The first of these, through which the empire comes into being, is the outflow of violence whereby the center conquers and dominates the outer circles: "These are the lands/peoples that I took hold of with this Persian army." Introducing similar lists at Susa and Naqš-i Rustam, Darius made much the same point, emphasizing the ability of the Persian center to project its force at a distance: "These are the lands/peoples that I seized *far from Persia*" (DNa §3, DSe §3).

Balancing the outflow of martial force and making its continuation possible is the reflux of wealth that empires extort through the threat of violence: "They feared me and brought me tribute." The payments established by Darius—which, if Herodotus's accounting at 3.89–97 is to be believed, amounted to some 14,560 (Euboic) talents of silver, not to mention traditional "gifts" that included 1,000 talents of frankincense from Arabia, 360 white horses from Cappadocia, and 500 Babylonian boys destined to become eunuchs, plus unspecified amounts of ebony and ivory from Ethiopia—made their way to Persia each year, which was itself exempt from tribute. Five inscriptions make reference to such extractions and show a historical progression that amounts to their normalization. Thus, the earliest text associates the payment of tribute with obedience to royal proclamations, the next in the series connects it to fear of the Persian army, and the three later passages treat it as part of obedience to the law while acknowledging that the law is an instrument for holding subject peoples in place (see table 5).

IV

The reciprocal exchange of outbound violence for inbound wealth is typical of all imperial formations, providing a political equivalent to Einstein's equation on the interchangeability of energy and matter. Political discourse, however, adds a mystifying wrinkle that is absent in the more sober discourse of physics. Thus, when those who define themselves as inhabiting the center also construe that site as more noble, more worthy, more moral than the periphery—as was true in Median, Persian, and general Iranian cosmology—they can theorize conquest as a benevolent act that brings benefits to the conquered.

All this helps us understand not only how the Achaemenians understood themselves and their subject peoples but also how they viewed those who lay beyond the (current) borders of their empire. Such people were wild, uncivilized, immoral, a threat to imperial tranquility, perhaps, but also in need of the good influence that could flow to them from the privileged center. While the Greeks (to choose the example about which we are best informed) may have conceived the process of being encompassed within the empire—as happened to the Ionian Greeks of Asia but not those of Europe—as a transition from freedom to tyranny, the Persians saw things differently. From their perspective, those fortunate enough to be encompassed, whether by voluntary submission or by conquest, were assisted in making the transition from lawlessness to law and from the Lie to truth.

The writing of history actually begins in the West when Herodotus—an Ionian Greek, born in Halicarnassus, a city under Persian rule—felt moved to narrate the wars between the Persians and the Greeks, which he took to be the most important event in human experience. His tale was meant to be both edifying and heroic, a proper successor to the epic poetry of Homer, and, in large measure, it celebrates the triumph of Greek virtues. It is, however, a complex text that reflects a multifaceted process of "inquiry" (the literal meaning of Greek *historiē*). From certain details—his catalog of the Persian army, for instance, or his detailed account of Darius's accession—it is

TABLE 5: Mention of Tribute in the Achaemenian Royal Inscriptions

DB §§7–8	DPe §2	DNa §3 (= DSe §3)	XPh §3
§7: Proclaims Darius the King:	Proclaims Darius the King:	Proclaims Darius the King:	Proclaims Xerxes the King:
These lands/peoples which came to me,	By the Wise Lord's will, these are the lands/peoples that I took hold of with this Persian army.	By the Wise Lord's will, these are the lands/peoples that I seized far from Persia.	By the Wise Lord's will, these are the lands/peoples far from Persia of which I was King.
by the Wise Lord's will they were subjects to me.	*They feared me*	I ruled over them.	I ruled over them.
They bore me tribute.	*and they bore me tribute.*	*They bore me tribute.*	*They bore me tribute.*
What was proclaimed to them by me, by day or by night, that was done.		That which was proclaimed to them by me, that they did.	That which was proclaimed to them by me, that they did.
§8: Proclaims Darius the King:			
Within these lands/peoples, that man who was loyal, him I treated well; he who was vulnerable to the Lie, him I punished well.			
By the Wise Lord's will, *these lands/peoples conducted themselves according to my law.*		*My law—that held them.*	*My law—that held them.*
Just as was proclaimed to them by me, just so they did.			

clear that Herodotus had access to Persian sources and informants. He is, moreover, a sympathetic narrator and a careful observer. Profoundly curious about the customs, religion, and distinctive practices of other peoples, he was as much an anthropologist, an ethnographer, a folklorist, and a historian of religions as he was the "father of history." What is more, occasionally he tells more than he knows he is telling.

Consider, for instance, his account of the first time a Persian king dealt with the Greeks of Europe, set in the spring of 546 BCE, as Cyrus was consolidating control over his conquests. Hoping to escape Cyrus's grasp, the Greek cities of Asia Minor sent ambassadors to Sparta, requesting military assistance. Anti-Persian, but wary of committing troops overseas, the Spartans refused, but they did send a fact-finding mission that took one Lakrines to Sardis, where Cyrus was then in residence. Rather haughtily, this man conveyed "a declaration of the Spartans to Cyrus," which stated: "Do not treat wantonly any city on Greek soil, for the Spartans will not permit it" (Herodotus 1.152).

By way of response, Cyrus asked who these Spartans were who spoke so boldly and how many of them there were. On getting his answer, he continued as follows:

> "I do not fear such men, *who have a place in the center of their city where people congregate, swearing oaths, and deceiving each other.* If I stay healthy, these people will have their own sufferings to chatter about, and not just those of the Ionians."
>
> (Herodotus 1.153)

Speeches in Herodotus are never quotations of what literally was said on a given occasion but the author's summation of what he takes to have been the actor's views on the salient issues. In this case, Herodotus goes beyond the speech itself and provides something of an ethnographic gloss to explain that the Persians possessed nothing comparable to the Greek agora and were not accustomed to haggling over prices. The latter point is open to question, but, this notwithstanding, it is the Cyrus of this episode who most exhibits the risks of ethnographic practice. Beginning with an astute observation— that the agora played a central role in Greek culture, as witnessed by the space allotted to it—he is subsequently led astray by the beliefs and mores of his own people, which he takes to be normative and through which he reads his data. Rather than recognizing the agora as an institution of civil society, one where contentiousness in the form of political debate and economic negotiation was turned to productive purpose, he treats it as a space of fraud and deception. Moreover, it stands at the spatial center of the Greek polis, where morality should be the greatest, but where the force of evil has penetrated and conquered. Seen through this optic, the existence of the agora constitutes prima facie evidence that the Lie flourishes in Greece: a situation that invites the benevolent intervention of an imperial power that defines itself as acting on behalf of morality, God, and creation.

V

The Achaemenian inscriptions provide very little information concerning Persian attitudes toward the Greeks, but the position assigned the latter in the lists of lands/peoples that were compiled at different times tells us some things worth knowing. Thus, in the earliest list (that of Bisitun, considered above), dated ca. 520, the Greeks appear among the empire's western subject peoples. From the term that is used (Old Persian *Yauna*) and the historical circumstances, it is clear these are the Ionian Greeks of Asia, who were conquered by Cyrus ca. 546. Later inscriptions introduce other types of Greeks, however, beginning with inscriptions at Persepolis and Susa that distinguish between "Greeks by the sea" and "Greeks beyond the sea" (DPe §2, DSe §2). The distinction between Asiatic and European Greeks (those *by* and those *beyond* the sea) seems a natural one, and the body of salt water that lay in between them provided a useful means to mark their division. One could well understand that the Persians might theorize the Asiatic Greeks as lying at the peripheries of the imperial circles, a locus that would describe their occasionally wild and rebellious nature or, to put it in reverse fashion, their ongoing need for Persian control and direction. Under such a construction, the sea marked the empire's outer reaches, beyond which point lay more savage, less moral, and still unconquered peoples, including the Greeks of Europe. All this is reasonable enough, but it is not what the inscriptions say. Rather, post-Bisitun, all inscriptions list both types of Greek—those by the sea *and* those beyond it—among the lands and peoples of the empire. How can this be so?

To understand, we must consider the events of 507, just after Athens had suffered a brief but humiliating military occupation by the Spartans. Responding to the ongoing danger from Sparta, the Athenian tyrant Cleisthenes sent ambassadors to Persian representatives in Sardis, hoping to negotiate an alliance. Herodotus describes the discussions that followed:

> When the messengers conveyed the things they had been authorized to say, Artaphrenes, son of Hystaspes, satrap of Sardis, asked them: "What kind of men are you, and what land do you inhabit, that you should need to become allies of the Persians?" Having heard the messengers' answer, he summarized things for them. If the Athenians would give earth and water to King Darius,

he would conclude an alliance with them, and, if they would not give these, he
ordered them to depart. The messengers spoke among themselves, *deciding on
their own* to give the earth and water so that the alliance could be made. On returning home, they received heavy accusations.

(Herodotus 5.73)

This passage is very carefully crafted. Written sometime in the 430s, when
Athenian power was at its height, the text attempts to obscure some decisions
taken at an earlier moment of weakness that had since become an embarrass-
ment. Still, it clearly acknowledges that Athenian ambassadors gave earth and
water to the Great King. The significance of this gesture was widely understood. As summarized in Kuhrt 1988: "Earth and water giving represented an
act acknowledging the superiority of the recipient, on the basis of which negotiation of actual obligations and benefits could proceed. These in practice
varied considerably but the underlying relationship was a binding one—
infringements allowed the Persian king or his representative to intervene
more drastically if such action appeared to be in the imperial interest" (98).

In most attested instances, it was the Persians who raised the question of
earth and water, offering potential enemies the choice of making this gift
or facing the consequences: a choice that let them enter the empire (quasi-)
voluntarily, under negotiable terms, instead of by conquest, with terms then
imposed by the victors. In this case, however, it was the Athenians who initi-
ated negotiations, and they did so as supplicants, begging needed support
from the Persians. The response received was precisely what one would have
expected, and it is hardly credible that the Athenian emissaries were unpre-
pared for it.

Uncomfortable with these implications, the text displaces responsibility
for Athenian submission from Cleisthenes to his ambassadors, whom it most
implausibly describes as having exceeded their authority. The passage's de-
nouement further distances the Athenian people from these acts, but there
is no evidence that the treaty was nullified or rejected. This is why "Greeks
beyond the sea" appeared in all the lists the Persians compiled after that date.

Within a few short years, however, circumstances had changed appreci-
ably. Athens no longer felt threatened by Sparta, Persia was meddling uncom-
fortably in Athenian affairs of state, and rebellion was brewing among the
Ionian cities of Asia Minor. When in the spring of 499 the Ionians asked Athens
for assistance, the assembly of the latter agreed and sent twenty ships full of
troops that helped the rebels in the sack of Sardis. "Those ships," Herodotus
declared, meaning to pronounce weighty historical judgment, "were the beginning of evils for the Greeks and the Barbarians" (5.97).

There is much more that can be said about why the Athenians undertook these actions and how the Persians responded with subsequent invasions of Greece (490 and 480–479). For the moment, however, it suffices to focus attention on the different ways in which each party understood the commitments of 507. To the Athenians, the gifts of earth and water were a gesture that helped them conclude an alliance of finite duration and utility. Having outlived its usefulness, that treaty now needed to be abrogated.

In contrast, from the Persian perspective, this was, not some arrangement of convenience, but a sacred compact. Iranian religion makes quite clear that, when two parties pledge to join themselves to one another in peace, those words have binding force. Speech acts of this sort—compacts, covenants, contracts, and the like—were considered the very basis of social order and were regarded as divine and, as such, inviolable. Indeed, the name of the old Indo-Iranian god Mithra means exactly this: "compact, covenant, contract." For a Persian, to lie under any circumstances was regarded as a cardinal sin: corrupt, corrupting, and utterly corrosive of order. But to lie when forging a bond of this sort—as the Athenians did—was the worst of all possible evils. Zoroastrian texts denounce those who would do such a thing as "liars to Mithra" or "those who lie when making a compact" (Avestan *Mithrō-drug*). Their deeds create havoc, but they also bring retribution. When, for example, treaties are violated, wars follow, and in those wars Mithra and associated gods punish those responsible for the violation.

The Achaemenian inscriptions do not articulate such a view, although Mithra is well attested in theophoric names. It thus fell to the king, aided—as always—by the Wise Lord, to set right such offenses. From the Persian perspective, the Athenians who reneged on their commitments of 507 had revealed themselves to be, not just liars, but liars of the worst sort, whose thoughts, words, and deeds had been infected by the powers of evil and, as such, posed a danger to the world order. This was hardly surprising, given their distance from the Persian center, from which perspective the proper response was to conquer and civilize them.

VI

It is not my intention to renarrate the familiar tale of the Persians and the Greeks, inverting the roles of hero and villain. Given the evidence presented above, however, it is not difficult to treat the Persians as the defenders of truth, justice, and morality. My goals, however, are these. First is to recover the story the Persians told themselves about this conflict and about the

Greeks in general. Second is to show that this story was a variant of the story they told whenever they made aggressive war, the goal of which was, in Darius's words, for "the Persian man [to] push back the enemy far from Persia" (DNa §4). Here, it is hardly accidental that the Old Persian word we translate as "enemy" (*paratara*) most literally means "the one farther out, the one more beyond." Just as the fifth column at Bisitun shows that the Achaemenians found it necessary to describe their Scythian enemies as "vulnerable to the Lie" before they could attack them, so they needed to construe the Greeks as "those who lie when making a compact" before they could launch their invasion. A Pahlavi text articulates the same idea in theological and cosmological terms:

> The Wise Lord did not consider it right and just to launch a first strike against the Lie when that other had not yet struck against the heavenly lights, to attack him when he had not yet attacked those lights, to force expiation for evil before the evil had occurred, to take vengeance before there was a cause for vengeance, he whose immutable name is beneficence and nonvengeance, he whose nature is firm and reliable.
>
> (*Dadestan i Denig* 36.13)

Finally, I would frame this as a general principle and suggest that all imperial powers find it easier to undertake projects of conquest when they are able to recode their aggression as benevolence and their victims as their beneficiaries. Typically, they do this by convincing themselves that they wage their wars, however bloody these may be, always on behalf of the highest values: values the other party neither understands nor respects but will learn—at considerable cost but to his own benefit—once victory has been won. The task becomes easier still when the king construes himself as God's chosen.

I

Somehow, Achaemenian kingship managed to include in its sustaining ideology both dynastic and charismatic elements, which often work against each other. Commitment to regular, orderly succession within a privileged family line (the dynastic principle) provided one important base of legitimacy, as evidenced by the concern for royal genealogies and the care with which certain actors manipulated them. We have seen, for instance, how Darius invented the Achaemenian line as an instrument through which he attached himself to Cyrus's family. Early in his career, Cyrus himself did much the same thing when he wanted to persuade his Median subjects that their new ruler was, not some foreign conqueror, but the rightful heir of their own royal family. Thus, while Cyrus's father and patriline were unambiguously Persian, Herodotus and others make his mother the daughter of Astyages, the Median king whom Cyrus overthrew. These stories—which surely originate in pro-Cyrus propaganda—also assert that Astyages had no sons (Herodotus 1.109), thereby construing the young Persian as simultaneously the proper dynastic successor of the Median king and a charismatic leader in his own right whose extraordinary personal abilities were made manifest in his military triumphs (see figure 7).

"Charisma," of course, meant something different in the ancient world than it has come to mean in modernity. Ever since Max Weber, social scientists and others have used the term to describe the exceptional, more or less ineffable qualities that allow certain individuals to exercise effective authority. As the word's etymology indicates, however—it comes from the Greek *charis,* "grace"—the

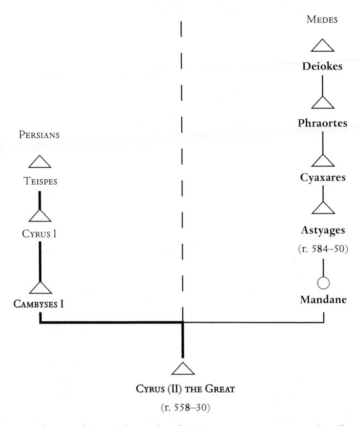

Figure 7: Dual nature of Cyrus's claim to kingship. Names appearing in caps and small caps are mentioned in the Cyrus Cylinder; those in boldface type appear in Herodotus 1.96–130. The thicker lines indicate relations mentioned in the Cyrus Cylinder, the thinner lines those in Herodotus; the dotted lines mark the ethnic division between the Persians and the Medes and suggest the interstitial identity constructed for Cyrus. A Persian according to normal patrilineal principles, he could also be construed as the rightful heir to the Median throne through his mother, given the absence of male issue in the family of Astyages (thus Herodotus 1.109).

idea of charisma has a theological grounding. Most literally, it denotes extraordinary gifts that come as a result of a god's grace and serve as marks legible to all that signal divine favor.

Claims that Cyrus possessed charisma in this stronger sense figure prominently in the legends circulated about him. Thus, the whole narrative is set in motion by two premonitory dreams attributed to Astyages and understood to convey divine revelations. In the first, the king saw his daughter, Mandane, "urinate so much that it filled his city and overflowed all of Asia." On the advice of the magian priests who served as dream interpreters, Astyages decided that it would be dangerous for Mandane to have a mate of equal status, so he married her to Cambyses, whose Persian identity made him much lower than a Mede. Presumably, the offspring of such a man would pose no threat (Herodotus 1.107). This failed to solve the problem, however, for, within a year of the marriage, Astyages was troubled by a second dream:

> He saw a vine grow from his daughter's vagina, and this vine spread over all Asia. Seeing this, he recounted it to the dream interpreters and sent for his daughter to be brought from the Persians, as she was pregnant. Once she arrived, he had her guarded, planning to kill her child, for the magi took his dream as a sign that his daughter's child would rule in his place.
>
> (Herodotus 1.108)

The story plays out as such tales always do. The child is born, narrowly escapes death, is abandoned, is raised by or among animals, then makes his way to the king's court, where he displays his innate excellence, thereby revealing his true nature and identity. After further adventures, he takes the throne, much as the dream prophesied. As in its countless other versions—Sargon, Moses, Jesus, Romulus and Remus, to name but a few—the plot has a fairy-tale quality to it. In all its episodes, one is meant to perceive a divine hand protecting the hero.

Beyond the stereotyped elements that recur in most versions of the narrative, several details make this variant unique and locate it within an Iranian context. First, there is the cowherd who saves Cyrus and raises him from infancy. Herodotus calls this man "Mitradates," an Iranian name that means "created by Mithra" or "under the law of Mithra," thus suggesting that the cowherd and his adoptive son fall under this deity's protection. Second, there is the scene that leads to Cyrus's recognition, which has him ten years old and playing with other boys in his village, who elect him their "king" as part of a game. Once crowned, he assigns roles to the others, congruent with the offices of the Median court: spear bearers, emissaries, palace builders, and the "eye of the king" (i.e., the chief of intelligence). Perhaps this simply shows that all boys know what kingship entails, but it is also possible to see Cyrus as virtually reinventing the royal order on the strength of some deep, innate understanding that he alone possesses. Subsequent action suggests that this is so. For example, when one of the boys—one who happens to be of noble birth—refuses to take orders from a cowherd, Cyrus has the lad seized and beaten. The boy complains to his father, the father complains to the king, and the king calls Cyrus before him. In the face of Astyages' anger, the precocious youngster defends his position. The others made him their king and judged him best suited for this honor. Although the boy who was beaten participated in this decision, he refused to obey Cyrus's orders, and those who defy kings must be taught a lesson. To teach such a lesson is tantamount to *dike* (justice), Cyrus maintains, and, beneath the Greek term, one can perceive a more Persian construct that brings together such notions as law, obedience, truth, and the threat of punishment. Further, Cyrus goes on to say that, if he was wrong in any way, he is himself prepared to accept punishment—i.e., justice—at the hands of the Median king (Herodotus 1.115).

So impressed was he by this child's extraordinary words, thoughts, and manner that Astyages recognized him as Mandane's son, his own grandchild, who had survived and become king, just as his dreams predicted (Herodotus 1.116). The scene is ironic and incredibly complex and involves three juxtaposed conclusions: (1) The children correctly recognize Cyrus's royal charisma, that is, the mysterious gift by means of which Cyrus understands all that kingship entails. (2) Astyages sees the same gift in Cyrus but misunderstands his service as the children's king to be the fulfillment of his own earlier dreams. The prophecy having been realized in this fashion, Astyages believes that the boy poses no further threat. (3) The audience for the story sees things more fully, realizing that the period of mock kingship is not a substitute for real kingship; rather, the former anticipates the latter. Having displayed his innate, extraordinary gifts in this preliminary role, Cyrus can be expected to assume the fullest form of royal power, dispensing with any who stand in his way, his still-obtuse grandfather included. Irresistible forces drive the action. One can call that force "charisma" or "the will of the gods": the two are one and the same.

II

The story proceeds as such stories must. Cyrus survives, returns home, grows to manhood, then organizes the Persians to overthrow the Medes. None of the Greek sources state that Cyrus had divine assistance when he defeated Astyages, although they all imply it. A direct assertion is found, however, in a Babylonian text written shortly after the events themselves. The passage in question—the so-called Dream of Nabonidus—treats a dream once more, this one attributed to Nabonidus, the last king of Babylon (r. 556–539).

In order to understand the dream, it is necessary to know that Nabonidus devoted much of his energy to extending Babylonian influence to the south, toward the Arabian Peninsula. He therefore promoted the worship of the moon god Sîn, whose cult was centered there. Among his most important initiatives toward that end was rebuilding Ehulhul, the temple of Sîn located in the city of Harran.

Such efforts led many to believe that, in his enthusiasm for Sîn, Nabonidus was slighting Marduk, traditionally the foremost god of Babylon, and the priests of Marduk were prime among those making that accusation. In the passage in question, the king tried to answer the charge, representing his policies as having originated with instructions that he received from Marduk himself. In the first year of his reign—so Nabonidus says—Marduk appeared to him in a dream, together with Sîn, and they ordered him to begin work on Ehulhul. There were obstacles, however, that made this difficult, and it is here that things become interesting:

> Respectfully, I said to Marduk, lord of the gods: "The Mede surrounds that temple you tell me to build, and his power is great." Marduk said to me: "The Mede of whom you spoke—he, his land, and the kings who march at his side will not exist." [Within a few years], *he raised up Cyrus, King of Anšan,* his young servant. With his small armies, Cyrus destroyed the numerous Medes. He captured Astyages, King of the Medes, and took him bound to his land. *This was by order of the Great Lord Marduk and Sîn, luminary of heaven and the underworld, whose orders cannot be altered.*

This text was written shortly after the Persians' victory of 550, which marks the emergence of Persia as a major power. Prior to that, Cyrus was the district king of a petty state subordinate to the Medes. It was the Medes, not the Persians, who threatened Babylonian interests before 550, and they were sufficiently formidable that Nabonidus was wary of confronting them. In this situation, Cyrus seemed the perfect answer to Nabonidus's prayers. The "Dream of Nabonidus" makes the same point in a different idiom by depicting the Persian as Marduk's chosen, which is to say the instrument through which Babylon's god put an end to Babylon's chief problem.

Composed comfortably after the fact, this dream omen also provided a way for Babylon to take credit for the victory won by Cyrus's troops. The Persian was nothing, the text argues, until Marduk chose him and raised him up. Only in the most superficial sense was he or his army responsible, for the ultimate author of the triumph was Marduk. And, as long as Marduk controlled such things, Babylon had nothing to fear.

Within ten years, however, circumstances had changed. Persian power had increased with further conquests, while Babylonian power had declined. What is more, internal rifts had opened up within the Babylonian elite. There were difficulties between Nabonidus and his son, Bel-shazzar, who governed the city during the years (553–543) his father resided in Teima, a city far to the south. More important, the conflict between the king and the Marduk priests became worse because, while he was resident in Teima, Nabonidus did not hold the Akitu ceremony, an annual ritual in which the king renewed his kingship by grasping the hands of Marduk's statue in the god's temple of

Esagila. The omission of this gesture, more than anything, scandalized the priests, leading them to believe, not just that Nabonidus was a bad king, but that he had lost all legitimate right to office by his failure to renew it. Some wished him overthrown, and, toward that end, they circulated accusations of all sorts that reached the ears of Cyrus, who, in 539, was turning his attention to Babylon. In the Cyrus Cylinder—a text written late that year by Cyrus's scribes—we can hear the Persians making use of the discourse that these disgruntled priests circulated against Nabonidus:

> An unworthy man has been installed in the kingship of his land. . . . Daily he spoke without reverence. In hatefulness he let the sacrificial rules be suspended. He ruined the cult. . . . He established the worship of Marduk, king of the gods, in other cities, but ended it in his own. Daily he did evil against his city. . . . His people were under the yoke without rest. He ruined them all. *On their complaints, the Lord of the gods became enraged and left their region.*
>
> (CB §§2–3)

This passage describes a situation of crisis, in which a whole series of grave offenses—religious above all, but also political and economic—have accumulated and compounded until the people cry out to their national god, a god as dissatisfied with the king as they are. In response to this expression of general misery, Marduk abandons his city, which is a way of saying (and understanding), first, that the city has lost its order, support, and security and, second, that the ruler is no longer a proper king, that his relation to Marduk is definitively broken.

Given that the city's relation to its god is normally mediated through the king, the question must arise: Is Babylon's relation to Marduk also definitively broken? Alternatively, at the level of narrative, one might ask: Did Marduk abandon Babylon, or did he abandon only Nabonidus? Did he leave forever, or is his absence only temporary? Having left the city, where did he go? Whom did he see, and what did he do? The answers were not long in coming:

> Marduk searched all lands, seeking, according to his heart's wish, a righteous ruler whose hand he would grasp. *He pronounced the name of Cyrus, King of Anšan.* He proclaimed his name for kingship of all the world. . . . Marduk, the Great Lord, who leads his people, looked joyfully at Cyrus's good deeds and righteous heart. He ordered him to go to his city, Babylon. He set him on the road to Babylon and marched at his side like a friend and companion. . . . Without conflict or battle, he let him enter Babylon, his city. He saved Babylon from oppression. Nabonidus, the King who did not worship, fell into his hands.
>
> (CB §§4–5)

This passage can be understood as a strategic reworking—and aggressive redeployment—of anti-Nabonidus propaganda developed by the Marduk priests, together with motifs that Cyrus found in the "Dream of Nabonidus," the text that first cast him in the role of Marduk's darling. In other ways, however, it breaks decisively with traditional Babylonian ideology, which not only connected Marduk and the city via the king's mediation but also defined all three elements of this system in the same terms. They were both good (i.e., pious, moral, successful) and Babylonian. What is more, these two criteria—moral and ethnic—are presented as so closely aligned as to be inextricable.

The Cyrus Cylinder revises this by systematically disarticulating the two criteria in the contrast it draws between Nabonidus (bad, but Babylonian) and Cyrus (just the reverse), then having Marduk choose between them (see figure 8). When the text has Marduk find Cyrus, sing his praise, take his hand, and lead him back to the city, it accomplishes two objectives, which in some ways are one and the same. First, like the "Dream of Nabonidus," it appropriates Cyrus, his excellence, and his accomplishments all on behalf of Marduk. Second, it appropriates Cyrus on behalf of Babylon, making him, in effect, an adoptive Babylonian. The fact that Cyrus entered the city without a battle is constituted as proof that the god has given the city to him and given

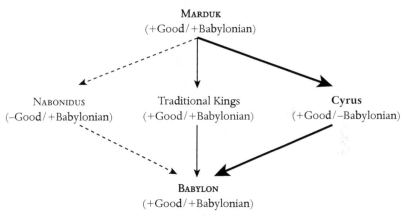

Figure 8: Events of 539, as narrated by the Cyrus Cylinder. The thinner lines represent the established Babylonian ideology of kingship, in which morality and ethnicity are consistently associated. The dotted lines represent the crisis that occurred when the Marduk priesthood concluded that Nabonidus had failed his religious and moral obligations and, thus, was an improper king. The thicker lines represent the action described in the text, wherein Marduk abandons Babylon, finds Cyrus, recognizes him as pious and moral, then brings him back to Babylon, where the people's reception ratifies him as their king. Caps and small caps indicate the alignment that was operative until 539. Boldface type indicates the configuration that replaced it after that date.

him to the city. The reaction attributed to the populace serves to ratify Marduk's decision: "All the people of Babylon, the whole of Sumer and Akkad, leaders and state officials, bowed before Cyrus and kissed his feet. They rejoiced at his kingship. Their faces shone. . . . They praised his name" (CB §6).

To claim that one's armies are welcomed as liberators is one of the great imperial fantasies and serves several related purposes. In the first place, it addresses needs of one's own, for it is far easier to commit the acts of violence that make conquest possible when one is convinced that the cause is, not greedy or base, but moral and divinely ordained. Second, it is helpful to propagate such a view among one's newly conquered subjects, for if they can be persuaded that the new master is a distinct improvement over their former rulers—better yet, that he comes to them courtesy of a loving god who sincerely cares for their welfare—they will be ever so much more likely to accept the yoke in relative quiescence.

Rarely, however, are occupying armies and foreign rulers received with appreciation, invested with legitimacy, or accepted as one's own. Sometimes, occupiers and the occupied cooperate in staging scenes that let the former preserve their fantasies—since there will always be toadies eager to ingratiate themselves while others mask their feelings with smiles and bide their time before taking action. That things were more complicated in Babylon than Cyrus's propagandists suggested (and perhaps believed) becomes clear from the string of rebellions that followed in 522, 521, 484, and 482, rebellions that sought to restore national independence and, in the first two cases at least, the native line of kings that ended with Nabonidus.

III

Others also showed interest in Cyrus's conquest of Babylon, perhaps none more so than that city's Jewish population, who had been taken there as captives in 586, when Nebuchadnezzar defeated Judah, destroyed the Temple, and ended the Davidic line of kings. Prophets like Isaiah and Jeremiah interpreted this catastrophe as God's chastisement for Israel's failings, but they also anticipated the day when God would accomplish Babylon's fall, then restore the Jews to their home and place their ancestral kings on the throne once more. In the 540s, hopes came to center on Cyrus, as reflected in Isa. 40–55 (the so-called Second or Deutero-Isaiah), which was written during that period.

In some ways, this text resembles the "Dream of Nabonidus" and the Cyrus Cylinder, particularly in its attempt to give YHWH credit for Persian triumphs and to represent these as fulfilling the Lord's promises to his people. That task was complicated, however, by the fact that God's purported instrument was, not the rightful heir in the line of David, as Jews commonly expected, but a foreign king previously unknown. To normalize this unexpected turn of events, the text—which served Persian interests at least as well as those of the Jews—has YHWH introduce Cyrus in these terms: "He is my shepherd, and he shall fulfill all my purpose" (Isa. 44:28). More fully, in a text often referred to as the Cyrus Oracle, the Lord instructs both the Persian king and the community of Israel:

> Thus says the LORD to his anointed, to Cyrus,
>   whose right hand I have grasped,
> to subdue nations before him
>   and ungird the loins of kings,
> to open doors before him
>   that gates may not be closed:
> "I will go before you
>   and level the mountains,
> I will break in pieces the doors of bronze
>   and cut asunder the bars of iron,
> I will give you the treasures of darkness
>   and the hoards in secret places,
> that you may know that it is I, the LORD,
>   the God of Israel, who call you by your name.
> For the sake of my servant Jacob,
>   and Israel my chosen,
> I call you by your name,
>   I surname you, though you do not know me.
> I am the LORD, and there is no other,
>   besides me there is no God;
>   I gird you, though you do not know me,
> that men may know, from the rising of the sun
>   and from the west, that there is none besides me;
>   I am the LORD, and there is no other.
> I form light and create darkness,
>   I make weal and create woe,
>   I am the LORD, who do all these things."

(Isa. 45:1–7)

Repeatedly, this passage insists that there is no other god than YHWH, which means that no other divine agency can account for the Persian's success. It also has YHWH claim responsibility for the creation of light *and* darkness, which serves to differentiate him from the dualistic traditions of Iran, where the qualities of light and darkness precede creation itself. The result is clear: although Persian by birth, Cyrus has been adopted once more, this time by the God of Israel, on behalf of his people.

Much like Marduk in the Cyrus Cylinder, Isaiah's YHWH grasps the Persian by the right hand (Isa. 45:1), marches before him (45:2), girds him for battle (45:5), grants him victory (45:1–3), calls him by name (45:4), and invests him with royal titles (45:1, 4), including one that has exceptional significance. At 45:1, Cyrus is called "YHWH's Anointed," "Anointed" being a term that denotes he whom God has chosen as the legitimate king of the Judean people. Initially applied to Saul, Israel's first king, it was thereafter used for David and his descendants. In the period of Babylonian captivity, it came to denote the savior, descended of David, who was expected to liberate Israel as its rightful king. In later, apocalyptic literature, the same title is used of the future hero who would overthrow occupying imperial powers—the Seleucids or Romans—and restore Israel's independence or, even more grandly, usher in the kingdom of heaven. This is why the term that we render "the Anointed"— Hebrew *māšîaḥ*, English *Messiah*—has such resonance, as does its translation in the Septuagint and New Testament: Greek *khristos*, English *Christ*.

In its original context, this is a term of national self-assertion that voices resentment of and resistance to all occupying powers. As a rule, the Bible never bestows the title "YHWH's Anointed" on anyone save a son of Israel's royal family. The sole exception is Cyrus (Isa. 45:1), who saved the Jews from captivity in Babylon but hardly restored independence. Rather, Israel and Judah became part of his empire and remained so until the Achaemenians yielded power to Alexander.

Receiving the title "YHWH's Anointed" clearly would have been useful to Cyrus since it conferred local legitimacy, connecting him to both the God and the royal lineage of Israel/Judea. The question, then, is why Deutero-Isaiah should have broken with tradition and bestowed it on him. Behind this choice, scholars have often perceived negotiations between the Persians and the Jews, in which, for example, the promise to rebuild the Temple in Jerusalem figured as a quid pro quo. Whatever the particulars may have been, the discursive strategy that Cyrus pursued in this case is consistent with that which we have observed elsewhere. Thus, representation of himself as YHWH's elect advanced the same kind of charismatic claims as did the Cyrus Cylinder's discussion of Marduk and Babylon. Similarly, asserting some connection to the Davidic lineage (even if only implicitly) provided a semblance of dynastic legitimation, much as his birth legends construed Cyrus as the heir to the Median kings.

In the mid-520s, Cambyses, Cyrus's son and successor, would employ much the same strategies to consolidate his conquest of Egypt. Egyptian documents show that he represented himself as a proper Pharaoh: a divine being, "Horus," "son of Ra," "beloved of the goddess Ouadjet." Legends preserved in Herodotus and Ctesias also show the kind of genealogical legerdemain with which we have become familiar. Thus, Cambyses circulated a story that, not only justified his invasion of Egypt, but also gave him—or his descendants—a dynastic right to the Egyptian throne. In one variant, the narrative recounts how Cambyses asked Apries, the last king of Egypt in the Saïte dynasty, to send one of his daughters to him. Apries, however, was reluctant, knowing that his daughter would become a concubine, not Cambyses' wife. Cognizant of Persian power, and fearing Cambyses' wrath should this request-cum-threat/provocation be denied, Apries decided to send a woman named Nitetis and say that she was his daughter when, in fact, she was the child of the former king, Amasis, whom Apries had killed and from whom he usurped the throne.

When Cambyses discovered what Apries had done, he knew him to be a liar. Herodotus describes Cambyses' anger, but this recodes as personal emotion a judgment grounded in the moral cosmology considered in chapter 2. The Egyptians being located beyond the empire's southwest border, it was only natural that they were subject to the Lie. Accordingly, they had need of the civilizing/moralizing/perfecting—and not just conquering—influence radiating out from the Persian center.

In addition, the story identified Apries as someone who had no dynastic right to be king and lied (once more) in representing himself as such. Further still, it connected Cambyses to the legitimate Saïte line via Nitetis, making any children she might bear him the true and proper heirs to this throne. Another variant goes further still and has Nitetis sent to Cyrus, making her Cambyses' mother and giving Cambyses the best claim to the Saïte throne (see figure 9).

In all this, one perceives another twist on the same general pattern as an Achaemenian king labored—with considerable ingenuity—to combine dynastic and charismatic arguments for the legitimacy of his rule.

IV

The materials considered thus far show how Cyrus and Cambyses enlisted the gods of the people they conquered to help forestall the possibility of native unrest and to legitimate their rule. Conceivably, the Teispid kings were eclectic and/or opportunistic in their theology, worshipping Marduk in Babylon, YHWH in Jerusalem, Horus and Ra in Memphis, Apollo in Miletus, and so on. Debate continues as to whether the policies they adopted toward the deities of their subject peoples showed a remarkably enlightened tolerance

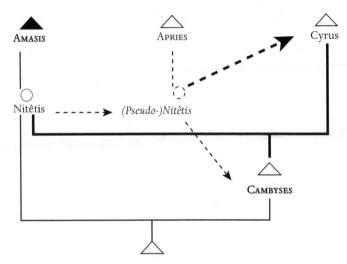

Figure 9: Narratives legitimating Cambyses as king of Egypt. Caps and small caps indicate Egyptian pharoahs. Boldface type shows those to whom these stories grant legitimacy. All variants agree that Apries slew Amasis, took his daughter Nitetis, and tried to pass her off as his own. Variant 1 (Herodotus 3.1 etc.), indicated by the thinner line, has him give her to Cambyses, thereby constituting the son that she will bear him as heir to the line of Amasis. In Variant 2 (Herodotus 3.2 etc.), indicated by the thicker line, Nitetis is given to Cyrus, thereby legitimating Cambyses. The dotted lines represent relations that the stories treat as intentional misrepresentations of fact. Italicization indicates characters who are similarly treated.

or were based on calculated self-interest. It is clear, however, that the early Persian kings showed little interest in imposing their beliefs. Indeed, as regards Cyrus and Cambyses, we have virtually no idea what their native beliefs might have been. In no surviving text or monument of either king does an Iranian deity appear.

Things are quite different when it comes to Darius, who introduced the Wise Lord at Bisitun, where he appears, not once or twice, but a full seventy-six times. While the text subtly acknowledges the existence of other deities, twice speaking of "the Wise Lord and the other gods who are," none of these other deities is named, and none will be named in any Achaemenian inscription until more than a century later, when Artaxerxes II (r. 404–359) named Mithra and Anahita alongside the Wise Lord, now occupying first place in a triad.

In most ways, the Bisitun text assumes that the reader will know who the Wise Lord is, but the Elamite version of this trilingual inscription adds a gloss intended for outsiders, identifying the Wise Lord as "god of the Iranians." The term it employs for this purpose (Elamite *har-ri-ya* [= Old Persian *ariya*,

"Aryan, Iranian"]) is a loanword taken from that with which Persians and Medes named themselves, their language, and their god: the three great bases of national identity.

From the Wise Lord's very first textual appearance, Darius emphasizes his own privileged relation to the deity:

> Proclaims Darius the King: By the Wise Lord's will I am King. The Wise Lord bestowed the kingship/kingdom on me.
>
> (DB §5)

The passage is brief but loaded. Here, Darius asserts that he is king by virtue of the Wise Lord's "will" (*vašna*), a term that can also be translated "grace," "favor," or "power." More than any of the other Achaemenians, Darius consistently grounded his claims to legitimacy in this phrase, and the reason is hardly mysterious, for his dynastic claim was weak. By his own admission, the line of Cyrus had died out in 522, and he gained the throne by assassinating his predecessor, who was, he insisted, an imposter ("Gaumata"), not Cyrus's son. The story is implausible, but, even if one gives Darius every benefit of the doubt, glaring anomalies still remain. Thus, as he acknowledged in a late inscription at Susa, in 522 Darius's father *and grandfather* were still alive, which means that these two men—and who knows how many others—had better claims to the kingship than he had.

Given these problems, Darius made a game effort to plead his cause in dynastic terms, but, like most usurpers, he was more inclined to stress the charismatic side of the argument. The formula "By the Wise Lord's will, I am King" is one of the chief ways in which he did this, announcing himself as God's chosen. In DB §5 (cited above), and a bit later in DB §13, he follows this formula with one that is, perhaps, even more significant, for it alludes to the ritual of royal investiture: "The Wise Lord bestowed the kingship/kingdom on me." Comparing different versions of this formula lets one trace the growth of Persian power and the empire's conception of itself. Thus, the earliest variants have the Wise Lord confer the land and people of Persia, that is, one province only. Later ones have him invest Darius with *xšaça,* a term that fuses the senses of "kingship" and "kingdom," denoting both royal power and the multiple provinces over which that power is exercised.

Toward the end of his reign, Darius apparently concluded that older words like *xšaça* were inadequate for the entity that God had bestowed on him. That domain was destined to keep expanding until it reached the world's outer limits. Only then would it realize the status implied in its new name: *būmi,* "earth/empire" (cf. chapter 1). When all space is unified under Achaemenian power, historical time will come to an end, the king's mission having been accomplished, God's will having been made real, and all cause of suffering/struggle/change having been effectively eliminated.

V

Whatever terminology might be used for the nature of the power and office conferred, performing the rituals of royal investiture was crucial, and, without this enactment of divine favor, legitimacy would always be lacking. Achaemenian discourse thus describes anyone who would assume royal office without such a ritual as having "seized" or "captured" the throne. Such a man might exercise illicit power for a time, but he was hardly a proper king. In claiming that title without ritual confirmation of divine favor, he misunderstood and misrepresented himself and his situation. His life, in effect, had become a Lie, and the effects on others were pernicious, for this lie undermined the social, political, and cosmic order, producing confusion, riot, and rebellion.

Skillfully deploying these themes and this vocabulary, the Bisitun text contrasted Gaumata's kingship with that of Darius, systematically constructing the latter as deriving from the Wise Lord and the former quite the opposite (see table 6).

VI

Bestowing kingship is one of several things the Wise Lord is typically said to do, but, in truth, the range of action attributed to him by the royal inscriptions is pretty small, with five verbs accounting for 93 percent of the total. All these take very few objects and occur in highly restrictive contexts. With one exception, moreover, all of them focus on relations with the king. In order of frequency, these verbs are the following:

1. *²dā-,* "to establish, set in place for the first time, create" (seventy-three occurrences, 39 percent of the total). This is the one verb not focused on the king, although the formulaic descriptions of the Wise Lord's creative activity—considered in the next chapter—have profound implications for him.

2. *pā-,* "to protect" (thirty-one occurrences, 17 percent of the total). This verb always appears in the imperative form, as part of the prayers that conclude many inscriptions. In these, the king always entreats the Wise Lord to protect him and something to which he feels closely connected. These include his house-

TABLE 6: Processes through Which Gaumata and Darius Became King

	Gaumata[a]	Darius[b]
Initial speech act	*He lied* to the people, saying thus: "I am Bardiya, the son of Cyrus, the brother of Cambyses."	*I prayed* to the Wise Lord for assistance.
Effect or response	*Then the people all became rebellious* from Cambyses. It went over to him—Persia and Media and the other lands/peoples.	*The Wise Lord bore me aid.*
Subsequent violent events	*Nine days had passed* of the month Garmapada [1 July 522] *when he seized the kingship/kingdom.* . . .	*Ten days had passed* of the month Bagayadi [29 September 522] *when I,* with a few men, *slew that Gaumata the Magus.* . . .
Fate of predecessor	*This kingship/kingdom, of which Gaumata the Magus deprived Cambyses,* this kingship/kingdom was our lineage's since long ago. Then *Gaumata the Magus deprived Cambyses of Persia and Media and the other lands/peoples.* He took them as his own. He made them his own possession.	*I deprived him of the kingship/kingdom.*
Assumption of office	*He became King.*	BY THE WISE LORD'S WILL I *became King.*
Ritual investiture		THE WISE LORD BESTOWED THE KINGSHIP/KINGDOM ON ME.

Note: In successive paragraphs, the Bisitun text contrasts the two, constructing the former as profane and illegitimate, the latter as just the reverse. Italicization calls attention to the most pointed items of the contrast. Caps and small caps indicate the most important items of all: the divine favor and sacred rituals associated with Darius and lacking for Gaumata.

[a] DB §§11–12.
[b] DB §13.

hold, his land/people, his kingship/kingdom, the things he has built, and also—on occasion—his father and the things his father has built.

3. *kar-,* "to make, do, build" (twenty-eight occurrences, 15 percent of the total). Although this verb is extremely broad in its semantics and can be used in countless ways, when the Wise Lord appears as its subject, the range is considerably narrowed. It occurs twenty-five times in variants of the sentence "The Wise Lord made X King."

4. *bar-,* "to bear, carry, bring" (twenty-eight occurrences, 15 percent of the total).

In the entire corpus, the Wise Lord is said to have delivered one thing only, always to the king or his armies. The item in question is "aid" or "support" (Old Persian *upastām*), specifically the kind of supernatural assistance that yields military victory, even for troops that are badly outnumbered.

5. *frā-bar-*, "to confer, convey, bestow" (fourteen occurrences, 7.5 percent of the total). As we have seen, this verb occurs only in the formula that describes rituals of royal investiture, and the beneficiary of such action is always the man who begins as God's chosen candidate and ends as the rightful king. That which the Wise Lord bestows varies from "this Persian land/people" in the earliest inscriptions to "this kingship/kingdom" for most of Darius's reign, to "this earth/empire" toward its end, but, in all cases, the king receives the ability to exercise legitimate power over this domain as a result of God's intervention and directly from his hand.

After creating the world, the Wise Lord thus seems to have had nothing to do, save the work of locating worthy candidates, installing them as king, securing their safety, and ensuring their victory over adversaries. Or so, at least, it seemed to the Achaemenian monarchs, who must have wondered from time to time just why God was so good to them.

VII

Cyrus described the process through which he won Marduk's favor thus: "Marduk searched all lands, seeking a righteous ruler according to his heart's wish. . . . He looked joyfully at Cyrus's good deeds and righteous heart" (CB §4). Darius similarly described moral considerations as the basis of his selection:

> Proclaims Darius the king: For this reason the Wise Lord bore me aid, he and the other gods that are: Because I was not vulnerable to the Lie, I was not a speaker of lies, I was not one whose actions are deceitful, neither I nor my family.
>
> (DB §63)

Although the Lie operates at the levels of thought, word, and deed, Darius was impervious at all three. One is reminded of the eschatological hero in Zoroastrian myth who bears the name "Truth Incarnate," of whom it is said:

> The comrades of victorious
> Truth Incarnate stride forth,
> Good in thought, good in speech,
> Good in deeds, good in religion.

Their tongues have not
The least bit of false speech in them.
[The demon] Furor, he of the bloody club, whose destiny is evil,
Flees before them.
With truth he will vanquish the evil Lie,
That creature of darkness, whose seed is evil.

(*Yašt* 19.95)

In similar fashion, Darius seems to suggest that the Wise Lord recognized him as the very antithesis of the Lie. Accordingly, God raised him to kingship and charged him with a restorative mission:

Proclaims Darius the King: When the Wise Lord saw this earth/empire seething in turmoil, then he bestowed it on me. He made me king. I am king. By the Wise Lord's will, I set things in their proper place.

(DNa §4)

To appreciate all that this passage entails, it is necessary to learn something about Achaemenian cosmology: more specifically, to ask how the Achaemenians construed the nature, structure, and purpose of creation.

Creation   4

When considering the actions most frequently attributed to the Wise Lord, I noted that only one of these—the most common of all—did not have the Persian king as its immediate object and beneficiary. This is the act denoted by the verb $^2d\bar{a}$-, which is usually translated "to create," but which has a somewhat more nuanced sense. Close analysis of its semantics suggests that it refers, not to material creation ex nihilo, but to the act of putting a set of entities in place for the first time and establishing their proper position within the ordered cosmos. This action is exalted and sacred, the verb appropriately solemn. No one save the Wise Lord is capable of creation in this sense, and no one else ever appears as this verb's grammatical subject. Moreover, this verb occurs only in the formulaic account of the world's foundation that is continually repeated.

In truth, the narrative of creation dominates later Achaemenian discourse, in terms of both its frequency and its emphatic placement at the beginning of every inscription in which it appears. Twenty-three inscriptions open in this fashion: ten attributed to Darius (r. 522–486), who modified the wording several times until he considered it perfect; nine more to Xerxes (486–465), who introduced only one, very minor change; and one each to Artaxerxes I (465–424), Darius II (423–404), Artaxerxes II (404–359), and Artaxerxes III (359–338), all of whom continued to repeat the wording faithfully. Thus, of the post-Bisitun inscriptions that have at least three paragraphs, almost three-quarters (twenty-three of thirty-two) begin with the myth of creation. While this may be the result of taking the principle of beginning at the beginning to its logical extreme, the salient position assigned to this narrative has other effects and motives. Most important, it invests all that follows with a cosmogonic consciousness: a concern for how the Creator conceived his world and what he intended for it.

While the creation accounts of the inscriptions are brief, their appearance of simplicity is misleading, as earlier studies have shown (above all Herrenschmidt 1977). Rather, their brevity is the product of a formulaic diction that is highly compressed and extremely efficient. While spare, each phrase conveys much information with great economy, not just through its precise wording, but also through its place in the overall structure. As an example, consider the most common account of creation:

> A great god is the Wise Lord, *who created this earth, who created that sky, who created mankind, who created happiness for mankind, who made Darius king:* one king over many, one commander over many.
>
> (DNa §1 etc.)

Five separate acts of creation are mentioned in this passage. All are understood as unambiguously good, having been accomplished by an absolutely benevolent creator who exists from eternity and is not himself created. The five creations are not equal in their age and status, however, since one is subtly set apart from the others. Thus, while the first four creations came into being at some unspecified moment in primordial eternity, the Wise Lord made Darius king at a precise historical moment: 29 September 522.

The text further distinguishes between the first four creations and the fifth through a detail of vocabulary. Thus, for the Wise Lord's initial creative acts, it uses the verb *ʾdā-*, whose semantics have already been considered. When it turns to his intervention in history via the election and investiture of Darius, it employs a less discriminating verb, *kar-*, which can take both humans and gods as its subject and can denote any act of doing, making, or shaping, including the most menial.

The point is clear. The Wise Lord's first four acts—all described with the same lofty verb and all located in prehistoric eternity—form a set, which can be referred to as *the original creation*. Once that original creation was complete, there followed an interval about which the texts are mostly silent. During this interval, the world seemed complete, and the Wise Lord ceased his creative labors. But something happened, something that roused the deity and forced him to take a new kind of action. From this perspective, making Darius king seems to have been something like a divine afterthought: the Wise Lord's response to some unexpected event or his attempt to redress some newly arisen problem.

II

Some obvious questions follow: What happened between the original creation and Darius's accession in September 522? What was the problem to which the new king construed himself as the Wise Lord's solution? Before addressing these questions, however, let us take a step back and look at the four original creations, paying particular attention to the logic that constituted them as a set. Here, we can begin by noting that the first two creations—earth and sky—are inanimate while mankind and happiness for mankind are not. Similarly, the first two items belong to nature, the second two to culture. Further still, earth and sky define the space in which living creatures emerge while also providing the material substance necessary for them to flourish.

Earth is the first of the natural/inanimate elements to be named and, presumably, the first to appear. The term used is *būmi*, which has been discussed earlier (see chapters 1 and 3). In its older, more concrete usage, this word denotes, not just soil, but the broad surface of the globe, including water and land. To have earth appear before heaven seems unusual, or at least counterintuitive, since most of the world's mythologies put heaven first, thereby recoding the precedence of deities over mortals and justifying the rule of the "high" over the "lowly." To invert that order—as all but one of the Old Persian variants do—can surely be no accident and must have had its motive. Here, the expansion of *būmi*'s semantics to include, not only "earth," but also "empire" is surely relevant. Thus, as Clarisse Herrenschmidt has observed, if the account of creation is always the first paragraph of any inscription in which it occurs, it is most frequently followed by an equally formulaic citation of four royal titles, listed in a sequence of increasing scope and grandeur. The combination of these two paragraphs produces a pattern that begins and ends with *būmi* (see figure 10). The effect is to suggest that all began when the Wise Lord created the earth, somehow knowing, even intending, that Darius, and his Achaemenian heirs, should, at some later time, become king over this earth-cum-empire. When that happens, his plan is accomplished.

The myth thus begins with the Wise Lord, who puts earth and then sky in their places. Earth will be the home of mankind, just as sky will become the deity's primary locus. If sky and God are above and earth and the human below, simple curiosity prompts one to ask: Is that all there is? Is there nothing below the below? The text is silent on that point, but its silence implies an answer: If anything lies below the earth, it is no part of God's creation.

Zoroastrian literature has something to say on this question and offers a hint worth pursuing. There, as we have seen (see chapter 2), the Wise Lord and the Evil Spirit—who is also called "the Foul Spirit" (*Gannāg Mēnōg*), "the Adversary" (*hamēstar, petyārag*), and, at times, "the Lie" (*druz*)—have existed

§1. A great god is the Wise Lord
a. **Who created this earth (būmi)**
b. Who created that heaven
c. Who created mankind
d. Who created happiness for mankind

Who made Darius king
One king over many, one commander over many

§2. I am Darius
a. Great King
b. King of Kings
c. King of lands / peoples (of all / many races)
d. **King in this great, far-reaching earth / empire (būmi)**

Figure 10: Correlation of cosmogony and royal titles in seventeen inscriptions. The term *būmi* opens and concludes this complex discourse but has its natural (i.e., strictly physical) denotation in the first instance and its cultural (i.e., sociopolitical) denotation in the second. Key items of the discourse are also correlated with one another by the adjective "great" (Old Persian *vazṛka*), which denotes the paramount item of a hierarchical set. Here, as elsewhere in the inscriptions, it is used for three objects only: among deities, the Wise Lord; among humans, the Achaemenian king; among polities, the empire.

independently of each other from time immemorial, one being located in the radiant above, the other in the darkness below. Their first encounter follows on the Wise Lord's original creation:

> The Creator of the world made the spiritual creation pure and undefiled. He made the material creation immortal, unaging, without hunger, without bondage, without sorrow, and without pain. That remained the state of things until there erupted from the darkness the Lie of wickedness, who is not a right chooser of wisdom, goodness, and beneficence. He is a wrecker, murderous, ignorant, deceitful, malicious, misleading, destructive, wasteful, and envious. . . . *From his own base, which is the very depth of darkness,* he established a boundary to the darkness and a border to the lights. He stared at the light and the undefiled creation of the Wise Lord with terror and demonic contemplation. In envy, full of vengeance, perfect in deceit, he sprang up to seize, destroy, smash, and ruin this well-made creation of the gods.
>
> (*Dadestan i Denig* 36.4–8)

III

Turning to the animate or cultural parts of the original creation, we find a situation no less complex. The first item—mankind—raises few problems, although we should note that the term used (Old Persian *martiya*) occurs in the singular, signaling the initial unity of the human species. Neither political, nor ethnic, nor even sexual differentiation is acknowledged, only humanity as such, and Zoroastrian versions of the cosmogony treat the world's various populations as having all been initially encompassed in the prototype of the species as created by the Wise Lord.

Returning to the Achaemenian inscriptions, the fourth item of the original creation is surely the most difficult to interpret, although its emphasis on the goodness of creator and creation alike is transparent and unmistakable. Still, it is no easy matter to sort out just what is meant by "happiness for mankind" (*šiyāti . . . martyahyā*), the sole abstraction in the set and a fairly unusual item in the world's mythologies of creation.

Several discussions have enhanced our understanding of how the Achaemenians theorized happiness. First, Herrenschmidt 1991 identified a noncosmogonic context in which the same term appeared. This is Darius's assertion: "If the Persian people were protected, their happiness [*šiyāti*] would be undisturbed for a long time" (DPe §3). This emphasis on protection prompts the question: What were the threats that menaced happiness, against which protection was necessary? When and how did they come into being? How did their appearance change the human condition, compromising the original state of happiness? Another inscription at Persepolis that stands immediately next to the one just cited helps answer some of these questions:

> May the Wise Lord protect this land/people from the enemy army, from famine, from the Lie. Against this land/people may the enemy army not come, nor famine, nor the Lie.
>
> (DPd §3)

Each of the three evils mentioned in this text involves the negation of some primary good. Thus, the enemy army disrupts peace, while famine is scarcity of food. Both threaten life, but most heinous of all is the Lie, which obviates truth and eats away at the moral, sociopolitical, and cosmic order necessary for all decent, civilized existence. Protection effectively negates these negations, thereby ensuring the three primary goods: peace, (abundant) food, and truth. It is this state that is construed as happiness.

As a principle of method, Herrenschmidt restricted her study to Achaemenian evidence. Others have extended their inquiries to consider the Avestan cognate terms *šyāta*, "happiness," and *š(y)ā-*, "to be happy," whose usage differs from that of Old Persian *šiyāti* in two important ways. The first of these is temporal, for Zoroastrians understood happiness as something that people can sometimes win in the present but that righteous souls usually receive postmortem. In contrast, the Achaemenians understood happiness

as the original and proper state of mankind, as per the Wise Lord's intentions. The appearance of enemy armies, famine, and the Lie—presumably
during the interval between the original creation and Darius's accession—
caused the loss of happiness as humanity's natural, god-given condition. Thereafter, people have to exert themselves if they are to gain happiness in this life,
and their effort also helps secure them a blessed state in the hereafter. To restore happiness as the general condition of all mankind, however, is something else: an extremely arduous undertaking.

One can schematize this temporal difference as follows. Both Avestan and
Achaemenian texts entertain happiness as a possibility and a desire that the
righteous can realize in both the present and the heavenly future. Beyond
this, however, the Achaemenian inscriptions also make it a feature of the
primordial past. In similar fashion, both the Avesta and the inscriptions identify two means to win happiness, truth and ritual speech, to which the inscriptions add a third, obedience to the law:

> You who come hereafter, if you should think, "May I be *happy* [*šiyāta*] when
> living and righteous when dead," conduct yourself according to that law that
> the Wise Lord established. Worship the Wise Lord with ritual speech accom-
> panied by truth. The man who conducts himself according to the law that the
> Wise Lord established and who worships the Wise Lord with ritual speech ac-
> companied by truth, he becomes happy when living and righteous when dead.
>
> (XPh §4d)

IV

Some of the later Zoroastrian texts written in Pahlavi also help nuance our understanding, particularly the cosmogonic accounts from which excerpts have
already been cited (see chapters 2 and 4). Using much the same terminology
as the Achaemenian inscriptions, these texts tell how, in the endless time before history, the Wise Lord established six—not four—perfect creations:

> The Wise Lord created six creations of the material world. First was sky, sec-
> ond water, third land, fourth plants, fifth animals, sixth man.
>
> (*Greater Bundahišn* 3.7 [TD² MS 33.2–5])

As table 7 shows, this list is quite close to that of the inscriptions. Three
items are identical (sky, earth, mankind), and a fourth match is implicit, the
Achaemenian inscriptions grouping water and land together under the head-

TABLE 7: The Order of Creation as Narrated in Achaemenian and Zoroastrian Sources

	Achaemenian[a]	Zoroastrian[b]	
1	Earth	Sky	1
		Water	2
2	Sky	Land	3
		Plants	4
		Animals	5
3	Mankind	Mankind	6
4	Happiness for mankind		

[a] DNa §1 etc.
[b] GBd 3.7 etc.

ing "earth" (*būmi*), the Pahlavi texts treating them separately (using the term *zamīg*, not *būm*, for "land").

Just as the Achaemenian account listed inanimate creations (earth and sky) before animate ones (mankind and happiness), the same pattern is evident in the Pahlavi texts, which add a further wrinkle. Thus, after the inanimate entities (sky, earth, and water), and before the animate ones (animals and mankind), a mediating entity appears: plants, which are living but have no soul. The Pahlavi sequence is also governed by a second organizing principle, the order of creation mirroring the food chain. Thus, beginning in the sky (creation no. 1), water (no. 2), in the form of rain, falls to the land (no. 3), which effectively eats or consumes it. Moisture metabolized by the soil causes the growth of plants (no. 4), which are eaters of water and earth. Animals (no. 5) then eat plants and water, while humans (no. 6) eat all the above.

This attention to processes of eating and being eaten calls to mind the analysis offered above suggesting that abundant food, along with peace and truth, was tantamount to happiness for mankind. It should also be understood that food is, not just the antithesis of famine, but the basis of life and health as well as—alongside sex—a prime source of sensuous pleasure. All this raises the possibility that the Achaemenian and Zoroastrian lists of original creations may be even closer than we originally imagined. For, just as earth in the first encompasses land and water in the second, so happiness for mankind may, similarly, encompass plants and animals (see figure 11).

Zoroastrian doctrine constituted the Wise Lord and his original creations as entirely good. Accordingly, the world's imperfections were understood to have appeared at a later moment, as the result of what is usually called "the Assault" (Pahlavi *ēbgat*) of the Evil Spirit. We have seen that the Evil Spirit is

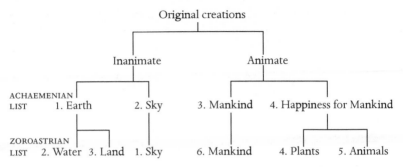

Figure 11: Achaemenian and Zoroastrian accounts of creation.

antithetical to the Wise Lord in all ways, and, here, two of the most important differences between them must be noted. First, while the Wise Lord is distinguished by his supremely creative power, the Evil Spirit is equally destructive. Envious of the original creation, he immediately wanted to annihilate it, and, toward that end, he engaged in a parodic version of (mis)creation that produced demons, vermin, diseases, vices, that is, all the things that attack, corrode, torment, afflict, and corrupt the better parts of existence. Second, in contrast to the Wise Lord, who is characterized by omniscience, the Evil Spirit is characterized by profound stupidity, as a result of which all his plans backfire and he is the ultimate victim of his own violence.

Given this, the demonic powers are incapable of destroying the good creation. Even so, the Assault had a number of lesser, but still grievous, effects. Among these were the introduction of mortality, the fragmentation of original unity, the commencement of historical time, and, more broadly, the transition from a perfect to an imperfect creation, one characterized by mixture and conflict.

Focusing on each of the original creations in sequence, texts like *Selections of Zad Spram* and the *Greater Bundahišn* delight in describing how the initially pure and simple nature of things was complicated and corrupted by the Evil Spirit. It is not that the Wise Lord's creations were destroyed, for such is beyond the Adversary's power. Rather, the Assault transformed the world from its original pristine unity, introducing a situation in which good and evil are mixed and coreside in all that exists. One can also describe this as a move from simplicity to duplicity, a state in which things are no longer (just) what they seem but harbor internal tensions and contradictions.

Thus, to cite one example, as initially created by the Wise Lord, the earth's surface was flat, soft, and level. The violence of the Assault disrupts and disfigures this smooth, gentle surface such that the earth acquires rocky mountains to go with (what now become) its plains and its valleys. As a result, some parts of the earth are more, and some parts less, supportive of the living parts of creation (plants, animals, humans). What is more, as some texts make clear, the distinction between mountains and valleys provides the model for social stratification and subsequent class conflict. In similar fashion, the Evil Spirit produced divisions between sweet and salt water, beneficent and poisonous plants, productive and predatory species of animals. The Assault also shattered the unity of the human species, dividing people into different nations, races, genders, and moral categories (including the distinction between the righteous and the liars).

Being omniscient, the Wise Lord foresaw all this, and, in effect, his original creation was the bait with which he lured the Evil Spirit from a space (the great, dark below) and a time (primordial eternity) in which he was utterly safe. Historical time and the earth's surface thus became the battleground on which good and evil continue their struggle until—at the end of the nine thousand years that the Wise Lord has appointed for this conflict—evil will be annihilated. In addition, three great events will occur over the course of the last millennium that restore the world's perfection. Each has its own title and marks a different aspect of the restorative process: "the Final Body" (*tan ī pasēn*), which restores individual bodies; "the Resurrection" (*ristāxēz*), which reunites the human species; and "the Renovation" (*frašgird* [Avestan *frašō-kərəti*, lit. "Wondermaking"]), which restores all nonhuman creations. These events being complete, history comes to an end, and perfection endures forever.

V

Although no Achaemenian text follows this story in all its details, many data show strong similarities, as, for instance, a bifurcation between beneficent and noxious creatures, sweet and salt water, mountains and plains, peace and conflict, purity and mixture. Some of these have been studied elsewhere (Herrenschmidt and Lincoln 2004), and some will be treated in subsequent chapters. Here, let us focus on the temporal structure that distinguishes between three ontologically different eras—primordial eternity, history, and final (or eschatological) eternity—and the cataclysmic transitions from one to the other.

We saw earlier that the Achaemenian cosmogony seemingly alludes to one such transition: the interval between the original creation and the moment the Wise Lord made Darius king, an interval that is implied but not narrated in the cosmogonic account. Fortunately, however, the Bisitun in-

scription—a text of quite a different genre—is very much concerned with
precisely the period that the mythic texts omit: that immediately preceding
Darius's accession. Its account begins with some basic information:

> A man named Cambyses, the son of Cyrus, of our lineage—he formerly was
> king here. The brother of that Cambyses was named Bardiya. He had the same
> mother and the same father as Cambyses.
>
> (DB §10)

Cambyses and Bardiya were, thus, full brothers, and they also had three
sisters. Cambyses was, presumably, the elder brother since (1) Cyrus named
him heir, (2) he married the sisters, and (3) he assumed the throne without
incident or opposition on his father's death in 530. From Greek sources, we
know that Cambyses and his sisters were childless, which means that Bardiya
was the only other male descendant of Cyrus. As such, he must have been regarded as the heir apparent when his brother left Persia for the conquest of
Egypt in 525.

Continuing his narrative, Darius purports to reveal a secret that explains
how a previously well-ordered world fell into terrible trouble:

> Afterward, Cambyses slew that Bardiya. When Cambyses slew Bardiya, it did
> not become known by the people that Bardiya was slain. Then Cambyses went
> off to Egypt. *When Cambyses went to Egypt, the people became vulnerable to the Lie,
> and the Lie grew greatly* throughout the land/people—in Persia and Media and
> the other lands/peoples.
>
> (DB §10)

According to Darius—whose highly interested and exceptionally shrewd
testimony is ideologically revealing, if not factually reliable—Cambyses thus
left home in spring 525, having committed a hideous crime. Contrary to our
assumptions, that crime was not his brother's murder, for kings were understood to hold the power of life and death over all their subjects. Keeping
Bardiya's execution a secret, however, was something else, for this effectively
misled the people. Neither truth nor lie, it was a royal half-truth that set in
motion a process of moral decay. Having misled his people and, thereby, produced a situation of misunderstanding, mistrust, and confusion, Cambyses
compounded this error by leaving Persia—the moral as well as the political
center of his empire—to embark on the conquest of Egypt. That project took
him to the outermost fringes of the empire, where he remained a full three
years, as things got steadily worse. The king being absent and the truth com-
promised, the people became restive, credulous, undependable.

These were the preconditions for insurrection and other mischief. Or, to put it in the idiom favored by Darius: "When Cambyses went to Egypt, the people became vulnerable to the Lie and the Lie grew greatly." If this elemental force of evil first began insinuating itself through a royal half-truth, it erupted with all its corrosive power in the proclamation that Darius attributed to an imposter and usurper:

> There was a man, a magus named Gaumata. He rose up from Paishiyauvada—a mountain named Arakadri, from there. Fourteen days in the month Viyaxna had passed when he rose up [11 March 522 BCE]. *He lied to the people,* saying thus: "I am Bardiya, the son of Cyrus, the brother of Cambyses." Then the people all became rebellious from Cambyses. It went over to him—Persia and Media and the other lands/peoples.
>
> (DB §11)

Several details are important. First, as a magus, the Gaumata of this story was doubly unqualified for kingship, for kings should be Persian nobles and magi were Median priests. Second, his insurrection began on a mountain, which—if the Zoroastrian contrast of plain and mountain holds good—is morally dubious space. Third, there is no hint that he had or claimed divine favor. Fourth, there is the understanding that rebellion is the act of a gullible, misguided people whose weaknesses have been exploited—and exacerbated—by an unscrupulous deceiver. Behind the deceiver stands the Lie, an elementary cosmic force whose outbreak brings consequences: tranquility shattered; happiness lost; the empire, indeed, the cosmos, plunged into chaotic disorder.

To rectify this is no easy matter, and Darius writes with the sense that the job remained incomplete. Even so, he claims to have begun the project of rectification and recovery on 29 September 522, when: "By the Wise Lord's will I became king" (DB §13).

Relentlessly historical in its discourse, the Bisitun inscription is concerned to narrate events that unfolded from early 525 (Bardiya's murder, Cambyses' departure for Egypt) through December 520 (Darius's consolidation of royal power, his defeat of nine rebels in nineteen battles, and his victory over the Scythians), all of which it constitutes as the pivot on which the fate of the cosmos turns.

Bisitun, however, is an exceptional text. Once Darius was firmly in power, none of his subsequent inscriptions concerned themselves much with historical events. Rather, as we have seen, most of them began with the myth of creation, after which they celebrated the king and his empire and also the mission and virtues of both. Still, there is overlap between these two different styles and genres, for the event that Bisitun makes its centerpiece is enshrined by the cosmogonic texts as the last act of creation, that is, when the Wise Lord made Darius king (DNa §1 etc.).

The historical discourse of Bisitun and the mythic discourse of the later inscriptions thus complement each other. Concerning the periods before and after history proper, Bisitun is silent, while the cosmogonic myth fills these gaps. Conversely, Bisitun describes the events that occurred during the interval that the cosmogonic texts imply but leave blank, the time between the Wise Lord's fourth and fifth acts of creation when happiness for mankind was lost. As Bisitun makes clear, this happened when the Lie manifested itself in a string of royal half-truths, popular confusion, deceptive imposters, and widespread revolts that put an end to truth, peace, and abundance.

Correlating Bisitun and the Achaemenian cosmogonies thus yields a tripartite temporal schema in which a period of primordial perfection is followed by one of historical crisis and struggle. The present moment stands inside that second era, but the worst of the crisis has ended, and one can anticipate that the forces of good will triumph, led by the Achaemenian king. When that is accomplished—as can be expected in the proximate future—a third era will begin: the eternity that follows after history has come to an end, when the Wise Lord's plan for the cosmos is accomplished, the Lie is destroyed, and perfect happiness will endure forever. All in all, we are very close to the temporal schema of the Pahlavi texts (see table 8).

VI

There is one last set of data to be considered. These data are variants on the cosmogonic narrative that occur in some later inscriptions of Darius and Xerxes. Apparently, these variants reflect scribal experimentation with the formulaic discourse and reveal two distinct phases (see table 9).

Both these experiments are attempts at summation that use the term *fraša* (wonder) to encompass several items of the creation treated separately in the standard formula. By introducing this term—which also figures prominently in Zoroastrian discourse—they try to convey how magnificent, how amazingly beautiful, how complete and perfect was the world that the Wise Lord created. Variant 1, the earlier attempt (that of DSs), thus uses *fraša* for the inanimate material creations, that is, earth and sky. Variant 2, the later attempt (introduced by Darius at DNb, copied by Xerxes at XPl), goes one step further to include humanity as well. Here, the original creation is theorized as consisting of two items only: a great "wonder" (*fraša*), which includes earth, sky, and mankind and "happiness for mankind" (*šiyāti . . . martyahyā*), which

TABLE 8: Periodization of Cosmic History in Three Different Eras, as Suggested in Darius's Inscriptions and Zoroastrian Scriptures

	DB §§10–55: Historical Discourse	DNa §1 etc.: Mythic Discourse	Pahlavi Texts: Zoroastrian Cosmology
Primordial eternity		Original creation. The Wise Lord creates earth, sky, mankind, and happiness for mankind, all perfect and good.	Original creation. The Wise Lord creates sky, water, earth, plant, animal, and mankind in 3,000 years, all perfect and good.
Historical time	Cambyses kills Bardiya in secret (early 525). Cambyses goes to Egypt (spring 525). People become vulnerable to the Lie, and the Lie grows greatly (525–522). Gaumata lies, calling himself Bardiya and claiming the throne (March 522). Death of Cambyses (June 522). Murder of Gaumata (Sept. 522). Darius ritually installed as king (Dec. 522). Darius suppresses nine rebellions and wins nineteen battles (Dec. 522–Dec. 521). Darius suppresses Elamite rebellion and conquers one group of Scythians (Dec. 521–Dec. 520).	Unspecified interval. Loss of perfection and happiness. The Wise Lord makes Darius King	Assault of the Evil Spirit. Original unity shattered. Perfection corrupted. Death, disease, suffering introduced. State of mixture commences. World and history as battleground between good and evil for 3,000 years.
Eschatological eternity	Expected triumph over the Lie. Establishment of stable world empire. Pax Persiana.	Expected triumph over the Lie. Perfection and happiness restored.	3,000 years of combat. Evil defeated. Final Body. Resurrection of dead. Cosmic Renovation.

TABLE 9: Variants on the Creation Account in Which Earth and Sky Are Replaced by the Term *Fraša* (Wonder)

	Standard Forumla[a]	Experiment: Phase 1[b]	Experiment: Phase 2[c]
1	A great god is the Wise Lord,	A great god is the Wise Lord,	A great god is the Wise Lord,
2	who created this earth,	who makes a wonder [*fraša*] on this earth,	who created this wonder [*fraša*] that is seen,
3	who created that sky,		
4	who created mankind,	who makes mankind on this earth,	
5	who created happiness for mankind. . . .	who makes happiness for mankind. . . .	who created happiness for mankind. . . .

[a] DNa §1 etc.
[b] DSs.
[c] DNb §7 and XPl §1.

is not spelled out any more here than it is elsewhere but would seem to include peace, food (plants and animals), and truth.

There is, however, another way in which the two experimental variants differ from each other, and, here, the first is more radical than the second. At issue are the verbs that they employ. Variant 2 uses the same verb as do all others, that which always denotes acts of divine creativity: Old Persian *²dā-* (to create, establish, set in place for the first time). Variant 1, in marked contrast, uses the less august and less specific verb *kar-* (to make, do, build), which can cover human as well as divine actions. What is more, its verbs are in the present tense, where all the other texts use the aorist or imperfect tense. Clearly, this suggests that creativity—that of mortals and immortals—is continuous and ongoing in the present, but it also has some more specific implications, to be considered in the next chapter.

In closing, I should return and say a bit about the way in which Zoroastrian texts treat the term *fraša*, although this topic deserves fuller treatment than is possible here. Briefly, a few Avestan passages give this word a cosmogonic sense similar to that of the Achaemenian inscriptions. Overwhelmingly, however, both Avestan and Pahlavi texts deploy *fraša* in eschatological contexts. Thus, as we have seen, *frašgird* (Avestan *frašō-kərəti*), or "Wonder-making," is the technical term that denotes the Renovation, that is, the purification and perfection of the natural world after evil has been conclusively defeated at the end of historical struggle.

That the same word should be used to describe the original and the final perfection of the material cosmos is not particularly surprising. In this fashion, the Zoroastrian texts make the point that the world's salvation from evil accomplishes nothing novel. Rather, it restores the state of ideal goodness intended—and initially realized—by the world's creator. The end and the beginning thus come together such that a wondrous cosmos, happiness for mankind, and the supremely benevolent deity Ahura Mazdā, the Wise Lord, fill the eternity of the future, just as they fill the eternity of the past. Evil, strife, conflict, turbulence, and corruption are acknowledged, to be sure, but confined to a very finite time between primordial and final perfection.

Microcosms, Wonders, Paradise 5

I

Zoroastrian myths treat unity as a prime feature of the Wise Lord's original creation. That the Creator established only one sky and only one earth is itself hardly surprising. But the texts also make the same point apropos of his later creations, the ones he endowed with life, insisting that he made only one plant, one animal, and one human, placing all three at the center of the earth, which happens to be in Iran. Each of the three specimens was perfect, moreover, until the Assault of the Evil Spirit. Since, however, the Evil Spirit was no more omnipotent than the Wise Lord, he could no more annihilate these primordial beings than the Wise Lord could keep them entirely safe from harm.

As a result of this collision between an irresistible force and an immovable object, the creations were corrupted and fragmented, but still extant and enduring. With the Assault, primordial eternity and perfection came to an end. In its wake, the cosmos passed into a morally ambiguous, conflict-ridden state characterized by the mixture of good and evil that marks our present age. That condition will persist through historical time, but not forever, since historical time is finite in its duration. At history's end, sometimes calculated as nine thousand years and sometimes as six thousand years after the Assault, the Wise Lord and the forces of good will triumph in their struggle, and the drama of their victory—which involves the definitive conquest of evil, the resurrection of the dead, and a final ordeal that cleanses all people of their sins and pollution—is known as *frašgird*, a term that is usually translated as "the Renovation" but that literally means "Wondermaking."

Among the great theological themes that the Pahlavi texts ponder is the question of mortality, which they treat through a dialectical narrative worthy of Lévi-Strauss and Hegel. Thus, they posit as thesis that the Wise Lord intended his first plant, animal, and human to have been immortal, as antithesis that the Evil Spirit brought death to each one. Mediation between absolute life and total destruction is, then, established when immortality shifts from the level of the individual to that of the species, via processes of sexual reproduction.

Sexual differentiation implies a loss of original unity, however, and the myths connect this development to others that continue the move from the one to the many. Thus, when the first plant, animal, and human died, their seeds and bodily matter were preserved, and, through different processes (each one equally circuitous and inventive), these gave rise to the myriad species (or races) that, in later generations, are found scattered over the earth's surface. Collectively, the various species inherit all the properties that were concentrated in the original beings, but each species is understood to represent only a partial instantiation of that primordial whole. As such, it inherited a subset of the qualities possessed by its original ancestor. Being finite, the various species are deficient and flawed, the desirable qualities that one lacks having been distributed to other descendants. What is more, each species is marred in some measure by the admixture of evil.

Diversity, then—like mortality—characterizes history and the state of mixture. It also constitutes a problem that needs to be solved if perfection is to be regained. At the level of the human, this occurs as part of the Renovation: an eschatological reunion when, having been purged of their imperfections, all the resurrected dead gather at a central place where they will live together in perfect love and harmony.

II

As we have already observed, the Achaemenian inscriptions have relatively little to say regarding the Assault and the world's fall from perfection into the state of mixture. DB §10 simply states that, when Cambyses went to Egypt in 525 BCE, "the Lie became great." Apparently, the force of corruption was already present in the world prior to that moment, albeit less active and potent. The rest of the Bisitun text makes clear that, in subsequent years, the Lie grew rapidly, manifesting itself in numerous rebellions. Most immediately, these upheavals were precipitated by the deceitful speech of ambitious pretenders who misrepresented their identity, lineage, and claim to legitimate power. Such untruths became effective, however, only when they reached a public already "vulnerable to the Lie" (*arika*). From this explosive conjunction of falsehood and credulity, there follow other manifestations of the Lie: popular unrest, military insurrection, lawlessness, and usurpation.

During the turbulent year 522–521, Darius put down nine different rebellions of this sort, which affected no fewer than fourteen provinces of the empire, some of them repeatedly. Although two of these risings involved attempts to seize control of the empire, the other seven did not. Rather, these began when local leaders—usually sons of the old royal line or displaced nobles who could pass themselves off as such—perceived a moment of Persian weakness and sought to exploit it. Evoking older identities and sentiments of affinity, they sought to extricate their people from imperial domination and to recover their lost independence. From their own perspective, they acted as heroes of what would later be called "nationalism." Darius, however, understood them as instruments of the Lie, who threatened the empire with dissolution. That which earlier Persian kings (i.e., Cyrus and Cambyses) had painstakingly built up, these rebels now wished to tear apart. As in the Zoroastrian myths, this construction of historical conflict pits unity against diversity, truth against the Lie, with the empire defending the interests of God, morality, and progress.

III

In a crucial scene from what is, in effect, the earliest historical analysis of imperialism, Herodotus describes Xerxes in the moment he told the Persian nobles of his intention to invade Greece (ca. 483 BCE). To begin, the new king said that it was the hallmark of Persian ancestral culture never to remain at peace. Rather, ever since Cyrus seized power from the Medes, the Persians had brought ever more peoples and territories under their dominion, and this, he asserted, was as God would have it. He anticipated the conquest of Greece as a continuation of this process, which would also let him gain glory and avenge the grave wrongs that the Greeks had committed against his father. None of this was an end in itself but simply part of a larger project:

> If we subdue them and their neighbors . . . we will produce a Persian earth bordering on Zeus's heaven, for the sun will look down on no land that is neighbor to ours. Rather, having marched through all Europe together with you, I will make them all one land. For I learn thus: no city of men nor race of people will be left to oppose us in battle when those of whom I spoke have been removed.
>
> (Herodotus 7.8)

The words themselves surely belong to Herodotus, not Xerxes, and the implicit critique of Persian expansionism as hubristically insatiable reflects a Greek perspective. That notwithstanding, this passage preserves Achaemenian religious beliefs attested in the royal inscriptions, beliefs that structured and helped motivate their imperial campaigns of conquest. In chapter 2, we saw, for instance, how Persian constructions of space—more specifically, the relation of center and periphery—informed the outward projection of force, and chapter 3 made similar points regarding the Achaemenians' views of their divinely ordained mission.

To these themes, the Herodotean passage adds three others with which we are not yet equally familiar. First is the global nature of imperial ambition: the goal of establishing a "Persian earth," one in which "no city of men nor race of people will be left to oppose us." Second is the goal of consolidating the world's diverse populations in a single, unified and unifying entity tantamount to the empire: "I will make them all one land." These points seem consistent with the Zoroastrian materials considered earlier in this chapter, which treat human (as well as plant and animal) diversity as a problem to be overcome. Third is the desire to create a single earth, nestled peacefully under a single sky, just as the Wise Lord made them: "We will produce a Persian earth bordering on Zeus's heaven." Thus, a cosmological dimension is added to the quest for political unity, connecting it to the Achaemenian cosmogony treated in chapter 4.

Here, it becomes important to appreciate a crucial step in the development of Achaemenian ideology, one that was touched on briefly in chapter 1. As Clarisse Herrenschmidt was the first to realize, Persian power grew so rapidly that the early kings had no adequate term to describe the political entity that their conquests brought into existence. Thus, until some years into the reign of Darius (522–484), the highest level of social integration that could be named in Old Persian was the "kingdom" (*xšaça*) or the "land/people" (*dahyu*), the former of which applies primarily to Persia and its surrounding areas, the latter to individual provinces of the empire. The Persians had no prior name, however, for an aggregate of lands/peoples with one uniquely privileged land/people situated at its center, ruling over the others, extracting wealth from them, enjoying superior moral status, and constantly seeking to extend its power over ever more distant lands/peoples—that is, the kind of formation that we would call an "empire." Only in Darius's later inscriptions did they solve this problem in ingenious fashion, modifying the semantic range of an older word to meet the needs of the new situation.

The word they chose—Old Persian *būmi*—had enormous resonance and holds considerable interest. In ancient Indo-Iranian usage, it denoted "earth, soil," that is, the globe and its physical substance. In Achaemenian discourse,

the word retains the sense of "soil" on a few rare occasions, but its other occurrences all fall in one of two contexts. In eighteen different inscriptions, as
we have seen, it appears in cosmogonic accounts, most often in the formula:
"A great god is the Wise Lord, who created *this earth* [*imām būmīm*], who created that sky. . . ." Even more often (thirty-eight times), it appears in the royal
title that Darius introduced to denote the highest level of sociopolitical integration over which he held sway: "King in *this empire* [*ahyāya būmiyā*]." When
one seeks to correlate these two contexts, the point becomes clear: The "earth"
that the Wise Lord originally created has now become the "empire" that he
entrusts to the Achaemenian king, presumably as the result of postcosmo-
gonic events that created the need for such kingship. The empire is, thus,
ideally coextensive with the earth. Although political realities may leave
portions of the globe outside the Great King's control, God has given these
to him, no less than the others. It thus becomes his task to recover what is
rightfully his, by the grace of God.

Such ideas are confirmed in one last passage, one that connects the myth
of an ideal creation to the view of history as a mixed state. With remarkable
economy, it describes how the Wise Lord responded to the corruption of his
perfect world by conferring responsibility for the fallen earth now become
empire on the Achaemenian king:

> Proclaims Darius the King: *When the Wise Lord saw this earth/empire* [*imām*
> *būmīm*] *seething in turmoil, then he bestowed it on me.* He made me king. I am king.
> By the Wise Lord's will, I set things in place. What I proclaimed to them they
> did according to my desire. If you should wonder, "How many are the lands/
> peoples that King Darius held?" look at the pictures of those who bear the
> throne. Then you will learn, then it becomes known: "The spear of the Persian
> man went far." Then it becomes known: "The Persian man has pushed back
> the enemy far from Persia."
>
> (DNa §4)

Darius placed this text at the site of his tomb in Naqš-i Rustam. Here, he
described the problem that he was made king to solve: the turbulence of rebellion, a state of affairs, provoked by the Lie, that shatters the world's ideal
state by disrupting its tranquility, unity, and happiness. Going further, Darius
described his success in restoring order ("I set things in place"), enforcing the
law ("What I proclaimed to them they did"), and conquering distant peoples
("The spear of the Persian man went far. . . . The Persian man has pushed
back the enemy far from Persia"). As the crowning image of what he accomplished, however, he called attention to the relief sculpture that accompanies
this inscription (see figure 12).

Figure 12: Relief sculpture at Darius's tomb, Naqš-i Rustam.
Drawing by Sir Henry Creswicke Rawlinson, ca. 1850.

Holding a bow—the weapon that projects power at a distance—and facing the Wise Lord and a fire temple, Darius towers at the top of the composition. The inscription directs one's attention elsewhere, however, to "the pictures of those who bear the throne," for it is by counting these diminutive
figures that one can answer the question, "How many are the lands/peoples
that King Darius held?" Captions beneath each of the throne bearers make
clear why this is so, as each one represents a different land/people. Thirty in
all, they match the lands/peoples listed in the inscription (DNa §3), and comparison to the list of Bisitun (DB §6) lets one measure the empire's growth
under Darius's kingship, a period in which seven new lands/peoples were
added, mostly at the northwest, southwest, and southeast frontiers.

The throne-bearer relief is, in effect, a trope of empire and a microcosmic
representation of its current political power and geographic expanse. It is,
however, a snapshot taken at a specific moment in time, meant to be compared with similar snapshots taken at earlier moments as well as with the
ideal toward which the empire aspires. Read thus, it depicts the extent to
which the empire as it is *extant in history* has realized its true identity (and ultimate ambition) to become the empire *as world*. New throne bearers mark

progress toward that goal, but the imperial project remains incomplete—and the world remains troubled—as long as there remain lands/peoples falling outside the picture.

IV

Alongside the throne-bearer image, the Achaemenians had several other favored models that they constructed as microcosmic representations of the empire as world. One of the more important was the palace that Darius built at Susa shortly after consolidating his hold on the kingship (521 and thereafter). Ancient authors report that Susa was the most beautifully adorned of all the Achaemenian palaces, and Darius described it with a term that he used for no other product of human hands. The word in question is Old Persian *fraša*, "wonder" or "marvel," which—as was noted in the previous chapter—also appears in some experimental variants of the creation myth. One of these experiments was placed at Susa itself and, thus, holds prime importance for the question: What did it mean for Darius to call his palace there a "wonder"?

> A great god is the Wise Lord, who makes a wonder on this earth, who makes mankind on this earth, who makes happiness for mankind, who makes good horses and good chariots. On me he bestowed them. May the Wise Lord protect me and what has been made [*or:* built] by me.
>
> (DSs)

When I considered this passage in chapter 4, I observed how the word *fraša* replaces the material elements of the cosmos (earth and sky) that figure in other versions of the cosmogony. A "wonder" thus includes all the inanimate material substance of the universe, in its original, pure and pristine condition, untainted by the corruption introduced by the Assault.

I also noted that—in contrast to all the others—this variant employs the unmarked verb *kar-* (to make, do, build) for the Wise Lord's creative acts and uses it in the present tense. By way of explanation, I suggested that this usage conveyed the sense that the work of creation is ongoing and that (certain) humans participate in it. The last sentence of the text just quoted confirms this interpretation, but lets one improve on it. Here, Darius identifies himself as the kind of human who does just that when he says: "May the Wise Lord protect me and what has been made [*or:* built] by me," for the verb with which he denotes his own products and accomplishments is *kar-*, the same verb he just used for the Wise Lord's creation of the world as wonder.

In the full corpus of Achaemenian inscriptions, various actors appear as subjects of this verb. Some of them are capable of making or doing bad things only. The Lie, for instance, can make lands/peoples rebellious (DB §54), as can men who falsely pass themselves off as kings (DB §52). Rebellious provinces can make an undeserving man their chief, an action that invariably leads him—and them—to disaster (DB §§38, 71). Other actors are capable of good works, but only in mediated fashion, that is, when they are carrying out the orders of the rightful king. This is clearest when generals make battle (DB §§25, 33, 35, etc.), but it is also true when construction workers dig foundations for buildings designed by the king (DSf §3f) or when subject peoples do as they are told (DB §7, DNa §§3, 4, DSe §3, XPh §3).

Only the Wise Lord and the king are able to make, do, or build things on their own authority and have this come out well. Some of the king's creative action takes the form of changing someone's status by, for example, "making" him a crown prince (XPf §4) or a general (DB §§25, 33, 41, etc.), and in this he mirrors the Wise Lord's ability to "make" a king (DNa §1, DSe §1, DSi §1, DSm §1 etc.). Like a general, the king can "make" battles (DB §52), and he can also "make" an example of defeated rebels by the tortures he inflicts on them (DB §§32, 33, 43), a theme to which we will return in chapter 6. His material acts of creation, however, chiefly take the form of construction projects, and numerous passages use the verb *kar-* to describe the Achaemenian ruler's role in building palaces, colonnades, reception halls, defensive walls, and so forth. Only one human product is ever described as a "wonder," however: the palace that Darius erected at Susa:

> Proclaims Darius the King: By the Wise Lord's will, a great wonder was planned at Susa. A great wonder was made [*or:* built].
>
> (DSz §13)

Five different inscriptions at Susa name its palace a "wonder." All but one use the verb *kar-* and specify that the project was carried out "by the Wise Lord's will." The fifth inscription leaves this last point implicit, but, in another of its paragraphs, it goes on to describe how the collaboration between God and the king was accomplished: "The Wise Lord bore me help. That which was planned by me, that he made well-made [*or:* well-built] by me. All that I made [*or:* built], I made [*or:* built] by the Wise Lord's will" (DSf §§3d–3e).

Darius's discourse at Susa differs from that of all other Achaemenian inscriptions in ways that can hardly be coincidental. Nowhere else is the Wise Lord's material creation (heaven and earth) described as a "wonder." Nowhere else is his creative action described with the verb "to make, build." Nowhere else is any human product described as a "wonder." And nowhere else is anything ever described as "well-made" or "well-built." All these details are orchestrated to produce the impression that, when Darius built the palace at Susa, his actions paralleled the Wise Lord's creation of heaven and earth. The relation implied between Susa and the world is that of microcosm and macrocosm, and this understanding informed the process of its construction as well as the way in which it was perceived.

Three inscriptions (DSf, DSz, and DSaa) are usually referred to as *foundation charters* for this palace, and they tell very much the same story. All three list the materials that went into it, and all three are particularly concerned with those materials considered the most beautiful and costly: gold, silver, gems, exotic woods, ivory, and marble. All these materials, moreover, come from different lands/peoples, who contributed their finest goods and their most highly skilled labor to realize the project. The completed palace was, thus, the site at which the rarest, most exotic, most gorgeous of the earth's substances were perfected and reunited:

> I worshipped the Wise Lord. The Wise Lord bore me help. That which was planned by me, that he made well-made [*or:* well-built] by me. All that I made [*or:* built], I made [*or:* built] by the Wise Lord's will. *This is the palace I made* [*or: built*] *at Susa: its ornamentation was brought from afar.* . . . This timber of cedar was borne from a mountain named Lebanon. The Assyrian people bore it to Babylon, and, from Babylon, the Carians and Ionians bore it to Susa. Cypress was borne from Gandhara and Carmania. Gold was borne from Lydia and Bactria. That was wrought here. Gems of lapis lazuli and carnelian, which were wrought here, were borne from Sogdiana. The gems of turquoise were borne from Chorasmia. That was wrought here. Silver and ebony were borne from Egypt. The ornamentation with which the fortress is adorned was borne from Ionia. The ivory that was wrought here was borne from Ethiopia, India, and Arachosia. The stone columns that were wrought here were borne from a village in Elam named Abiradus. The stonemasons who worked the stone were Ionians and Sardians. The goldsmiths who worked the gold were Medes and Egyptians. The men who worked the wood were Lydians and Egyptians. The men who made the bricks were Babylonians. The men who adorned the fortress were Medes and Egyptians. Proclaims Darius the King: *In Susa a great wonder was planned. A great wonder it was.*

(DSf §§3d–4)

Extensive though this version of the foundation charter is, it names only seventeen lands/peoples, while another variant (DSaa) has twenty-three, but even that one falls a bit short of the twenty-seven lands/peoples of the empire listed in DSe §3. Clearly, the lists aspire to completeness, but, even were all the imperial provinces represented, the goal of completion would still be deferred. The Achaemenians' ultimate ambition was to unite all the world's lands/peoples under their rule, at which point all the best materials would flow to the center for perfection by all the most skilled hands. Finally, these materials would be combined—better, reunited—to produce a structure of incomparable beauty and elegance that replicates the primordial wonder created by the Wise Lord. Just as the expanse of the empire at any given moment announces and anticipates the goal of merging empire and world, so the current magnificence of Susa announces and anticipates the ultimate goal of palace as site and instrument for restoration of the world's original material perfection.

V

The royal banquet table provided another model of the same ideals and processes, for on it were countless exquisite dishes, gathered from every part of the empire. The Greeks mistook this for excess and luxury, but the Persians hardly saw it as a fall into corruption. On the contrary, their intention was to reverse the fall by restoring the original unity of matter, perfection of all things, and happiness of mankind. Even so, the sumptuous Achaemenian banquets only anticipated the ultimate goal, which waited at history's end. Thus, a famous story tells that, when Xerxes was served a plate of Athenian figs (a delicacy so highly regarded that its export was illegal), the king refused them, proclaiming that he would eat such fruit only when he had conquered Athens—which, insofar as the king's table mirrored the empire, is to say that only when the empire encompassed the world would the banquet be perfect and complete.

The famous Apadana reliefs at Persepolis were crafted to make the same general point (see figure 13). Here, delegations from every land/people of the empire converge on the enthroned king, bearing tribute of every sort. Members of the various delegations are depicted with meticulous attention to details of dress, coiffure, and physiognomy, with the result that their ethnic identity is immediately legible. Their diversity and particularity are subsumed, however, in the overall composition, which shows the king and his capital as the site at which all varieties of the human species are effectively reunited. The same is true of animals, for each of the delegations bears a different kind of beast in tribute. The unique nature and specific identity of these beasts thus serve as an index of their donors' ethnicity—the humped bull (*Bos indicus*) of the Gandharans, the two-humped camel of the Bactrians, the large-tailed sheep of the Cilicians, and so forth. Brought together under the auspices of the Achaemenian king, however, these specimens represent the

Figure 13: Relief sculptures representing three of the twenty-three delegations that bear tribute to the Achaemenian king, as depicted on the steps approaching the Apadana at Persepolis. At the top, Scythians lead in a horse; in the middle, Gandharans bring a humped bull (*Bos indicus*); and, at the bottom, Cilicians bring long-tailed sheep. (Photos: R.E.F. [top, middle]; Ricciarini-Prato [bottom].)

totality of animal characteristics and possibilities, reunited through the workings of the empire: workings that consisted of a centrifugal drive (conquest
and expansion) and a centripetal pull (extraction and tribute).

VI

These animals did not remain at the capital, and many were destined to stock
an institution unique to the Medes and Persians and renowned throughout
antiquity. These were the animal parks and walled gardens that bore the
name *paridaida* (cf. Median *paridaiza*, Avestan *pairidaēza*), a name that countless other languages adopted to describe these extraordinary places, having
no words of their own adequate to the task. The same word ultimately entered most European languages via Greek and now serves as the standard
word for "paradise." In its Persian original, however, it most literally meant
"walled enclosure" and, more broadly, "walled garden or game park," although it was not without religious significance, as we will see. Such estab-
lishments were built throughout the empire, always in the most climatically
favored surroundings, that is, those whose ideal mix of warmth and moisture
could make all forms of life flourish. Walls were built to isolate this terrain
from its surroundings, after which cultural improvements—irrigation and
shade—were introduced to further perfect the environment. Some of these
paradisal enclosures specialized in animals, which they kept for display and
for hunting, others specialized in plants, and some had both. But, in all cases,
the intent was to create a space of perfect comfort and radiant beauty, filled
with plants and/or animals of every imaginable type.

  This insistence on broad representation particularly impressed the Greek
authors who left the fullest descriptions of Achaemenian parks and gardens.
Thus, for example, Xenophon depicts Astyages, the last king of the Medes,
promising to fill his paradise with animals "of every species" (*Cyropaedia*
1.3.14) for Cyrus's entertainment. Other authors tell that the paradises at
Persepolis, Celaenae (in Phrygia), Dascyleium (in Lydia), and elsewhere were
similarly well stocked. Xenophon's testimony regarding plants is even more
emphatic, for he describes a paradise garden in Syria as "possessing all that
the seasons bring forth" (*Anabasis* 1.4.10), another one at Sittake (on the
Tigris) as "thick with every sort of tree" (2.4.14), and others as "full of everything good and beautiful that the earth cares to grow" (*Œconomicus* 4.13–14).
When imagining the wonders of Atlantis, where everything grew in abundance, Diodorus Siculus was still careful to distinguish simple gardens (Greek
kêpeia) from paradise gardens, which he described as "full of plants, with
trees of every species" (5.19.2).

While some texts describe an all-embracing totality, others recount mere abundance, and it is hard to tell whether this reflects a difference in the authors' attention and rhetoric or something more subtle: that is, an ideology positing that a paradise should aspire to include all species, and trusting that this ideal would be achieved at history's end, but accepting that, until the empire had encompassed the globe, one would have to settle for something less than totality and perfection.

VII

A Pahlavi text titled *Arda Wiraz Namag,* often considered a source for Dante, describes the protagonist's ecstatic journeys through a series of heavens and hells. His final vision of the highest heaven reads as follows:

> I saw the best world of the truthful, which is light, all-bliss, and abundance. And there were many fragrant flowers of every color, all in bloom and radiant, full of glory. *And there was all-happiness and all-peace,* of which a person cannot know satiety.
>
> (*Arda Wiraz Namag* 19.19–20.3)

Not only does this celestial realm include many features reminiscent of the paradise gardens—flourishing vegetative life, flowers of every variety, perfumed fragrance, fabulous beauty, etc.—but it also contains the precise features constitutive of the happiness that the Wise Lord fashioned for mankind as part of his original creation. As we saw in chapter 4, the Achaemenians theorized that state as depending on the negation of three menaces: the enemy army, famine, and the Lie. As this passage takes pains to show, all three are emphatically absent from heaven (see table 10).

Even were these details not part of the description, it would still be clear that, in heaven, the righteous dead recover the ideal happiness that was lost with the Assault. Not only are "all-bliss" and "all-happiness" identified as prime qualities of the celestial realm, but the latter term echoes the Achaemenian cosmogony (Pahlavi *šādīh,* "happiness," being cognate to Old Persian *šiyāti*). Old Persian data also suggest that the paradises that the Achaemenians built on earth were meant to offer a foretaste of the delights awaiting the righteous after death and at history's end. Thus, the only paradise whose name has been preserved bore this very same title: "All-happiness" (**Vispa-šiyāti*).

Achaemenian gardens thus seem to complement and parallel the wonder built at Susa. If the latter aspired to perfect and reunite all the world's inanimate matter, thereby restoring the Wise Lord's first two creations (earth and

TABLE 10: Heaven and the Recovery of Primordial Happiness: Correspondences between Achaemenian Cosmogony and the Personal Eschatology Described in Zoroastrian Sources

Three Menaces That Destroy Happiness[a]	Menaces Obviated[b]	Characteristics of the Highest Heaven[c]
Enemy army	Peace	"All-peace"
Famine	Abundance	"Abundance"
The Lie	Truth	"The best world of the truthful"

[a] DPd §3.
[b] Necessary for the restoration of happiness.
[c] As described in the *Arda Wiraz Namag*.

heaven) to their pristine condition, the paradise did similar service as regards the last piece of his original cosmos: happiness for mankind. Such happiness includes both abstract qualities (peace and truth) and the living beings (plants and animals) that provide humans with food (which sustains life) and sensory pleasure (via their fragrance, appearance, and taste).

Perfect happiness existed at the dawn of creation, and it will come again when history ends. It may also await the truthful and righteous after death, although Zoroastrian sources have more to say on this than do the Achaemenian inscriptions. With a single exception—a very unusual inscription by Xerxes—the latter corpus is much more concerned with the king's responsibility to perfect the world than with the individual's responsibility to perfect himself and win heavenly reward. Perfecting the world meant, as we have repeatedly seen, defeating the Lie and conquering all peoples in order to reunite humanity—as well as the kinds of matter found in their soil, their foodstuffs, plants, and animals. Viewed through this optic, the imperial project of global expansion acquired a rosy glow. One was concerned, not to enrich one's self, but to do God's work, restore primordial wholeness, and set right an afflicted cosmos.

We are normally accustomed to view such arguments as legitimations and rationalizations: the discursive instruments through which guilty actors pretty up the record and soothe their conscience after the dirty work is done. Surely, it can be so. Yet it is also possible that constructions of this sort enter earlier in the game, actively motivating—and not just excusing—at least some of the actors and some of their acts. As a case in point, consider a passage from Herodotus that shows Xerxes having second thoughts about the invasion of Greece. At this, Mardonius, his close kinsman and chief adviser, entered the discussion. Alternately flattering Xerxes, reasoning with him, and shaming the young monarch, Mardonius urged him to seek justice, vengeance, and glory by making war on Greek soil. Beyond these well-rehearsed arguments, however, he introduced another line of persuasion: one that may strike us as unexpected, perhaps, but one with which the Achaemenians are likely to have been familiar:

> He repeatedly made an addition to the argument, saying that Europe was a very beautiful place and bore cultivated trees of every sort, a land high in excellence and worthy to be possessed by the king alone among mortals.
>
> (Herodotus 7.5)

The first phrase of this text is remarkably subtle and contains quite a mixed message. On the one hand, it characterizes Mardonius's argument as a remark made in passing: a "[parenthetical] addition" (*parenthêkên*) tossed in as a coda or afterthought. On the other hand, it uses the iterative verb *poieesketo,* the grammatical form used for habitual and repeated actions, suggesting that this was no casual utterance, however much Mardonius wished to mask its import by framing it as a side comment. Hardly insignificant, the point that he harped on in this fashion is fully consistent with the ideology of paradise, for he noted that Europe and its many fine trees—the Athenian fig, for instance—were not yet part of the empire. In that measure, the salvific project that the Wise Lord had entrusted to the Achaemenian kings remained incomplete. This situation might be rectified, however, by the conquest of Greece, after which those exotic trees could be reunited with others in a Persian paradise garden.

The Dark Side of Paradise   **6**

Although no Persian descriptions of the Achaemenian pleasure parks survive, the etymology of Old Persian *paridaida*, Median **paridaiza*, and related terms makes clear that the defining feature of these structures was a wall that separated the space inside from the surrounding environment. In other contexts, walls might serve a military function, and they could also mark concentrations of wealth, power, and status, as when palace walls enclosed treasuries, temples, or royal complexes. At times, walls themselves become symbolic objects, as at Ecbatana, whose seven concentric walls offered a model of the planetary spheres and the cosmos itself, or the citadel of Persepolis, where massive, irregularly shaped stones were fitted together perfectly without any mortar to form an image of the empire itself, in which different lands/peoples were harmoniously conjoined while preserving their individual identity. Further, the king was obliged to restore any of these walls that fell into disrepair, thereby renewing the order that they both preserved and created.

The Avestan cognate of *paridaida* also denotes a walled enclosure, but, in many ways, the structure to which it refers is the opposite of the Achaemenian paradise. The term occurs only once, in a passage that answers the question: What place should be assigned to a corpse bearer who, as a result of his sustained contact with dead bodies, has become hopelessly polluted? The answer, attributed to the Wise Lord himself, is that this man should be taken to the driest, most desolate place on earth, a spot devoid of plants and animals, to be immured within an encircling wall (*pairidaēza*).

There, pious Mazdā worshippers are expected to give him food and clothing while maintaining a safe distance and keeping him at least thirty paces
from fire, water, and plants, all sacred entities created by the Wise Lord. For
the duration of his life, the former corpse bearer remains inside these walls
until he dies of old age and decrepitude. Then, his righteous survivors will
pray: "May he renounce every evil thought, evil word, and evil deed!" And,
if he has committed no further sins, he will at last be free of pollution (*Videvdat* 3.15–21).

In both the Achaemenian and the Zoroastrian paradise, walls thus separate the world outside, which is constituted as the existential norm, from an
internal space that stands in marked contrast to it. The two traditions differ,
however, on the nature of that contrast. Thus, the Achaemenian interior is a
space of perfection, characterized by warmth and moisture (the qualities that
make life flourish), abundant, infinitely varied plants and animals (key components of happiness), and intense sensory pleasure (visual and olfactory),
all of which are signs and products of the Wise Lord's benevolence. In contrast, the Zoroastrian enclosure contains the very opposite qualities: dryness
and cold, death and decay, scarcity and deprivation, and suffering, guilt, and
pollution, all of which entered the world with the Assault of the Evil Spirit
(see table 11).

TABLE 11: Conditions inside and outside the Achaemenian and Zoroastrian Versions of
"Paradise"

	Inside Walls	Outside Walls
Achaemenian	+	−
(as per Greek sources)	Warm, moist environment conducive to life. Abundant plants and animals of every species. Open to king and nobles. Peace, relaxation, and sensuous pleasure. "All-happiness" (Persepolis Treasury Tablets, nos. 49 and 59).	Normal existence.
Avestan	−	+
(*Videvdat* 3.15–21)	Cold, dry environment hostile to life. Devoid of plants, animals, and righteous humans. Sole inhabitant is the corpse bearer, utterly polluted by contact with death. Isolation, suffering, and gradual atonement, processes ended by death. "The very poorest and most run down of places" (*Videvdat* 3.19).	Normal existence.

II

If this Zoroastrian paradise can be understood as a logical inversion of its Persian counterpart, there is another Achaemenian datum that it resembles in more direct fashion. This is the ordeal of the hollowed-out troughs that was mentioned briefly in chapter 1. Here, another kind of barrier—that of the troughs themselves—delineates an internal space—one of pollution, corruption, darkness, and death—that it holds separate from the world outside. We are almost at the point where we can revisit the troughs and comprehend their significance. But, first, a bit of background.

The sole attested use of the troughs immediately followed the battle of Cunaxa (3 September 401). There, Artaxerxes II defeated a rebellion led by his brother, Cyrus the Younger, who died under murky circumstances. Some said that Artaxerxes himself slew Cyrus, and the king clearly favored this version. Other stories circulated, however, including one told by Ctesias, a Greek physician at the royal court who claimed to have been an eyewitness. His account, as preserved in Plutarch's summary, involved the following sequence of events: (1) Cyrus wounded Artaxerxes, who withdrew for medical attention (which Ctesias himself administered). (2) Darkness and the loss of his diadem conspired to conceal Cyrus's identity. (3) A Persian soldier by the name of Mithridates wounded Cyrus in the temple and knocked him from his horse, without knowing whom he struck. (4) A lowborn Carian struck him in the back of the leg, again without knowing who he was. (5) Falling, Cyrus hit his wounded head on a rock and died.

In this narrative, responsibility for the rebel prince's death is anything but clear and could be attributed to Mithridates, to the Carian, or simply to fate in the form of the rock. Excluded, however, is Artaxerxes. Nevertheless, we are told that the king believed that he had personally slain his brother and wanted all men to know this, his position being consistent with representation of the battle as a victory of rightful authority over rebellion, of truth over the Lie. Accordingly, when Artaxerxes distributed rewards to Mithridates and the Carian, he did so handsomely, but defined their contributions in ways that denied them credit for Cyrus's death.

The Carian, for his part, refused the king's gifts and cried out loudly that "he, and no one else, killed Cyrus," an indisputable overstatement of the facts since it ignored Mithridates' contribution. From the royal perspective, the Carian's self-serving claims were a manifestation of the Lie and, accordingly, an invitation to ethicocosmic disaster in the form of further rebellion.

Consistent with this view, Artaxerxes ordered the Carian beheaded, but the queen mother, Parysatis, requested that she be permitted to deal with him. This granted, she had her servants gouge out his eyes and drip molten brass in his ears until he was dead. Attacking the eyes and ears of a liar might be ways to dramatize, even rectify, his failures of perception and communication, but the use of molten metal is, perhaps, even more significant. Zoroastrian sources, including some of the most ancient, describe judicial ordeals involving this substance:

> What satisfaction do you give the two parties through your bright fire,
>   O Wise One,
> Through the molten metal to give a sign among the living?
> To destroy the liar, you make the truthful person flourish.

Later texts provide a fuller description, making clear that such ordeals were expected to differentiate liars from the truthful since the effects of the metal would vary with the moral status of those to whom it was applied:

> This is the way to propitiate molten metal: One makes the heart so pure and holy that, when they put molten metal on one's body, it does not burn. Adurbad, son of Mahraspand, followed this practice. When they put molten metal on his body and heart, which was pure, it was as pleasant to him as if they milked milk on him. When they put molten metal on the body and heart of liars and sinners, it burns, and they die.

Such practices were theorized not only as a means of inquiry, designed to determine who spoke the truth and who did not, but also an instrument of world purification, the fiery metal eliminating the lies and liars it revealed. Other texts gave eschatological associations to such ordeals by imagining a last judgment in which—as a culminating part of the Renovation—the resurrected dead wade through a river of molten metal that burns off their sins and impurities over the course of three days. Having thus been restored to their original state of moral and physical perfection, all people then enter eternal bliss, consistent with the intentions of the Wise Lord, who, in his absolute benevolence, could not imagine consigning any of his creatures to eternal damnation. To be sure, considerations of justice demand that sinners suffer in ways the righteous do not, but their suffering ends when this final ordeal is completed: "To one who is truthful, the metal seems like he is walking in warm milk; to the liar, the same metal seems like he is walking in molten metal" (*Greater Bundahišn* 34.19).

Parysatis thus construed her treatment of the Carian soldier as part of the great historical struggle to vanquish the Lie and restore primordial "happiness" (*šiyāti*). Indeed, her very name is consistent with such an understanding, for it means nothing other than "Much Happiness" (Old Persian **Paru-šiyāti*).

III

For his part, Mithridates accepted the king's gifts and initially kept silent, albeit with some resentment. One night at a banquet, however, under the influence of drink and provoked by Parysatis's chief eunuch, he asserted that Cyrus died of the wound that he himself inflicted. Less exaggerated than the Carian's claim, this was still an overstatement since it ignored the fact that only when the wound was exacerbated by Cyrus's fall on the rock did it prove fatal. Be that as it may, the eunuch relayed Mithridates' words to Parysatis, and she to Artaxerxes, who ordered the following treatment:

> Taking two troughs that were made to fit closely together, they laid Mithridates on his back inside one of them. Then they fit the other on top so the man's head, hands, and feet stuck out while it covered the rest of his body. They gave him food, pricking his eyes to force him when he resisted. They also poured milk mixed with honey into his mouth, and they poured it over his face. Then they turned his eyes constantly toward the sun, and a multitude of flies settled down, covering his face. Meanwhile, inside, the man did what it is necessary for people to do when they have drunk and eaten. Worms and maggots boiled up from the decay and putrefaction of his excrement, and these ate away his body, boring into his interior. When he was dead and the top was removed, people saw his flesh all eaten away and swarms of such animals surrounding his vitals, eating them and leeching at them. Thus, Mithridates was gradually destroyed over seventeen days, until he finally died.

The text offers no interpretation, being content to let the episode speak for itself. Even so, there are questions one might like to ask. First, how did the Persians involved in these proceedings construe them, and what did they mean to accomplish in this fashion? Second, why was this specific procedure considered appropriate for Mithridates? Third, what were spectators meant to observe, and what conclusions were they supposed to draw? None of these can be answered with absolute certainty. Still, drawing on evidence from the Achaemenian inscriptions, Herodotus, and Zoroastrian scriptures, we can venture some interpretations with a high degree of confidence.

IV

How did the Persians involved in these proceedings construe them, and what did they mean to accomplish in this fashion?

Although this hypothesis will later need some refinement, let us start by assuming that the things done to Mithridates were meant as a form of punishment. If so, Artaxerxes was simply following the instructions that Darius left for his successors:

> Proclaims Darius the king: "You who may later be king here: Protect yourself boldly from the Lie! The man who is a liar, punish him so he is well-punished, if you would think thus: 'Let my land/people be secure.'"

(DB §55)

> Proclaims Darius the king: "You who may later be king here: That man who is a liar and he who is a deceit-doer, do not be a friend to them. Punish them so they are well-punished."

(DB §64)

Although the Old Persian verb *fraθ-* is conventionally translated "to punish," as in these passages, close study reveals some unexpected subtleties. To begin, its cognates in all other Indo-Iranian languages mean "to ask," and this is still evident in the Old Persian compound *pati-fraθ-*, "to read," which treats reading as a process of inquiry, through which one learns something of value through close scrutiny and careful examination. If the uncompounded verb retained some of the same sense, conceivably the action it described was not punitive, with the infliction of pain as its goal, but interrogatory, pain being only the means to another end: that of obtaining information.

Such a view finds confirmation in the Akkadian and Elamite translations of Old Persian *fraθ-*. The former employ a verb that means "to investigate, prosecute"; the latter are even more striking, for they use an idiomatic phrase that elsewhere describes the extraction of oil from sesame. While strange (to us), the metaphor is extraordinarily apt, for, in both the agricultural and the judicial context, it describes the systematic application of pressure to squeeze the very essence out of something—or someone. The goal of such operations was not punishment in the sense of vengeance, chastisement, or retribution. Rather, these were inquisitorial proceedings or, more precisely, judiciary ordeals of the sort we considered apropos of the Carian. Within such ordeals, the imperial apparatus understood itself to be applying pressure that could strip away pretense and disclose the accused's innermost moral nature. If vindicated, the suspect could be released; if proved guilty, he would be destroyed in the process and the world cleansed of his transgressions. The goal was to establish truth and then—if necessary—to annihilate the Lie, thereby setting right the moral and cosmic order.

Infractions were not all treated with equal severity, however, and one test of whether a given criminal had been "well-punished" or "well-interrogated" was whether the king's response was commensurate to the offense in question. Further elaborating his principles of rule, Darius explained: "He who causes destruction, I interrogate/punish him according to the destruction caused" (DNb §2c). Seemingly, Artaxerxes adopted the same policy. Thus, a soldier whose boasts were false but who posed no threat to the king or the realm received the relatively mild rebuke of having three needles thrust through his tongue. The case of Mithridates, however, demanded stronger measures.

V

Why was this specific procedure considered appropriate for Mithridates?

Mithridates was, apparently, charged with having exaggerated his role in Cyrus's death and with slandering the king, whose veracity he thereby implicitly impugned. Both offenses would have been understood as instances of the Lie, but the latter one was particularly grievous as it struck directly at the sources of royal legitimacy and social order. Indeed, from Darius on down, kings in the Achaemenian line claimed that the Wise Lord had chosen them because they were antithetical to the Lie at every level of its activity: in thought, word, and deed. As Darius put it, speaking on behalf of the whole dynasty:

> For this reason the Wise Lord bore me aid, he and the other gods that are: Because I was not vulnerable to the Lie, I did not speak lies, I was not a deceit-doer, *neither I nor my lineage.*
>
> (DB §63)

Logically, the assertions of Mithridates and Artaxerxes were mutually exclusive. If one told the truth, then the other one lied. And, given the nature of Achaemenian ideology, if the king was a liar, the empire—no, the cosmos itself—stood on shifting sand. The ordeal of the troughs was, thus, designed to vindicate the king, reassure all others, and quiet the realm, by publicly convicting Mithridates of unspeakable corruption.

Herodotus reports that the Persians regarded lying as the most shameful of all actions. In Zoroastrian lists of capital crimes, it appears more prominently than any other offense and takes a multitude of forms, including perjury, heresy, slander, breach of contract, and rendering false judgment. Liars could expect stern requital, as a text comparing the postmortem torments of unrepentant sinners to the this-worldly punishments of capital criminals makes clear. Insofar as Mithridates refused to retract his story, royal authority would have considered him an unrepentant liar. Falling in both categories, he would, thus, have deserved such pains both in life and thereafter:

> If one dies in a state of sin, without penitence and unrepentant, one's soul goes to hell and receives the punishment of capital offenders. All the demons inflict heavy pain, trouble, *devouring, and many things like stench and biting, tearing, cutting in pieces,* all harm and misfortune. The offender's own choices created these things for him in hell, and there will be evils for him until the Renovation [*or:* Wondermaking].
>
> (*Dadestan i Denig* 40.4)

In hell—which exists only until the end of history, when the Lie is defeated and happiness regained—these torments are inflicted by demons, but, in all other ways, they mirror the pains that Mithridates suffered, complete with biting, tearing, devouring, cutting in pieces, and the stench of filth and corruption. Note also the specification that "the offender's own choices created these things for him," which is to say that he—and he alone—bears responsibility for his suffering. Other texts go further still, describing the demons that torment a sinner as the tangible product of his own moral choices and actions.

VI

What were spectators meant to observe, and what were they meant to conclude?

Several things, each fraught with deep significance. Let us take them in sequence, starting from the outermost, and working our way inward.

First were the king's soldiers or servants, who carried out the ordeal and whose conduct was irreproachable. Not only did they commit virtually no violence against the accused, but the whole business was organized to construe their actions as beneficent. Above all, they fed the accused milk and honey: the purest forms of nourishment, regularly associated with goodness, light, happiness, and peace. Note, for instance, the contrast drawn in the judicial and eschatological ordeals described above between milk (the sweetest, most soothing, most innocent of fluids) and molten metal (the most violent and destructive). That contrast is brought into alignment with other binaries—good and evil, truth and lie, pleasure and pain, purity and pollution—such that the persons associated with milk were understood to be righteous and the guilty were associated with substances of an antithetical sort: molten metal, on the one hand, and feces, on the other (see table 12).

The troughs themselves contrast accusers and accused, drawing a sharp line between them. Accusers stood outside, moving freely in the light above the suspect, who lay horizontal in the dark inside, below them and immobile.

TABLE 12: Ordeals Designed to Differentiate Liars and the Truthful

Processes of Interrogation	Truthful/Righteous	Liars
Judicial ordeals	Purity of heart protects one from pain and makes the metal feel like warm milk	Molten metal inflicts great pain and kills the evildoer
Eschatological ordeal	Wading through molten metal feels like walking in warm milk	Molten metal inflicts great pain, burning away sin and restoring one's original purity
Ordeal of the troughs	Those administering the ordeal feed milk and honey to the accused	The body of the accused transforms milk and honey into excrement, which breeds maggots that devour his flesh, inflicting great pain, killing the man, revealing his inner organs and nature

One can also understand the troughs to have differentiated feeders who gave abundantly from the man who took their food with reluctance—or, to put it in the most pointed terms, the putatively righteous from the presumptive liar.

Next, we should consider the flies on Mithridates' face. That the Achaemenians regarded such creatures with religious revulsion is clear from Herodotus's testimony that the magi, the chief priests of the dynasty, waged ceaseless war against ants, serpents, reptiles, and insects as part of their sacred duties. Zoroastrian priests are enjoined to act similarly, and each one is invested with a holy flyswatter of sorts, known as a "vermin-killer." Insects, reptiles, and a few other species (scorpions, mice, worms) are, in fact, grouped together in the category "vermin" (Avestan and Pahlavi *xrafstar*), which is antithetical to all good forms of animal life. In contrast to the latter, vermin were created by the Evil Spirit when he mixed his own bodily filth with the primordial darkness. Reflecting such origins, these creatures are aggressive, venomous, death dealing, and destructive. Although small, they travel in swarms and attack in great numbers, gnawing, biting, and poisoning their prey. Their colors relate them to darkness, just as their ravenous appetites and lack of intellect relate them to the demonic. They were brought into being just before history began to serve as shock troops in the Evil Spirit's attack on the Wise Lord's creation, when he himself took the form of a fly. The demon "Corpse" (*Nasu*), who is responsible for bodily decomposition, decay, and pollution, does the same, death being thus theorized as a repetition of the Assault, effected at the level of the individual organism:

> Just after death, when consciousness departs, the Lie named Corpse flies here
> from the north [i.e., the demonic direction of cold and dry], taking the form of
> a monstrous fly, knees forward, stinger behind, speckled all over, like the most
> horrid vermin.

To be sure, flies started the attack on Mithridates, but they did not finish
the process. The honor of actually killing him goes to the worms and maggots who teemed up out of his excrement. To appreciate the significance of
this, one must understand that Zoroastrian texts theorized digestion, not
simply as a metabolic, but as a moral process. Their analysis begins with the
observation that—like everything else in historical time—food is a mixed,
ambiguous entity, containing elements of both good and evil. Digestion, then,
is the analytic process that separates good substances from evil, transform-
ing the former into blood (which sustains all life, by virtue of its hot-moist nature), and sending this blood upward to the brain, the body's heavenly re-
gion. In contrast, the bad substances residually present in food as a result of
the Assault ("poisons," which are cold-dry in nature and, thus, antithetical to
life) are treated in converse fashion. This deadly matter is sent downward
and, finally, cast out in the form of excrement, whose dark color and foul
smell reveal its origin and nature:

> When someone dies, his sins and good deeds are calculated. All those who are
> pure go to heaven. All those who are liars are thrown into hell. Homologous
> to this is people's eating of food. All that is good goes to the brain, where it be-
> comes pure blood. All that is mixed with poison goes from the stomach to the
> intestine, and it is thrown outside through the anus, which is just like hell.

Such a theory raises some practical questions as regards Mithridates' ordeal. Thus, if excrement results from the evil substances present in food, and
if the food that Mithridates received was of the purest type, why did his body
produce so much excrement of such a vile, vermin-spawning sort? An important passage from another Zoroastrian text suggests an answer: "Bodily filth
[a category that includes excrement as its prime type] is entirely demonic; it
all comes from demons. The more one's body is inhabited by demons, the
more filth there is."

Here, we must recognize that things we tend to treat as abstractions—ap-
petite, greed, wrath, envy, and, above all, the Lie—Mazdaean theology per-
sonifies as demons, and this helps us solve our problem. Milk and honey ought
not produce so much excrement, and that is precisely the point. If the deadly
filth that poured from Mithridates was not the normal end product of such
foods, then its excessive quality must derive from his body itself, not the

things he ate. His reeking, vermin-laden excrement thus bore graphic witness to the corruption (moral and physical) of his body and the demons resident therein, chief of them all the Lie. What was squeezed from his body—in the most literal and graphic fashion—thus provided the means to convict him guilty on all charges.

VII

One last fact should be mentioned here. Old Persian discourse includes a number of terms—eleven, to be exact—that can designate evil in one fashion or another. These were used, however, in very unequal measure by various members of the Achaemenian dynasty (see table 13).

Ten of these terms are found in Darius's inscriptions, Xerxes used four, and none of the subsequent Achaemenians used any of them, save Artaxerxes II, who used one and one only. He did, however, use it on three different occasions, in contrast to Darius and Xerxes, each of whom used it once only in corpora that are much larger than his by far. For Darius, moreover, this term was only an adjective, while Xerxes turned it into a substantive, thereby endowing it with a sense of independent existence and agency. Artaxerxes, however, used it with wildly disproportionate frequency and made it a centerpiece of his discourse, repeatedly imploring: "May the Wise Lord, Anahita, and Mithra protect me from all that is foul/stinking." Conventionally translated "evil"—a bland impoverishment of its proper meaning—Old Persian *gastā* is derived

TABLE 13: Achaemenian Terminology for Evil: Usage by Different Kings (number of times)

	Darius	Xerxes	Artaxerxes II	Others
arika, "vulnerable to the Lie, gullible"	5	0	0	0
daiva, "evil god, demon"	0	3	0	0
duš-, "bad, mal-"	2	1	0	0
Drauga, "the Lie"	6	0	0	0
draujana, "liar"	4	0	0	0
gastā, "foul, stinking, malodorous"	1	1	*3*	0
hamiçiya, "rebellious"	48	0	0	0
miθah, "evil, hostile"	3	0	0	0
yaud-, "in commotion"	2	1	0	0
zūrah, "deceit"	1	0	0	0
zūra-kara, "deceit-doing"	2	0	0	0

from a root that means "to stink." When this sense is restored, we can understand that, with Artaxerxes II, an olfactory code came to dominate the Persian imaginary of evil, as witnessed, not only by his use of this word, but also by the ordeal that he inflicted on Mithridates.

VIII

In Ctesias's pages, the ordeal of Mithridates stands as a prime example of Oriental despotism, providing an indelible image of the potentate's delight in designing novel, refined, and titillating means to inflict exquisite pain on those who incurred his disfavor. Such bias is typical of his writing, and it has led many to discount the value of his testimony, notwithstanding the fact that, more than any other Greek author, Ctesias was able to observe the Achaemenian court firsthand. Interpretation, however, can sometimes be detached from reporting. By using other Iranian data, I hope to have shown that the ordeal of the troughs had a profound sense and significance that Ctesias failed to comprehend. Not simply a spectacular theater of cruelty, it was a legal procedure informed by and thoroughly grounded in religious principles that included such domains as ethics, cosmology, demonology, and salvation. Which only makes things that much worse.

What is most appalling in this ordeal is not the empire's willingness to perform disgustingly bestial acts or even its ability to justify those acts as necessary parts of its sacred mission. It is its capacity to coordinate even the most questionable practices with its animating discourse to produce results that are read as confirmation of its loftiest principles, even when the two stand in the starkest contradiction. Whatever he and his court may have believed, Artaxerxes was not God's agent, defending truth against the Lie, and struggling to restore primordial perfection. Rather, he was defending himself against gossip that undermined state propaganda that labored to establish his reputation and status as Cyrus's slayer, rightful king, and champion of truth. To do that, he made an object lesson of the unfortunate Mithridates and, above all, the latter's body. Onto such natural processes as digestion, elimination, and putrefaction—as well as the spawning and feeding habits of maggots, the vulnerability of flesh, and death itself—the imperial apparatus projected a set of religious beliefs in an extraordinarily prejudicial fashion. Ultimately, Mithridates' feces were constituted as conclusive proof of the Orwellian propositions that the truthful soldier was a lying wretch and that the lying king was the heroic embodiment of truth.

Given the materials considered over the course of in this book, I am led to differentiate two phases in the history of empire. The first—its incipient moment, the leitmotif of which is the pursuit of paradise—is one in which a nation or a people organizes and energizes itself for the conquest, domination, and exploitation of its neighbors. As its troops meet with success, its control expands outward, and it draws resources back to the center to fuel its further expansion. Few peoples have attempted such a venture, and even fewer have succeeded to any significant degree. To do so involves overcoming countless practical problems.

Among the most important of these is the fact that, before it can unleash the force necessary for expansive conquest, any group needs to overcome the inhibiting systems that normally hold such violence in check. These may include international law, calculations of political and economic costs, treaty obligations, and traditional considerations of morality and religion. Should a different style of religious ideology and orientation be developed, however, one that does not inhibit but actively licenses such violence, that can make an enormous difference.

One finds such developments in the discourse of the early Achaemenians. In the texts associated with Cyrus and, above all, with Darius, one finds the notion that not only force but also truth and virtue flow outward from a uniquely privileged center to reach and transform lesser, outlying peoples. Nor does wealth flow back to the center simply to enrich the emergent imperial power. Rather, the material substance previously scattered across the globe is reunited at the center, where it is used to transform and perfect the world according to God's original plan for creation. All this, moreover, is to be done at the direction of uniquely gifted and moral leaders, chosen by God for the purpose.

Three basic constructs thus characterize Achaemenian ideology, each one profoundly religious and brilliantly suited to represent the empire's most aggressive tendencies and its most audacious ambitions as righteous, sacred, and holy. It is as an ensemble, however, that the three are exceptionally potent, and this ensemble recurs—with contextual and dialectal variations, to be sure—in the discourse of most successful empires as a condition of their possibility. The three components, as we have repeatedly observed, are (1) a starkly dualistic ethics in which the opposition good/evil is aligned with that of self/other and correlated discriminatory binaries, (2) a theology of election that secures the ruler's legitimacy by constituting him as God's chosen agent, (3) and a sense of soteriological mission that represents imperial aggression as salvific action taken on behalf of divine principles, thereby recoding the empire's victims as its beneficiaries.

There is, however, a later moment in Achaemenian history—one for which the troughs may stand as leitmotif—when the empire finds it increasingly difficult to contain the contradiction between its discourse and its practice.

Having overcome the problem of moral hesitation by wrapping even its most distasteful actions in an ennobling, sanctifying discourse, the empire now faces the possibility of moral exhaustion, in which its animating discourse loses all credibility, by virtue of its complicit relation to those same repugnant actions. In order to avoid that danger, it becomes necessary for the leaders and foot soldiers of empire to repersuade themselves—ever more emphatically—not only that the discourse is true and worthy, but also that it is appropriately applied to the practices in question. Toward that end, they may find it useful to stage circular spectacles in which actions that would be considered brutish under any other circumstances produce results that (seem to) confirm the lofty principles that rendered them licit in the first place.

Contradictions between sacred discourse and bestial practice, as well as the dialectical relation between moral confidence and moral depravity, are built into the deep structure of empire, and, the longer imperial rule persists, the more episodes will accumulate in which these tensions manifest themselves painfully. Whenever this happens, further discursive operations will be launched that struggle to contain the contradiction in one fashion or another. Staunch denial is always a favorite tactic, as are euphemism, blurring the issues, invoking the divine, flogging scapegoats, slandering critics, and reasserting one's devotion to traditional ideals, all evidence to the contrary notwithstanding. Such operations become increasingly strained with repetition since a people's capacity to tolerate contradiction is distinctly more finite than is an empire's capacity to manifest them. Sooner or later, the day comes when the king is driven to brandish his critic's shit as evidence that the man was a demon, the king himself presumably being shitless and divine. The ordeal of the troughs shows just how extraordinarily ingenious, inventive, and self-confident an imperial apparatus can be in advancing so ridiculous and repulsive an argument. Indeed, in such desperate straits, it needs to have these gifts and more if it is to persuade itself—once again!—that it is doing God's work, leading good against evil, and recovering happiness for mankind.

Postscript: On Abu Ghraib and Some Related Contemporary Matters

I

Although the topic that concerns me most broadly is that of empire in general, I have kept the preceding discussion focused on Achaemenian data in the belief that the painstaking study of a single, well-chosen example can reveal more than a wide-ranging, but superficial, comparative survey. Still, it would be disingenuous to pretend that my thoughts have been riveted on ancient Persia with a single-mindedness equal to that of my text. As careful readers will, no doubt, have recognized, my anguish and outrage concerning the American imperial adventure in Iraq frequently bubble close to the surface.

At times, when working with the inscriptions of Cyrus, Darius, or Xerxes, I thought that I recognized quite a similar, religiously grounded apologia for empire in the official rhetoric of George W. Bush, as, for instance, in the opening and closing passages of his "Mission Accomplished" address, delivered 1 May 2003 on board the USS *Abraham Lincoln*. Here, the same themes that I have repeatedly identified—ethical dualism, a theology of election, and a sense of soteriological mission—are all patently evident:

> Thank you all very much. Admiral Kelly, Captain Card, officers and sailors of the USS *Abraham Lincoln,* my fellow Americans: Major combat operations in Iraq have ended. In the battle of Iraq, the United States and our allies have prevailed. And now our coalition is engaged in securing and reconstructing that country. In this battle, *we have fought for the cause of liberty, and for the peace of the world.* Our

nation and our coalition are proud of this accomplishment—yet, it is you, the members of the United States military, who achieved it. Your courage, your willingness to face danger for your country and for each other, made this day possible. Because of you, our nation is more secure. Because of you, *the tyrant has fallen, and Iraq is free.* . . .

We are mindful, as well, that some good men and women are not making the journey home. . . . Every name, every life is a loss to our military, to our nation, and to the loved ones who grieve. Those we lost were last seen on duty. *Their final act on this Earth was to fight a great evil and bring liberty to others. All of you—all in this generation of our military—have taken up the highest calling of history.* You're defending your country, and protecting the innocent from harm. And *wherever you go, you carry a message of hope—a message that is ancient and ever new. In the words of the prophet Isaiah, "To the captives, 'come out'—and to those in darkness, 'be free.'"* Thank you for serving our country and our cause. May God bless you all, and may God continue to bless America.

Here, as in many of his speeches, Mr. Bush implicitly advanced a well-structured syllogism, in which two premises—(1) that, in its wars, the United States pursues the cause of freedom and (2) that this cause originates, not with the United States, but with God himself—interact to suggest an implicit conclusion: that the United States is God's chosen instrument for the accomplishment of his purpose for all humanity. In this speech, however, Mr. Bush went further still, and it is important to note that the passage from Isaiah that is paraphrased toward the end of the address (Isa. 61:1) contains a claim of messianic status closely related to that advanced elsewhere in Isaiah on behalf of Cyrus (see Isa. 45:1), a claim considered in chapter 3. The full verse thus identifies the speaker of these hopes as nothing less than God's Anointed (Hebrew *māšîaḥ*, English *Messiah*, i.e., king and savior):

> The Spirit of the Lord GOD is upon me
>   *because the LORD* has anointed me
> to bring good tidings to the afflicted;
>   he has sent me to bind up the brokenhearted,
> to proclaim liberty to the captives
>   and the opening of the prison to those who are bound.
>
>   (Isa. 61:1)

Even more rousing than these words were the dramatic accompanying visuals, as the victorious leader swooped down from the heavens in an S-3B Viking jet, made a precision landing on the aircraft carrier's deck, strutted forth in a perfectly tailored flight suit, and fraternized with military personnel before making his historic address. The stage management of the event was perfect, and White House advance teams spent several days on board the *Lincoln* to organize all details of the spectacle.

Although this went virtually unmentioned, when Mr. Bush's plane set down, the *Abraham Lincoln* was a scant 50 kilometers offshore from San Diego and had been making lazy circles at sea for fifteen hours in order to stay in position. The president's landing was, thus, unnecessary in practical terms, for he could easily have greeted the crew on their return to base. In that context, however, he would have represented civilian life, domesticity, government, and the home front welcoming military personnel back from war. As staged, the event conveyed the impression of a warrior president and a triumphant hero descended from the clouds, master of air, land, and sea. The delay also resulted from the advance team's desire to time the president's speech so that it could be set in "magic hour light . . . so that Mr. Bush would be bathed in a golden glow." Camera angles were also carefully controlled so that the huge "Mission Accomplished" banner would be prominent in the background while the skyline of San Diego would never appear.

II

Mr. Bush's *Top Gun* landing became one of two iconic images of the Iraq War in its early phases. The other preceded it by three weeks, and the president acknowledged this when he said: "In the images of falling statues, we have witnessed the arrival of a new era." His allusion identified the 9 April 2003 toppling of Saddam Hussein's statue in Baghdad with the heroic history of iconoclasm, from Abraham shattering his father's idols to the treatment of Lenin's image after the fall of communism: an image of religious truth overcoming superstition, atheism, and tyranny. Quickly seized on by electronic and print media, the action at Baghdad's central Firdos Square (the Arabic *firdos* means "paradise" and is derived from the Iranian terms discussed in chapter 5) was initially construed as a spontaneous popular event, one in which the jubilant Iraqi people enacted their newly won liberty by toppling the image of the tyrant.

Although initial commentary was close to rapturous, some images complicated matters and exposed the operation to criticism. Thus, several critics called attention to pictures of U.S. Marine Corporal Edward Chin, who draped the statue's face in the U.S. flag when attaching chains to haul it down. Some of the crowd voiced disapproval of this, and marine officers ordered the flag's replacement with an Iraqi banner. Still, damage was done since this brief incident suggested that events were hardly spontaneous, but under American control. The subsequent release of long-shot photographs of the event confirmed this impression, revealing that Firdos Square was nearly empty when the statue came down, having been sealed off by American troops and tanks. Investigation showed that this was done after a Marine Corps colonel specializing in psychological operations identified the statue as a "target of opportunity" and developed a plan to exploit it. A small number of dependable Iraqis—most of them affiliated with Ahmed Chelabi's Iraqi National Congress, an expatriate group particularly favored by the U.S. Department of Defense—were then admitted to the square, having been recruited to play the role of "the crowd." In this performance, they were directed by psyop officers using bullhorns who also selected the most effective photograph angles.

III

Both the episodes discussed this far were carefully structured to play on codes of verticality, contrasting the high and the low. The first was an attempt to exalt the American national self via its lofty, airborne, charismatic president (see figure 14); the second was a complementary effort to denigrate Iraq—or, more precisely, its defeated ruling stratum—via the fallen statue of its former dictator (see figure 15).

A third iconic episode expanded on the latter construction by following the trajectory of Saddam Hussein's fall, not only to the earth's surface, but into an underworld of sorts where the former dictator cowered like an animal until captured. This, of course, was the "spider hole," from which he was taken on 13 December 2003. The name given to this small, subterranean refuge is a military term (like the more familiar "foxhole") that normally denotes a shallow blind from which ambushes are launched, but it was applied to Saddam's bunker by General Ricardo Sanchez in his press conference announcing the capture. Conceivably a minor slip of the tongue, but also conceivably deliberate, the "spider hole" misnomer was indelibly fixed in the public imagination and helped cement the humiliating images of Mr. Hussein as a thoroughly defeated man, reduced to a lowly, filthy, vermin-infested existence (see figure 16).

IV

Unlike the photographs from the USS *Lincoln*, Firdos Square, and the spider hole, those made by members of the 372nd Military Police Company at the

Figure 14: George W. Bush waves as he walks with U.S. Navy Lieutenant Ryan Phillips
on the tarmac to a Navy S-3B Viking jet at North Island Naval Station in Coronado, CA,
1 May 2003. Bush flew in the navigator's seat to the deck of the carrier USS *Abraham Lincoln*
to deliver a speech to the nation. (AP/Wide World Photos/Denis Poroy: APA6750920.)

Abu Ghraib prison complex between October and December 2003 were not
intended for propaganda purposes, nor were they part of a program to man-
age public opinion. Still, they have their relevance to this discussion.

For all the notoriety of these pictures, the nature of their content has received relatively little serious scrutiny. Many have speculated that the MPs
acted under orders—real or implicit—to soften up prisoners for interrogation. Some have compared the pictures themselves to trophy shots taken by
hunters. Only a few of those involved have spoken for the record, the most
important being Private First Class Lynndie England, who offered the vulgar
Nietzscheanism: "It was just for fun." Not so different was the judgment of
Special Agent Tyler Pieron, who looked into events at Abu Ghraib for the

Figure 15: Photograph that creates the impression of U.S. soldiers watching Iraqi civilians topple a statue of Saddam Hussein in downtown Baghdad, 9 April 2003. In actuality, the statue was brought down by U.S. Marines using heavy equipment as a small and select group of Iraqi expatriates watched. (AP/Wide World Photos/Jerome Delay: APA6721809.)

Criminal Investigation Division and maintained that the MPs did these things "simply because they could."

Roughly twenty pictures have been made public at the time I write, and others, including videotapes, are still classified, notwithstanding court rulings mandating their release. To look at these images with any degree of analytic dispassion is not easy, yet close study shows that they deploy—in a fashion more blunt and obscene and much less concerned with theological niceties—the same basic codes as do the more official spectacles that we have been considering. What they reveal is that, not only did humble foot soldiers absorb the symbolic constructs that their superiors used to justify imperial aggression, but they also became capable of reproducing these with the limited means at their disposal.

Like children overexposed to Hollywood westerns who learn to mount crude versions of "cowboys and Indians" on their own, the soldiers at Abu Ghraib staged and restaged variant scenarios, all of which delineate the difference between "us" and "them." In these small-scale tableaux, low-level GIs endlessly repersuaded themselves of the basic truths: We are high; they are low. We are clean; they are dirty. We are strong and brave; they are weak

and cowardly. We are lordly; they are virtually animals. We are God's chosen; they are estranged from everything divine. In the vast majority of the
pictures that have been published, the Iraqis are naked and close to the floor.
In virtually all, they are—or have been made to seem—humiliated, de-
moralized, craven, and base, thoroughly dominated by America's superior
power (see figure 17).

For all that it may seem counterintuitive, I am persuaded that the mini-
dramas staged at Abu Ghraib were not designed to degrade the Iraqi prisoners. Rather, like the treatment of Mithridates by Artaxerxes' soldiers, they
were designed to confirm the captors' worst suspicions concerning the Iraqis,
whom they had been trained to regard as "terrorists," as "fanatics," as "die-
hard Baathists," or, simply, as Arabs and Muslims, but, in any event, as *always
already* degraded. The point was to establish that such people got what they
deserved and deserved what they got, being exactly what "we" always knew
them to be.

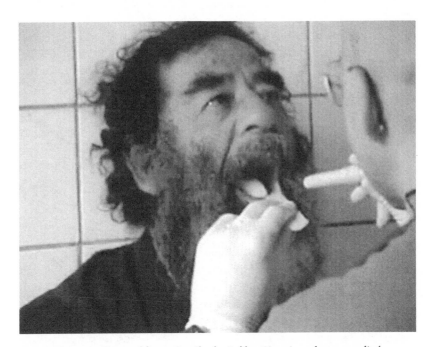

Figure 16: Captured former Iraqi leader Saddam Hussein undergoes medical
examinations in Baghdad, 14 December 2003. The U.S. administrator in Iraq,
L. Paul Bremer, confirmed the capture of Hussein in a dirt hole under a
farmhouse near his hometown of Tikrit, eight months after the fall of
Baghdad. (AP/Wide World Photos/U.S. Military via APTN: APA7063239.)

Figure 17: An Associated Press photograph showing Private First Class Lynndie
England holding a leash attached to an unnamed Iraqi prisoner in late 2003 at the
Abu Ghraib prison in Iraq. (AP/Wide World Photos: APA30582840.)

V

Conceivably, the guards at Abu Ghraib may represent a late moment in the
history of an empire, or they may simply have found themselves at a stress
point, the accumulated pressure of events disclosing deep contradictions in
the empire's traditional animating verities. At such times, even the lowliest
grunts may feel the need to repersuade themselves that they and their leaders are good, their enemies bad, their own cause righteous, even divine (although there is precious little evidence of overtly religious concerns in the
photographs from Abu Ghraib). At relatively recent moments in this empire's history, propositions of this sort gave its leaders and soldiers the moral
confidence needed for the project of conquest. But continued moral confidence is also necessary for the preservation of empire, and this can be difficult to sustain. For, the longer an empire endures, the more often its person-

nel are called on to engage in acts that, under other circumstances, they would consider unjustified, even repugnant. However sincere the Achaemenian pursuit of paradise may initially have been, sooner or later troops presumably came to suspect that impaling rebels did not produce happiness for mankind. Similarly, it is difficult to reconcile the grim realities of interrogation and guard duty at Guantanamo, Abu Ghraib, or secret prisons still undiscovered with a lofty discourse of "freedom," however elastically the latter term may be taken.

Circumstances of this sort put soldiers to a severe test. In such moments, the maintenance of imperial power depends on their ability to sustain or regenerate certain core beliefs, in spite of brutal experiences that threaten to demolish everything they have been taught to hold dear. To repersuade

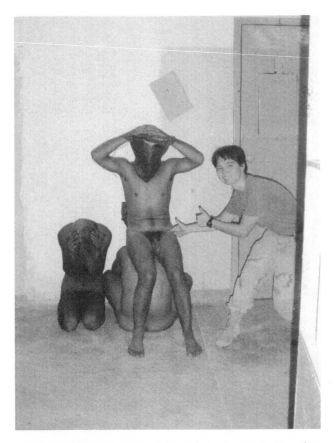

Figure 18: An Associated Press photograph showing Private First Class Lynndie England posing with unnamed naked prisoners in late 2003 at Abu Ghraib. (AP/Wide World Photos: APA30582873.)

themselves in extremis, they may stage all manner of spectacles emphatically reasserting the conventional, but severely embattled, articles of faith. Some of these demonstrations are, no doubt, elegant, sincere, and aesthetically appealing: the paradisal side of the story. Others, like those at Abu Ghraib and the late Achaemenian ordeal of the troughs, are infernal exercises in circular logic the results of which are desperately construed as confirmation of their increasingly shaky presuppositions.

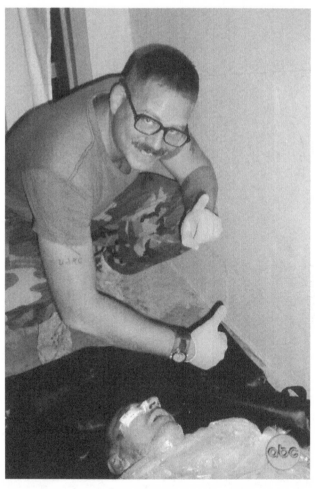

Figure 19: An undated photograph obtained by ABC News, allegedly taken by Sergeant Charles Frederick, showing Sergeant Charles Graner of the 372nd Military Police Company posing with the body of the Iraqi prisoner Manadel al-Jamadi, who was beaten to death during interrogation and packed in ice at Abu Ghraib. (AP/Wide World Photos/ABC News: APA7758991.)

Figure 20: On board the USS *Abraham Lincoln* off the California coast on 1 May 2003, George W. Bush flashes a thumbs-up after declaring the end of major combat in Iraq. (AP/Wide World Photos/J. Scott Applewhite: APA6751630.)

In all cases, however, the goal is the same: to restore flagging moral confidence so that troops can continue to commit the atrocities and engage in the depravities on which an empire depends. The sign that such operations have succeeded is a cocky posture, a knowing smile, and a jubilant thumbs-up signal (see figures 18–20).

Notes

PREFACE

The contemporary question of empire. Empire became a fashionable topic with Negri and Hardt 2000. Since then, there has followed a raft of publications, including Hahn and Heiss 2001, Howe 2002, Joxe 2002, Lal 2002, O'Hara 2003, Johnson 2004, Khalidi 2004, Passavant and Dean 2004, Magstadt 2004, and Vidal 2004.

Recent studies of religious politics and political religion in empires. See, among others, Rostworowski de Diez Canseco 1983, Conrad and Demarest 1984, Wechsler 1985, Tanner 1993, Miller 1994, Hempton 1996, Lucrezi 1996, Clauss 1999, van der Veer 2001, Wills 2001, Gradel 2002, Holloway 2002, Rabassa and Stepper 2002, and Coreth 2004.

Research on Achaemenian Persia over the last twenty-five years. The culminating synthesis of contemporary knowledge is Briant 1996. Other major contributions include Dandamaev 1976 and 1989, Hinz 1976, Root 1979, Sancisi-Weerdenburg 1980, Frei and Koch 1984, Dandamaev and Lukonin 1989, and Wiesehöfer 1996. The volumes of *Achaemenid History*, which began to appear in 1987, have also consistently advanced the discussion. None of these works make religion a major focus, although Briant and Root have interesting discussions at numerous points. The major works on religion that have come out over the same period, while erudite and learned, make little attempt to relate religious data to broader issues of society, history, and culture. The most important are Koch 1977, Boyce 1982, Schwartz 1985, Kellens 1991, Jong 1997, and Stausberg 2002: 157–86.

Paucity of work on religion. The relevant items are listed in Weber and Wiesehöfer 1996: 462–63. Herrenschmidt 1980 provided an excellent summary of the state of the question as of that date. Some modification would now be necessary, but considerably less than one might expect.

Herrenschmidt on cosmogony. Herrenschmidt 1977. Also relevant and extremely important are Herrenschmidt 1976, 1979a, 1979b, 1987a, 1990, and 1991.

Molé on eschatological renovation. Molé 1963: 34–36, 86–120, 412–18, and passim. See also Lincoln 1996.

Hostile reactions to Molé. Publication of Molé 1960 prompted a sharp exchange, involving Duchesne-Guillemin 1961 and Molé 1961. Respectful on some points, but quite critical and condescendingly dismissive on others, was Gnoli 1964, but Gnoli 1965 was considerably more aggressive. Meanwhile, Duchesne-Guillemin 1966 and 1966–67 renewed that author's objections. I have the account of Benveniste's reaction and Molé's death from knowledgeable Parisian colleagues.

Kings and kingship. In addition to Ahn 1992, see Gnoli 1972 and 1984, Schmitt 1977, Root 1979, Sancisi-Weerdenburg 1981, Kuhrt 1984, Panaino 2000, and Westenholz 2000.

1. INTRODUCTION

I

Paradise gardens. See chapter 5. Recent literature includes Tuplin 1996, Bremmer 1999, Hultgård 2000, and Lincoln 2003a and 2003c.

Artaxerxes II and the torture of the hollowed-out troughs. For the full account, see chapter 6. The episode was first reported in Ctesias (preserved in Plutarch, *Artaxerxes* 16.1–4).

Iconographic evidence. Root 1979 remains the classic study. The most innovative research in recent years has shifted attention from the well-known monuments to the much more intimate genre of cylinder seals. See, among others, Dusinberre 1997, Garrison 2000, Garrison and Root 2001, Kaptan 2002, and Root 2003.

II

Achaemenian history. The most comprehensive study is Briant 1996 (English translation: Briant 2002), which is nothing short of magisterial. Also excellent are Gershevitch 1985, Dandamaev 1989, Dandamaev and Lukonin 1989, Wiesehöfer 1996.

Cyrus and his Median predecessors. The most important sources are Herodotus 1.107–30, Xenophon, *Cyropaedia* (which contain a good deal of legendary material), and a Babylonian text often called the "Dream of Nabonidus." These will be discussed more fully in chapter 3.

Darius and Cyrus's daughters. According to Herodotus 3.88, after obtaining royal power, Darius married Atossa and Artystone, both daughters of Cyrus by Cassandane. The former had previously been wife to her two royal brothers, Cambyses and Bardiya. At the same time, Darius also married Parmys, the daughter of Bardiya and granddaughter of Cyrus. Atossa's role in the succession of Xerxes is narrated at Herodotus 7.2–3 and confirmed in an inscription of Xerxes at Persepolis (XPf §4). See further Briant 1996: 143–45.

The Cyrus Cylinder. The current standard edition of the text is Schaudig 2001: 550–56.

Royal titles. See Herrenschmidt 1976, Kienast 1979, Ahn 1992: 217–21, 259–65.

Names of Cyrus and his ancestors. The lack of plausible etymologies was first noted in Andreas 1904, and the importance of this problem has often been emphasized since then, most recently in Kellens 2002: 422–25. Attempts, like those in Eilers 1964 and 1974, to provide an Indo-Iranian origin for the name "Cyrus" can produce no Iranian evidence in support of their claims and lean on a few obscure Indic data that they overvalue and misinterpret.

The Bisitun inscription. The standard critical edition is now Schmitt 1991a for the Old Persian text. The Akkadian and Elamite versions have been published separately in Voigtlander 1978 and Grillot-Susini, Herrenschmidt, and Malbran-Labat 1993, respectively. Excellent translations of all the inscriptions are available in Kent 1953, Asmussen 1960, Schmitt 1991a and 2000, and Lecoq 1997.

The genealogies of Cyrus and Darius. These texts and the issues they raise have received a great deal of attention recently, most of it skeptical. See Tichy 1983, Miroschedji 1985: 280–83, Briant 1996: 26–27 and 122–24, Waters 1996 and 2004, Rollinger 1998, Kellens

2002: 417–34, Frye 2003, and Potts 2005. Less suspicious of Darius (and more suspicious of Cyrus) is Vallat 1997. Herodotus 7.11 produces an alternate line of descent, equally consistent with Darius's wishes, but lacking division into two branches.

The inscriptions of (Pseudo-)Cyrus at Pasargadae. These inscriptions have been suspect almost since their discovery. The reasons are developed most fully in Nylander 1967 and Stronach 1997 and 2000.

III

Nabonidus's titles. The opening passage of the Ehulhul Cylinder (see Schaudig 2001: 415–16) reads: "I am Nabonidus, Great King, Mighty King, King of the World, King of Babylon, King of the four quarters, caretaker of Esagila and Ezida."

Nabonidus. Most extensively, see Beaulieu 1989 and D'Agostino 1994, which build on Tadmor 1965. The texts attributed to Nabonidus are collected in Schaudig 2001.

Babylonian priests and the Cyrus Cylinder. For a fuller discussion of the issues, see Harmatta 1971a, Kuhrt 1990b, and Kratz 2002: 148–51.

Cyrus as "King of Anšan." A cylinder seal found at the so-called Cyrus Door at Ur, first published in Dougherty 1923 and available in Schaudig 2001: 549, reads as follows: "I am Cyrus, King of the World, *King of Anšan,* son of Cambyses, King of Anšan. The great gods filled my hands with all lands. I let the land dwell as a peaceful dwelling." See further Bollweg 1988.

Elam. See Amiet 1979 and Miroschedji 1990. The division of Elam seems indicated, e.g., in the neo-Elamite king Shutruk-Nahhunte's designation of himself as "King of Anšan *and* Susa" in inscriptions dating from the end of the eighth century. The texts were published in König 1965: nos. 71–73.

Anšan. Early Persian history is made difficult by the paucity of documentary evidence, which has been interpreted differently in Miroschedji 1985, Rollinger 1999b, and Potts 2005, which have displaced the older accounts of Hansman 1972 and 1985.

Parsa, Parsua, and/or Parsuma. All these forms appear in Akkadian texts, beginning with the annals of Shalmaneser III (r. 858–824), as do forms with the nominative suffix *-š,* although some of the occurrences treat a population in the Zagros and others a people in Fars. For discussion of the details, see Waters 1999 and the bolder treatment of Rollinger 1999b.

Cyrus's early victories. Harmatta 1971b, Balcer 1984: 95–117, Mallowan 1985, Dandamaev 1989: 1–65.

Appropriation of titles. Kienast 1979.

Appropriation of royal ideology from the ancient Near East. The first to insist on the importance of this process were Harmatta 1971a and Gnoli 1974. Since then, many have pursued it further, including Kienast 1979, Root 1979, Skjærvø 1999: 14–27, Panaino 2000, Westenholz 2000, and Pongratz-Leisten 2002.

Legends surrounding Cyrus. Herodotus (1.95) claims knowledge of three other versions of the romance of Cyrus, versions that he chose to omit, in addition to the material that he included (1.107–30). Those other versions have been studied in Aly 1921, Binder 1964, Drews 1974, Cizek 1975, and Accame 1982.

Sargon. See Drews 1974, Lewis 1980, and Kuhrt 2003.

Median-Persian relations. The cultural and linguistic proximity of the Persians and the Medes has been stressed in Harmatta 1971b: 9–14, Lecoq 1974a, Graf 1984, Tuplin 1994, and others.

Herodotus's *Medikos logos.* Critical questions have been posed in Helm 1983, Brown 1988, and Sancisi-Weerdenburg 1988 and 1994. More optimistic are Scurlock 1990, Flusin 1999, and Kienast 1999.

Pasargadae. Stronach 1978, 1985b, and 1989 (the last focused on the garden).

Cyrus's death. Discussed in Herodotus 1.208–14. See Francfort 1985, Dandamaev 1989: 66–69, and Sancisi-Weerdenburg 1985.

Cambyses as regent and successor to his father's throne. Petschow 1988, Dandamaev 1989: 56–60, Peat 1989. On the rites of royal succession, see Briant 1991. Herodotus (2.208) has Cyrus designate Cambyses his heir on the eve of his final campaign but follows this with a portentous dream (1.209–10) in which the king sees Darius—then still a young man—dominating Europe and Asia.

Cambyses in Egypt. Herodotus's account is found in 2.1 and 3.1–38 and 61–66. On the actualities of Persian conquest and rule, as best these can be ascertained from other records, see Posener 1936, Vorbichler 1981, and Bresciani 1985. On Cambyses' attempts to construct himself and his rule as legitimate in Egyptian terms, see Atkinson 1956. On the role of propagandistic sources in shaping the Herodotean portrait, see Hofmann and Vorbichler 1980, Brown 1982, Gammie 1986, and Lloyd 1988. More sympathetic to Herodotus is Depuydt 1995. On Cambyses' religious policies, see Farina 1929.

Bardiya's usurpation. The dramatic events of 522 are narrated most fully in DB §§10–14 and Herodotus 3.30 and 3.61–79. Variants are also found in Ctesias, *Persica* 12 (preserved in Photius) and Pompeius Trogus (preserved in Justinus). Following Darius's official account, these maintain it was not actually Bardiya who took the throne but an imposter. In the past, historians accepted this uncritically, and some continue to do so, including Hinz 1976: 122–45, Wiesehöfer 1978, and Gershevitch 1979. Starting with Olmstead 1948: 107–10, however, and following on the publication of the decisive Bickerman and Tadmor 1978, the majority now view this critically, as part of the propaganda campaign with which Darius sought to legitimate himself and to evade any charges of regicide.

Bardiya's tax relief. Herodotus 3.67, on which see Dandamaev 1976: 134–35 and Briant 1996: 117–18.

Cambyses' death. DB §11 states that Cambyses "died his own death" (*uvamṛšiyuš amariyatā*), a phrase that seems to denote a death that is not violent. The effect of this is to free Bardiya *and all others* from suspicion of regicide. A potential beneficiary was Darius himself, who was then serving as Cambyses' spear bearer in Egypt (Herodotus 3.139). See Schulze 1912, Schaeder 1946, Asmussen 1968, Herrmann 1978, and Walser 1983. The Egyptian Demotic Chronicle, Verso, col. C, lines 7–8 (on which see Bresciani 1981), asserts that Cambyses caused his own death, depicting this as divine retribution. Herodotus 3.64 is similar.

Bardiya's death and Darius's accession. The most important primary sources are DB §§13 and 68, Herodotus 3.68–88, and Aeschylus, *Persians* 775–77. See Dandamaev 1976 and 1989: 103–13, Gschnitzer 1977, Wiesehöfer 1978, Balcer 1987, and Briant 1996: 119–27.

IV

Rebellions of 522–521. These are recounted in DB §§15–50, with summary comments at §§51–59. The Babylonian version of the text (Voigtlander 1978) contains casualty figures that are omitted from the Old Persian. Dandamaev 1989: 114–31, Briant 1996: 127–35.

Executions and tortures. The most extreme punishments are detailed at DB §§32–33: "Fravarti was captured. He was led before me. I cut off his nose, his ears, and his tongue, and I put out one of his eyes. He was held bound at my gate. All the army/people saw him. Then I impaled him in Ecbatana, and the men who were his foremost followers I hung in Ecbatana" (DB §32). Briant 1996: 135–36 has discussed these punishments as a propagandistic display of royal power. Pirart 1996 has treated them in terms of human sacrifice.

Rebels' ideology and its delegitimation. The claims that the rebels made for themselves appear at DB §§11, 16, 22, 24, 33, 38, 40, 49, and 52 and in the minor inscriptions (DBa–DBj) that serve as captions to the Bisitun relief sculpture discussed in chapter 2. See further Lincoln 2005. On religious aspects of the Bisitun text, see Pirart 2002.

"The Lie." On the opposition of truth and lie as the central, organizing construct of Mazdaean religions, see Widengren 1965: 142–43, Boyce 1982: 120–23, Schwartz 1985: 685–86, and, most important, Bucci 1983 and Skjærvø 2003.

Invention of the Old Persian script and dissemination of the Bisitun text. DB §70 reads as follows: "Proclaims Darius the King: By the Wise Lord's will, this is the form of script that I made. Further, it was in Iranian [lit. Aryan], and it was inscribed in clay and on parchment. And, further, I made my signature. And, further, I made the lineage. And this was written and read to me. Afterward, I dispatched this form of script everywhere through the lands/peoples. The people/army worked together [on it]." The Elamite version adds a highly significant phrase, stating: "I made a script of another sort, in Iranian [lit. Aryan], *that previously did not exist."* For discussion of this passage and its implications, see Lecoq 1974b, Herrenschmidt 1989a, and Mayrhofer 1989. The Aramaic version of the Bisitun text, on papyrus and intended for broad circulation, has been published in Greenfield and Porten 1982.

Dualism. Boyce 1982: 118–24, Hasenfratz 1983, Herrenschmidt and Lincoln 2004.

Acceptance of Bardiya. See the texts collected in Graziani 1991.

Magus. Some authors have seen religious conflict in the struggle between Darius and "Gaumata the Magus," emphasizing the testimony of Herodotus 3.79. Such views have relevance only if one accepts the veracity of Darius's account. If "Gaumata" is a construct of Darius's propaganda, his identity as a magus serves to identify him as doubly unfit for the kingship: once as a Mede and not a Persian, again as a priest and not a noble.

Bisitun as propaganda and the invention of Gaumata. The fullest discussions are Dandamaev 1976, Bickerman and Tadmor 1978, Herrenschmidt 1982, Balcer 1987, Dandamaev 1989: 83–113, Zawadzki 1994, and Briant 1996: 109–27. Herodotus does not know the name "Gaumata." In his version, the dissembling magus bears the same name as the dead prince whose identity he assumed, both being called "Smerdis," a Greek transformation—along with Mardos (Aeschylus, *Persians* 774)—of Old Persian *Bardiya*.

V

Bisitun's fifth column and Darius's Scythian invasion. Harmatta 1976, Kellens 1987, Dandamaev 1989: 136–40.

Old Persian *arika* and vulnerability to the Lie. Lincoln 2003c: lecture 3.

Further events of Darius's reign. Hinz 1976: 168–219, Dandamaev 1989: 141–77, Briant 1992a and 1996: 151–73. Particularly good on the Ionian revolt is Tozzi 1978.

Susa and Persepolis. On Susa, see Boucharlat 1990 and Muscarella, Caubet, and Tallon 1992. On Persepolis, see Schmidt 1953–70, Roaf 1990, and Root 1990.

Earliest inscription at Persepolis. The chronology is established at Schmitt 2000: 56, with the text itself given at Schmitt 2000: 58.

Herrenschmidt. Herrenschmidt presented her perspective on these texts and her principles of method in her earliest publications: 1976, 1977, and 1979a.

Old Persian *naiba*. As numerous authors have observed, this replaces an older, equally weighty term that survives in Sanskrit *vasu* and Avestan *vohu* but in Old Persian is present only as an element in proper names (e.g., *Vahyaz-dāta, Daraya-va[h]uš*). See Kent 1953: 9 and 192, Molé 1963: 32–33, and Skjærvø 1999: 11. On the presence of the older term in the (throne) name of Darius, see Kellens and Pirart 1988–91: 1:40–41 and Schmitt 1990.

"Whose horses are good, whose people are good." This phrase (or formulaic variants of it) occurs eight times in the Achaemenian inscriptions. Three times it describes Persia (AmH §2, AsH §2, DPd §2), four times the kingship/kingdom that Darius received from the Wise Lord (DSf §3a, DSm §2, DSp, DZc §1), and once the Wise Lord's creation (DSs; cf. DZc §1). It is associated with the term *naiba* at DSp and with a prayer for protection at AsH §2 and DSs.

Happiness. Menasce 1940, Kellens 1969 and 1995: 34–38, Herrenschmidt 1991. See further chapter 4.

Darius as God's near-equal partner. This point has been noted in Lecoq 1997: 227.

Three menaces. Since Benveniste 1938, this set has been regarded as one of the few pieces of Old Persian data consistent with Georges Dumézil's theory of "the Indo-European tri-functional ideology" (Dumézil 1958, 1961). Panaino 1986, however, militates against such an interpretation.

Enemy army. The term used (Old Persian *hainā*) has demonic associations and stands in contrast to that used for one's own army (*kāra*). See Kellens 1976: 113–32. Recognition that the older Iranian languages instantiate the dualistic outlook in religion and culture at the level of their vocabulary begins with Güntert 1914.

VI

Xerxes' modification of Darius's formula. Kienast 1979, Wiesehöfer 1996: 257.

Earth and empire. Herrenschmidt 1976: 42–44, 47–49, 64–65. It is worth noting that this term does not appear in the Bisitun inscription. The titles claimed there include one using the nominative case ("Great King"), one the locative ("King in Persia"), and two the genitive ("King of Kings," "King of lands/peoples"). In Darius's later texts, that using the locative, which placed him "in Persia," is replaced by another locative, of a more imperial nature, holding final position in the set, rather than the more modest second spot: "in this earth/empire." Darius also introduces the same term (*būmi*) in the cosmogonic myths considered in chapter 4. Of particular interest is his claim to have received the world from the Wise Lord and to have perfected it on his behalf: "When the Wise Lord made me King in this earth/empire, by the Wise Lord's will, *I made all good* [*naiba*]" (DSi §2).

Set of four titles. Herrenschmidt 1976: 39–45.

VII

Greek sources. For general discussions, see Cantarella 1965, Drews 1973, Briant 1982, Lewis 1985, Konstan 1987, Sancisi-Weerdenburg and Kuhrt 1987, and Georges 1994. On Aeschylus, see Jouanna 1981, Belloni 1986, and Hall 1989. On Xenophon, see Hirsch 1985, Tatum 1989, and Tuplin 1990 and 2003. On Ctesias, see Momigliano 1969, Bigwood 1978, Sancisi-Weerdenburg 1987, and Lenfant 1996. The literature on Herodotus is enormous. Among the more important items are Fornara 1971, Hegyi 1973, Murray 1987 and 2001, Cartledge 1990, Tourraix 1995, Rollinger 2000, Thomas 2000, and Luraghi 2001. The commentary in Asheri and Medaglia 2000 is preferable to all others for the way it accommodates a Persian as well as a Greek perspective.

Luxury. Sancisi-Weerdenburg 1987, Briant 1989a and 1996: 311–13.

Banquet table. Lavish meals hosted by the Great King are described in Xenophon, *Agesilaus* 9.3, Athenaeus, *Deipnosophistae* 67a and 145b–146a, and, most extensively, Polyaenus 4.3.32. See Lewis 1987, Sancisi-Weerdenburg 1995, Briant 1996: 297–306, and Dalby 2000. On symbolic practices of redistribution more broadly, see Sancisi-Weerdenburg 1980: 145–83.

Bestowal of kingship and the king's mediating position. On the relation between rituals of royal investiture, in which the Wise Lord bestows kingship and kingdom (the semantics of Old Persian *xšaça* encompass both senses [Benveniste 1969: 2:19–20]) on the new king, and the latter's consequent ability to call on that deity for protection and support, see Herrenschmidt 1979a and 1990.

Comparative use of Zoroastrian texts. See, most recently, the important studies Kellens 1997 and Skjærvø 1999 and 2005.

Zoroastrianism of the Achaemenians. Discussions include Benveniste 1929, Molé 1963: 26–36, Gnoli 1964, 1974, 1985, and 1988, Widengren 1965: 117–55, Duchesne-Guillemin 1972, Kellens 1976, 1983, 1991, and 2002, Bianchi 1977 and 1988, Duleba 1977, Koch 1977 and 1991, Herrenschmidt 1980, 1987a, and 1990, Boyce 1982 and 1988, Schwartz 1985, Dandamaev and Lukonin 1989: 320–66, Skjærvø 1999, Pirart 2002, and Stausberg 2002: 157–86. That some persons present at the Achaemenian court considered themselves Zoroastrians is now made certain by the discovery of a seal dating to the fourth century with an Aramaic inscription that reads *zrtštrš*, i.e., *zaraθuštriš*, "Follower of Zarathustra." See further Schmitt 1997: 922–24.

Walled enclosures. Lincoln 2003c: lecture 4.

Mazdaean tradition. Use of this term implies the view that "the Wise Lord" was, not an innovation introduced by Zarathustra, but an older Iranian deity embraced by Zoroastrians and others. Achaemenians from Darius on would constitute a branch of this tradition that developed independently of the Zoroastrian branch. The Medes might constitute yet a third branch, to judge from onomastic evidence. (Two Median princes named Mašdakku paid tribute to Sargon II in 715. On those two princes, see Lommel 1931 and Mayrhofer 1973: 195.) A deity named Assara Mazaš also appears in a list of gods' names from the library of Assurbanipal (III R 66, col. 11, 24), as has been recognized since Hommel 1899. See also Kent 1933.

2. CENTER AND PERIPHERY

I

Bisitun relief. Excellent photographs of the relief are available in Schmitt 1991a: pls. 1, 2, 29, 32b, 33a, 33b, and 34; line drawings in pls. 4 and 5. The best discussions include Luschby 1968, Root 1979: 182–226, and Westenholz 2000.

Assyrian prototypes. The most important influences on the Bisitun composition were the Victory Stela of Naram-Sîn and the rock-cut relief of Annubanini at Sar-i Pul. Both date to the third millennium, but they would have been readily available to Darius's artists since the former was in Susa (the Elamites having carried it off ca. 1165) and the latter was located in the immediate vicinity of Bisitun.

Crown. Technically, this is known as a "polos" crown, on the significance of which, see Luschby 1968: 81–82, Azarpay 1972, Gall 1974, and Calmeyer 1977.

The Wise Lord. For identification of the figure in the winged lozenge, see Lecoq 1984, pace Shahbazi 1974 and 1980. On the deity's nature, see Lommel 1930: 10–17 and Boyce 1975: 192–98. No other deity is mentioned in any Achaemenian inscription prior to the time of Artaxerxes II (r. 404–359), but Darius's statement that the Wise Lord is "greatest of the gods" (DPd §1, DPh §2, DSf §3a, etc.) and his request for help from the Wise Lord "with other gods" (DB §§62, 63, DPd §3, DSe §6, etc.) make clear that this is not a monotheistic system.

Proffered ring and raised hand. Root 1979: 172–76, Choksy 1990.

Greater Bundahišn. The best manuscript of this text is Anklesaria 1908, conventionally cited as TD² MS. The only complete translation is Anklesaria 1956, which is badly flawed, but a translation of and commentary on this passage can be found in Zaehner 1955: 278–79 (transliteration), 285–88 (commentary), and 312–13 (translation).

Selections of Zad Spram. The standard edition is Gignoux and Tafazzoli 1993.

Ethnic representations. Stereotyped portraits of subject peoples appear, not only at Bisitun, but also in scenes of throne bearers and tribute bearers at other sites. See, among others, Walser 1966, Hinz 1969: 95–114, Goldman 1974, Roaf 1974, Root 1979: 227–84, Koch 1983, Stronach 1985a, Jamzadeh 1992, Vogelsang 1992: 94–119, 132–65, Hachmann 1995, and Jacobs 1997.

II

Inscription at Suez. All inscriptions from sites other than Bisitun, Persepolis, and Naqš-i Rustam are found in Kent 1953.

Old Persian *dahyu.* Lecoq 1990a.

Dominant class-ethnicity. Briant 1987, 1988, 1996.

Lists of lands/peoples. Herrenschmidt 1976: 52–60, Goukowsky 1978: 222–24, Calmeyer 1982, 1983a, and 1987, Briant 1996: 185–91, Jacobs 2003.

Persia listed first. Thus DB §6, DSe §3, DNe, and A¹Pb.

Persia as "good" (*naiba*). DPd §2. Persia is also the only land/people described as having "good men" and "good horses," which signals, not only its inherent military capacities, but also a more fundamental flourishing of life (AmH §2, AsH §2).

The Medes, Elamites, and Babylonians. As further evidence of the privilege accorded these peoples, one should note that the Achaemenian inscriptions were generally produced in trilingual fashion for precisely these groups: Elamite, Akkadian (the language of Babylon), and Old Persian (sufficiently close to Median as to be immediately comprehensible).

Orientation to the cardinal directions. The tendency to theorize space in this fashion is also evident in two inscriptions that define the empire in terms of its (current) outermost limits to the northeast, southwest, southeast, and northwest in sequence:

> Proclaims Darius the King: This is the kingship/kingdom that I hold, from the Scythians, those who are beyond Sogdiana, thence to Ethiopia; from India, thence to Lydia. The Wise Lord, greatest of the gods, conferred this on me.
>
> (DPd §2, DH §2)

The speech assigned to Artabanus in Herodotus 7.18 has much the same structure. There, Artabanus associates the limits of the empire with the failed military campaigns of successive kings: Cyrus's expedition against the Massagetae to the northeast (1.211–14), Cambyses' against the Ethiopians and Ammonians to the southwest (3.25–26), and Darius's against the Scythians to the northwest (4.121–42). In warning Xerxes against a Greek invasion, however, he breaks with this structure, which would require a limit to the southeast (India, perhaps), not another check in the northwest. See further Jamzadeh 1993.

III

Reciprocal processes constitutive of empire. Claessen 1989.

Force at a distance. Also noteworthy is Darius's boast at DNa §4:: "'The spear of a Persian man has gone forth into faraway regions. . . . A Persian man fought against the enemy far from Persia."

Lands/peoples seized far from Persia. Xerxes adopted this same formula, but he modified the verb phrase to reflect the fact that he had made no conquests himself, simply continuing to rule over territories won by his father and others. Thus: "By the Wise Lord's will, these are the lands/peoples far from Persia *of which I was King*" (XPh §3).

Herodotus on tribute. See the commentary in Dandamaev 1972, Descat 1985, Briant 1996: 399–433, Asheri and Medaglia 2000: 305–7, and Jacobs 2003 and the essays in Briant and Herrenschmidt 1989, especially Descat 1989 and Sancisi-Weerdenburg 1989.

Persian exemption. Herodotus 3.97. See also Wiesehöfer 1989 and Sancisi-Weerdenburg 1998. Gschnitzer 1988 attempts to minimize the importance of privileges accorded Persia as the empire's basis and center.

Inscriptions referring to tribute. These formulas have received inadequate attention to date. On the significance of the Old Persian term *bāji*, which denotes "tribute" or, more literally, "the (king's) portion," see Herrenschmidt 1989b and Sancisi-Weerdenburg 1998. I hope to say more on this topic in the future.

Law. On the significance of the king's law—which is also the Wise Lord's law—as a religious and political instrument, see Bucci 1972 and 1983, Frei and Koch 1984: 63–65, and Herrenschmidt 1987a.

IV

Median, Persian, and Iranian cosmology. The tendency to theorize the world as a set of concentric circles in which the moral status of residents covaries with their proximity to the center is evident in the Median capital city of Ecbatana, said to have been surrounded by seven circular walls, ever higher as they approach the center, and each of a different color, the innermost two being coated in silver and gold, respectively. Inside the final, golden wall were the palace and treasury, at the center of which was the king (Herodotus 1.98–99). The Avesta also treats the world as having a central realm surrounded by others that are lesser, there being either five (*Yašt* 13.143–45), seven (*Videvdat* 19.39, *Vispered* 10.1, *Yašt* 10.89), or sixteen (*Videvdat* 1) such realms in all. The system of seven predominates in the Pahlavi texts (*Selections of Zad Spram* 3.33–35, *Greater Bundahišn* 8 [TD² MS 74.9–76.6], *Dadestan i Denig* 36.5–7, *Bahman Yašt* 3.47, *Denkard* 3.29). In the Zoroastrian texts, creation regularly takes place at the center of the world. See further Shahbazi 1983 and Daryaee 2002.

Greek perspectives on the Persian Wars. Construction of the wars in terms of the binary oppositions Greece/Persia, Europe/Asia, democracy/tyranny, freedom/slavery, individual/ mass, etc., as pioneered by Herodotus, has, until recently, informed much that is written on the topic, the classic example being Burn 1962.

Herodotus and the Homeric epic. Nagy 1987.

Herodotus's Persian sources. The classic discussion is Wells 1907. More recently and extensively, see Drews 1973, Hegyi 1973, Armayor 1978, Dandamaev 1985, Lewis 1985, and Murray 1987.

Lakrines and the Spartan embassy to Sardis. Most historians accept that such an embassy did take place. Thus, e.g., Lewis 1977: 62 and Murray 1988: 464.

Speeches in Herodotus. On the particular value of those Herodotean speeches dealing with the Ionian revolt, see Solmsen 1943.

Persians and the Greek agora. Xenophon, *Cyropaedia* 1.2.2 expands on this theme in a way that treats the Greek agora, not only as a space of the Lie, but also as a space of disorder where evil threatens to intermingle with good, contaminating the latter: "The Persians have a place called the 'free agora' [*eleuthera agora*], where the royal palace and other magistracies are located. But marketers [*hoi agoraioi*], their wares, their cries and vulgarities are removed from that spot to another place, lest their tumult mix with the fair order [*eukosmia*] of those who are well-reared." On the theme of mixture in Zoroastrianism, see Schmidt 1996.

V

Achaemenian inscriptions and the Greeks. On the way the Ionian Greeks were represented in official Persian discourse (inscriptional and iconographic), see Calmeyer 1983b, Klinkott 2001, Sancisi-Weerdenburg 2001a and 2001b, and Kuhrt 2002: esp. 19–22.

Cyrus's conquest of the Ionians. The Ionians, who had been under Lydian rule, offered to submit to Cyrus once he had defeated the Lydians (Herodotus 1.141, with reference to 1.76). Refusing this as opportunistic, Cyrus insisted that they submit unconditionally, which set off conflict lasting for some years and ending in Persian triumph (1.141–69). See La Bua 1977 and 1980, Boffo 1983, and Walser 1984: 12–15.

Greeks "by" and "beyond" the sea. This distinction appears in three inscriptions (DPe §2, DSe §2, XPh §3), none of which accompanies a relief sculpture. Where lists are connected to such reliefs, the terminology changes, such that "Greeks who wear the *petasos* [a kind of hat]" replaces "Greeks beyond the sea" (DSm §2, DNa §3, A'P). As Sancisi-Weerdenburg 2001b: 324–30 recognized, this description let one connect the text to a figure in the relief, identifiable through his hat.

Salt water. Zoroastrian texts treat fresh water as an original creation of the Wise Lord, thus pure and perfect. Salt water resulted from the corruption of this substance by the Assault of the Evil Spirit (thus, e.g., *Greater Bundahišn* 6B [TD² MS 61.10–65.11] or 3.7–25). Some pieces of evidence suggest that Achaemenians made the same distinction (see Herrenschmidt and Lincoln 2004).

Events of 507. The Spartans' occupation of the Acropolis, their expulsion of Cleisthenes and dissolution of the Athenian assembly are related in Herodotus 5.72. See Orlin 1976, Williams 1982, and Horsley 1986.

Artaphrenes. This was the half brother of Darius, whom Aeschylus, *Persians* 776 credits with having slain Bardiya. From 513 on, he was the Persian satrap in Sardis, the most important center of the western empire. For a summary of what is known about him, see Balcer 1993: 71–73.

Earth and water. Herodotus describes ten instances in which the demand for such gifts arises. These have been studied most extensively in Kuhrt 1988.

Displacement of responsibility in the Herodotean text. See Raubitschek 1964, Orlin 1976, and Kuhrt 1988: 91–92.

Athenian assistance to the Ionian rebels and participation in the sack of Sardis. Herodotus 5.96–103 is our only source for these events. The conclusions that Darius drew about Athens are recounted at 5.105. Tozzi 1978 remains the best general history of the rebellion, but see also Hegyi 1966, Lateiner 1982, Wallinga 1984, Murray 1988, Lang 1988, and Georges 2000.

Differing perspectives on the treaty of 507. Orlin 1976, Walser 1984: 31–35.

Mithra. The meaning of this deity's name was established in Meillet 1907, which has been the basis for all subsequent discussion. More recent literature includes Dumézil 1948, Thieme 1957 and 1975, Gershevitch 1959, and Schmidt 1978. According to the Avesta, when treaties have been violated, Mithra renders ineffectual the armies and weapons of those who have lied to him (*Yašt* 10.20, 10.23, and 10.62). In addition, he unleashes the deity Verethragna, the incarnation of aggressive force, "who shatters, rips apart, tramples, and disrupts the battle formations . . . of men who lie in their treaties" (*Yašt* 14.62–63; cf. *Yašt* 10.70–72, 14.47). On this deity, see Charpentier 1911, Benveniste and Renou 1934, and Lommel 1939.

Mithra in theophoric names. Mayrhofer 1973: 201–7 lists more than twenty names compounded on that of Mithra. Onomastics notwithstanding, Mithra was not mentioned by name in any Achaemenian inscription until the reign of Artaxerxes II (404–359). See the discussion in Briant 1996: 695–96 and 1024–25.

VI

Old Persian *paratara*, "enemy." Wackernagel 1932: 29–30, accepted in Mayrhofer 1956–76: 2:214–15, Brandenstein and Mayrhofer 1964: 137, and Schmitt 2000: 32, pace Benveniste

1945: 63–64. The word appears in this passage only, and its interpretation is made difficult by differences in the Elamite and Akkadian versions of the text.

Discursive prelude to invasions. Note also Herodotus's description of Darius's plan to exploit the Athenians' offense as "a pretext for subjugating those [other] Greeks who had not given him earth and water" (Herodotus 6.94).

Dadestan i Denig. The Pahlavi text is found in Anklesaria n.d., transcription, translation, and commentary in Jaafari-Dehaghi 1998.

3. GOD'S CHOSEN

I

Ideology of kingship. The best works on the topic are Root 1979 and Ahn 1992. Older studies include Widengren 1959 and 1974, Duchesne-Guillemin 1963 and 1979, Frye 1964, Gnoli 1972 and 1984, Filippani-Ronconi 1974, Schmitt 1977, Herrenschmidt 1979b, Sancisi-Weerdenburg 1981, and Kuhrt 1984.

Dynastic principle. See, e.g., Cyrus's description of his family as "a lineage enduring in its kingship" (CB §7) or Darius's assertion that "from long ago our family has been royal" (DB §3). Herodotus 1.125 treats the Achaemenians as a royal clan within the Pasargadae tribe, which was the highest ranking among the Persians. The name "Pasargadae" is obviously related to the capital city founded by Cyrus.

Invention of the Achaemenian line. See chapter 1 and the literature cited there. It is possibly worth mentioning that Darius gave the name "Achaemenes" to one of his younger sons, as mentioned in Herodotus 3.12, 7.7, and a few other places.

Cyrus's genealogy. The best treatment of these materials is Jacobs 1996. See also Accame 1982 and Sancisi-Weerdenburg 1982.

Legends preserved in Herodotus. Herodotus 1.107–30. Variants are also found in Charon of Lampsacus (FGH 262F14, FGH 687bF2), Xenophon, *Cyropaedia,* Diodorus Siculus 9.22.1, Aelian, *Varia historia* 12.42, and elsewhere. In book 9 of his lost *Persika* (summary preserved in Photius), Ctesias denied that Cyrus was the grandson of Astyages and connected the families differently by having Cyrus marry Amytis, another daughter of Astyages, after conquering her father. These legends have been studied in Aly 1921, Binder 1964, Drews 1974, Cizek 1975, Accame 1982, and Kuhrt 2003.

Charisma in antiquity. The term is rare in Greek literature but occurs quite frequently in the New Testament, as at 1 Cor. 12.4, Rom. 6.23, etc. For its extrabiblical usage, see Taeger 1957–60.

Royal dreams as divine revelation. The pattern is a common one in the ancient Near East, as attested in a wealth of Egyptian, Mesopotamian, and biblical data, which have been treated in, among others, Saporetti 1996, Butler 1998, Husser 1999, and Szpakowska 2003. Among the Achaemenians, Cyrus (Herodotus 1.209) and Xerxes (7.12–19) are also credited with premonitory dreams, on which see Evans 1961, Lieshout 1970, Gärtner 1983, and Köhnken 1988.

Astyages' dreams. These have received less attention than one might expect. The fullest studies are Bichler 1985 and Pelling 1996.

Mandane. She appears in Herodotus 1.107–11, Charon of Lampsacus (FGH 262F14, 687bF2), Xenophon, *Cyropaedia* 1.2.1–3.13, and elsewhere. For full references, see Balcer 1993: 49. Her name appears to be formed on an Akkadian ethnonym for the Medes: (*Umman-*)*Manda.* On the significance of this term, see Komoroczy 1977 and Zawadzki 1988.

Fairy-tale plot. Such tales have been much studied: Rank 1922, Raglan 1937, Campbell 1949, Binder 1964.

Mitradates. The name appears at Herodotus 1.110. For its occurrence in Iranian sources and its meaning, see Mayrhofer 1973: nos. 8.321, 8.1126, and 8.1169 and Justi 1895 / 1963: 209–13.

Eye of the king and other offices. Schaeder 1934, Lommel 1953, Olmstead 1968, Balcer 1977, Briant 1996: 272–73. The lance bearer is a particularly high-ranking office and is given special mention in one of the minor inscriptions of Darius at Naqš-i Rustam (DNc).

Reinventing the royal order. Median myths of the origin of kingship center on Deiokes, who instituted justice first, then built kingship on it (Herodotus 1.96–101). Cyrus, as a child, is, thus, repeating this invention of justice and kingship, which the story construes as the sociopolitical instantiation of his innermost essence and nature. On Deiokes, see Palomar 1987, Panaino 2003, and Meier et al. 2004.

Justice. Old Persian has no term that is fully comparable to Greek *dike* (or, for that matter, to English *justice*). The closest equivalents would be *arta*, "truth," understood as the principle that sustains the world order, *rāstam*, "right," and *dāta*, "law." A passage in the inscription placed at Darius's tomb in Naqš-i Rustam also summarizes principles that correspond roughly to the ideas of equity contained in our notion of the just:

> Proclaims Darius the King: By the Wise Lord's will, I am the sort of person who is a friend to one who is right. I am not a friend to one who is evil. It is not my desire that the weak man should have evil done to him on account of the powerful. It is not my desire that the powerful man should have evil done to him on account of the weak. That which is right is my desire. I am not friend to a lying man. I am not given to anger. That which comes into being from me in anger I hold firmly under control with my mind. I am firmly ruling over what is my own. The man who cooperates, according to his cooperation I protect him. He who does damage, according to his damage I punish him. It is not my desire that a man should do damage. Nor is it my desire that, when one does damage, he should not be punished.
>
> (DNb §§2a–2c)

II

Nabonidus and his policies. All subsequent studies depend on (or occasionally contest) the chronology established in Tadmor 1965. The most important recent studies are Beaulieu 1989, Kuhrt 1990b, D'Agostino 1994, Sack 1997, Weisberg 1997, and Kratz 2002.

The "Dream of Nabonidus." The text is found in Schaudig 2001: 416–17 (text), 427–28 (notes), 436–37 (translation). It is discussed in Beaulieu 1989: 107–10, where the translation (108) omits the last sentence quoted here. The bracketed clause in my translation— "Within a few years"—reflects a problematic phrase in the original that seems to place Cyrus's defeat of the Medes in the third year of Nabonidus's reign, i.e., 553 BCE, instead of the sixth, as actually occurred. This has occasioned considerable debate, debate that is still unresolved, but the details are not important for our interests.

Bel-shazzar. Bel-shazzar held effective power in Babylon from 553 until 543, when his father returned to the city. In the biblical book of Daniel, Bel-shazzar appears as the last king of Babylon, his role being conflated with that of Nabonidus. See further Dougherty 1929, Lambert 1972, Hasel 1981, Shea 1982, Grabbe 1988, and Yamauchi 1996: 85–87.

Nabonidus, Marduk, and Sîn. Beaulieu 1989, Kuhrt 1990b, D'Agostino 1994, Kratz 2002.

Akitu ritual. The standard account of this ceremony has long been Pallis 1926, now replaced by Bidmead 2002. See also Black 1981 and Smith 1982.

Accusations circulated by the Marduk priests. The most important texts are the "Nabonidus Chronicle," available in Grayson 1975: 104–11, and the "Verse Account of Nabonidus," a translation of which is found in Pritchard 1969: 312–15. Also relevant is the memorial written for Nabonidus's mother, Adda Guppi, in Pritchard 1969: 311–12. For discussion, see Beaulieu 1989, Kuhrt 1990b, and Kratz 2002.

The Cyrus Cylinder. The current standard edition of the text is Schaudig 2001: 550–56. The most important studies are Harmatta 1971a, von Soden 1983, and Kuhrt 1983.

Disarticulating goodness and nationality. The force of the argument is to make morality both necessary and sufficient for kingship while national identity is rendered (almost) irrelevant, with the result that the Persian Cyrus can claim the Babylonian throne. If nationality is truly irrelevant, however, the implications go far beyond Babylon, as is acknowledged in the grandest title Marduk bestows on his chosen: "He proclaimed his name for kingship *of all the world*" (CB §4).

Entry into Babylon without battle. Herodotus 1.188–91, Xenophon, *Cyropaedia* 7.5.7–32, and Daniel 5 tell a somewhat different story, in which the city was taken by surprise at the time of an unspecified festival, with a certain measure of violence. The best evidence, however, is that of the Babylonian Chronicle 3.12–23 (Grayson 1975: 109ff.), which tells that, in September 539, Persian troops crushed the Babylonians at Opis, a city on the Tigris, and met only token resistance thereafter, entering Babylon a few weeks later. Cyrus himself was not present then but made a triumphal entry in late October. The archaeological record shows no evidence of major destruction. See Dandamaev 1989: 42–49 and Briant 1996: 50–53.

Imperial fantasies. Lincoln 2004b.

Staging scenes. For the general principle, see Scott 1990.

Babylonian revolts. The revolts of 522 and 521 are described in DB §§16, 18–20, and 49–50, those of 484 and 482 in classical sources that include Herodotus 1.183, Arrian, *Anabasis* 3.16.4 and 7.17.2, Diodorus Siculus 2.9.9 and 17.112, Strabo 16.1.5, and Aelian, *Varia historia* 13.3. See generally Liagre-Böhl 1962 and 1968, Kuhrt and Sherwin-White 1987, Dandamaev 1989: 183–87, Briant 1992b, and Rollinger 1999a. On the situation of Babylon in the later empire, see Kuhrt 1987a and 1990a, Haerinck 1997, and Wiesehöfer 2002.

III

Second Isaiah. Smith 1944 remains a point of reference for all subsequent discussion. See also Smith 1963, Koch 1972, Netzer 1974, Kratz 1991 and 2002, and Laato 1992.

Creation of light and darkness. This point was first made in Smith 1963. For examples of how light and darkness are treated in Iranian cosmology, see the texts cited in chapter 2.

YHWH's Anointed. Mowinckel 1956 remains fundamental. See also Vaux 1971, Cross 1973: 241–73, Doermann 1987, Schreiber 2000, Waschke 2001, and Fried 2002.

The Anointed/the Messiah/the Christ. Mowinckel 1956.

A son of Israel's royal family. The same applies to New Testament usage of the title "the Christ." Note, e.g., how the Gospel of Matthew begins by tracing the genealogy of Jesus back to Abraham via twenty-eight generations (1:1–17). David stands at the center of this account, as the text emphasizes (1:17): fourteen generations from Abraham to David, fourteen from David to Jesus. Luke 3:23–38 has a different genealogy, one that extends back to Adam but in which David is once more a central figure (3:31).

Negotiations between Persians and Jews. Most recently and convincingly, Fried 2002 and 2004: 177–83.

Cambyses as Horus, son of Ra, and beloved of the goddess Ouadjet. The relevant texts are cited and discussed in Bresciani 1985: 503–7 and Briant 1996: 67–70. See also Posener 1936 and Atkinson 1956.

Cambyses, Apries, and Nitetis. The variant in which Apries sends Nitetis to Cambyses is found in Herodotus 3.1 and Ctesias (preserved in Athenaeus, *Deipnosophistae* 560de).

"Nitetis" is apparently a theophoric name of Egyptian origin, including reference to the goddess Neith (Auberger 1991: 159).

Egyptian variant of the Nitetis story. Herodotus 3.2, Deinon and Lycias of Naucratis (both preserved in Athenaeus, *Deipnosophistae* 560–61), and Polyaenus 8.29. Herodotus rejects this version as not credible but explains its appeal to Egyptians.

IV

Apollo in Miletus. Boffo 1983: 63–64, Briant 1996: 48 and the literature cited at 911. Such evidence as there is suggests a policy of respect and tolerance, rather than active appropriation.

Tolerance or self-interest. Scholarly opinion was deeply influenced for many years by the favorable portrait of Cyrus and the Achaemenians found in the Hebrew Bible and tended to reflect Israel's view that Cyrus introduced a religious tolerance unknown previously. More recently, Duchesne-Guillemin 1967, Dandamaev 1975, Tozzi 1977, Briant 1986, Firpo 1986, and Kuhrt and Sherwin-White 1987 are inclined to see this as a deliberate political strategy, emphasizing the destruction in Greece and Babylon of religious sites associated with resistance to Persian rule. For discussion of Israel and Judea as an atypical case, see Ahn 2002. For the sources of Cyrus's highly favorable reputation, see Wiesehöfer 1987.

Imposition of beliefs. Particularly astute is the judgment in Herrenschmidt 1987a, which argues that the Achaemenians were more interested in imposing their law than their religion, in part because the two categories were thoroughly imbricated, the king's law being the instantiation of the Wise Lord's intentions for creation. A very small number of passages from the inscriptions of post-Teispid kings show an attempt to stamp out some beliefs and encourage others. See, in particular, DB §§14 and 72–73 (= 75–76) and XPh §4b.

Beliefs of Cyrus and Cambyses. Duchesne-Guillemin 1974 tried to argue that Cyrus was a devotee of Mithra, and Boyce 1988 insisted that he was an orthodox Zoroastrian who worshipped the Wise Lord. Most experts would concur with the prudent judgment in Briant 1996: 106: "Beginning with such poor information, it seems foolhardy to want to reconstruct what Cyrus's religion might have been."

Other gods. The phrase appears at DB §§62 and 63. It is this mention of deities in the plural that prompts the Elamite gloss discussed below. Later inscriptions acknowledge that the Wise Lord is the paramount figure in a polytheistic system by designating him "greatest of the gods," without naming any of the others (thus AsH §2, DPd §1, DPh §2, DSf §3a, DSp, DH §2, XE §1, XV §1, A²Hc §1). Whether the unnamed deities are the gods of conquered peoples or part of an Iranian pantheon is difficult to say, but the research reported in Koch 1977, 1991, and 1992: 276–86 has shown the importance of Elamite, Babylonian, and Median gods at Persepolis, alongside others of Iranian origin.

Triad of the Wise Lord, Mithra, and Anahita. This appears at A²Sa, A²Sd §2, A²Ha §2. Artaxerxes' decision to introduce these deities—both of whom are well attested in the Avesta and (in the case of Mithra) also in Vedic India—has been much discussed: Gershevitch 1959: 18–21, Widengren 1965: 118–22, Boyce 1982: 216–21, Schwartz 1985: 670–71, Dandamaev and Lukonin 1989: 327–29, Briant 1996: 695–96 and 1024–25. Phonologically, the form in which Mithra's name appears would seem to be Median or Avestan in origin since Old Persian *Miça would be expected, as noted in, among others, Meillet and Benveniste 1931: 12 and Brandenstein and Mayrhofer 1964: 133.

Elamite gloss. The phrase is added to the Elamite version of DB §§62 and 63 (DB [Elam.] §§50 and 51 in the numeration employed in Grillot-Susini, Herrenschmidt, and Malbran-Labat 1993: 36 [translation at 57]). Elamite *har-ri-ya-* reflects Old Persian *ariya-*, "Iranian, Aryan," the term that Darius uses for the language he speaks (DB §70), the god he worships (DB [Elam.] §§62, 63), and the ethnic group to which he belongs (DSe §2, DNa §2). This is a self-referential ethnonym of great antiquity, as evidenced by its cognates in Avestan *airya* and Vedic *arya*. The Medes also called themselves by the same term, as reflected by the testimony of Herodotus 7.62: "In ancient times, the Medes were called *Arioi* [Iranians, Aryans] by everyone, until Medea came to the Arioi from Athens and they changed their name." Compare 1.101, where he identifies six Median tribes, including one named Arizantoi (from **Arya-zantu*, "of Iranian/Aryan birth"). Eudemus of Rhodes confirms this testimony, in a passage cited by Damascius, in which he refers to the "Iranian/Aryan tribe" (*to areion genos*). The passage is available in Clemen 1920: 95. See further Gnoli 1983, Lamberterie 1989, and Schmitt 1991b. The significance of the term **arya* has been much debated, often in the context of racist ideology concerning the category of the "Aryan." On this, see Wiesehöfer 1988 and 1990. The fullest discussion to date of this word's history and significance in an Iranian context is to be found in Gnoli 1989 and 1993.

By the Wise Lord's will. Lincoln 1996. For the meaning of Old Persian *vašna*, see also Mayrhofer 1956–76: 3:170, Szemerenyi 1975: 325–43, and Skalmowski 1988. Darius uses this formula thirty-six times at Bisitun and twenty-three times elsewhere, for 74 percent of all occurrences. Of his successors, only Xerxes employs it with any frequency (thirteen times, 17 percent). It occurs eight times (10 percent) in the inscriptions of all others from Ariaramnes to Artaxerxes II, the last of whom accounts for half of these.

Survival of Darius's father and grandfather. DSf §3b: "By the Wise Lord's will, my father, Hystaspes, and my grandfather, Arsames, were both living when the Wise Lord made me King in this earth/empire." Note how Darius employs the same formula we have been considering—"by the Wise Lord's will"—to code this potentially embarrassing fact as a sign of divine charisma, rather than a dynastic anomaly. Xerxes makes the same point but attributes things to the Wise Lord's "desire" (*kāma*), rather than his "will." On the problematic nature of Darius's dynastic claims, as acknowledged in these passages, see Dandamaev 1989: 107–8 and Briant 1996: 122–23.

Darius's game effort. Darius's invention of the "Achaemenian" royal line is discussed in chapter 1. Note also his assertion in DB §§3–4, immediately after he has treated his genealogy: "Therefore we are proclaimed Achaemenians. From long ago we are noble. From long ago our lineage has been royal. There are eight of my lineage who were kings before. I am the ninth."

Usurpers and legitimation. Near Eastern precedents for the strategy and rhetoric employed by Darius have been discussed in Kuhrt 1987b and Zawadzki 1994. Compare Strohm 1998, with reference to Lancastrian England.

Ritual of royal investiture. Herrenschmidt 1979a and 1979b, Briant 1991.

Old Persian *xšaça*. Thus Benveniste 1969: 19, Herrenschmidt 1979b, and Kellens 2002: 437–40, pace Gnoli 1972.

Old Persian *būmi*. Herrenschmidt 1976: 42–45, 1977: 38–47. On revisions to the formula of royal investiture, see Herrenschmidt 1976, 1979a, and 1979b.

Earth, empire, and the project of world conquest. The speech that Herodotus attributed to Xerxes when leading his troops across the Hellespont shows a certain understanding of Persian ideology and aspirations, albeit recoded to reflect a critical Greek perspective:

> If we subdue them and their neighbors . . . we will produce a Persian earth bordering on Zeus's heaven, for the sun will look down on no land that is neighbor to ours. Rather, having marched through all Europe together with you, I will make them all one land.

(7.8)

V

Seizing or stealing the kingship. The verb used is Old Persian *grab-*, which has much the same sense as its English cognate. It is used for three of those whom the Bisitun inscription treats as rebels: Gaumata (DB §11, cf. §12), Nidintu-Bel (§16), and Arxa (§49).

VI

²dā-, **"to establish, create."** On the semantics of this verb, Herrenschmidt 1984: 151–55, Bianchi 1988: 192–93, and Kellens 1989. This verb appears in the following formulaic descriptions of the cosmogony: DNa §1, DNb §1, DSe §1, DSf §1, DSp, DSt §1, DZc §1, DE §1, XPa §1, XPb §1, XPc §1, XPd §1, XPf §1, XPh §1, XE §1, XV §1, A¹Pa §1, A²Hc §1, A³Pa §1. DPd §1 and DSf §3a use *²dā-* to describe the action of establishing Darius as king, which is more often conveyed by the verb *kar-* (discussed below).

pā-, **"to protect."** The prayer formula occurs with the first-person pronoun *mām* as its object at AsH §2, DPh §2, DNa §5, DSe §6, DSf §4, DSj §3, DSs, DSt §2, DH §2, XPa §4, XPb §3, XPc §3, XPd §3, XPf §5, XPg, XPh §5, XSc §2, XV §3, A¹Pa §3, A²Sa, A²Sd §2, A²Ha §2, A²Hc §3, A³Pa §4. The king to be protected is identified by name in DSn and D²Sa, and DPd §3 asks protection for no one specific person but, rather, for the Persian land/people. These data should be compared to Herodotus 1.132: "The Persians pray, not for blessings to come to the sacrificer himself, but for good to come to all Persians *and to the king,* for each man thinks himself included in the phrase 'all the Persians.'"

kar-, **"to make, do, build."** When the Wise Lord is the subject governing this verb, it almost always takes a double accusative, where *X* is a noun or pronoun denoting the person whom the deity makes into a king. The formula appears with a first-person accusative pronoun at AsH §2, DSf §3a, DSf §3b, and DSi §2 and with the king's name at DNa §1, DSe §1, DSf §1, DSt §1, DZc §1, DE §1, XPa §1, XPb §1, XPc §1, XPd §1, XPf §1, XPh §1, XE §1, XV §1, A¹Pa §1, A²Hc §1, and A³Pa §1. All the variants that include the king's name occur as the final sentence of a cosmogonic narrative. The significance of this is discussed in chapter 4. Three occurrences of the Wise Lord together with *kar-* are anomalous: DB §54, where God makes rebellious lands/peoples fall into Darius's hand; DB §66, a prayer that asks God to make things good for anyone who reads the inscription respectfully; and DSs, where *kar-* is used to describe the acts of creation in a context where one normally expects *²dā-*.

bar-, **"to bear, carry, bring."** Arsames, Darius, and Xerxes report "The Wise Lord bore me aid" at AmH §3, DB §§9, 13, 18, 19, 25, 26, 27, 28, 29, 30, 31, 33, 35, 36, 38, 41, 42, 45, 50, 62, 63, DPd §3, DNa §5, DSf §3d, XPh §§4a, and 4c. The same idea was voiced as a prayer and request at DSk §2.

frā-bar-, **"to confer, convey, bestow."** The Wise Lord is said to bestow "this Persian land/ people" on the new king at AmH §2, AsH §2, and DPd §2; "this kingship/kingdom" at DB §5, DB §9, DB §13, DPh §2, DSf §3a, DSm §2, DSp, DH §2, and A²Hc §3; and "this earth/empire" at DNa §4. The anomalous wording of DSs describes bestowal of the whole creation.

VII

Thought, word, and deed. This is a formulaic set in Iranian discourse. See further Schlerath 1974.

"Truth Incarnate." The hero's name in Avestan is *Astvat-ərəta,* lit. "Truth that has bones." The overdetermined image of bones serves to assert, not only that the truth in question has assumed bodily existence, but that it is lodged in that part of the body that is pure, eternal, and powerful (the contrast of bone and flesh being a trope well established in Iranian thought). A postmortem son of Zarathustra, born from the sea at the center of the world, Truth Incarnate appears at *Yašt* 19.92–96 and 13.129. See further Lommel 1930:

215–19 and 1970: 389–93, Kellens 1974: 209, Boyce 1975: 282–83, Mayrhofer 1979: 22–23, and Hintze 1994: 371–72.

Seething with rebellion. The most concrete meaning of the term employed (Old Persian *yaud-*) is "boiling," and it points to commotion that is out of control. That this term was used more specifically to describe processes of rebellion, and to delegitimate these processes by casting them in unfavorable terms, is apparent from its use here and at DSe §4 and XPh §4a. As Lecoq 1997: 220 and Skjærvø 1999: 43–44 realized, further evidence is supplied from an Avestan text that employs a cognate term (*yaoz-*) in very similar fashion: "From now on, Mithra of Wide Pastures will promote all the foremost authorities of the lands and will pacify those lands seething in rebellion" (*Yašt* 13.95, on which see also Gershevitch 1959: 27).

4. CREATION

I

Nature of creative action. Gnoli 1963, Herrenschmidt 1984: 151–55, Kellens 1989.

Achaemenian narrative of creation. The myth is recounted in the first paragraph of the following inscriptions: DNa, DNb, DPg, DSe, DSf, DSs, DSt, DSab, DE, DZc, XPa, XPb, XPc, XPd, XPf, XPh, XPl, XE, XV, A¹Pa, D²Ha, A²Hc, and A¹Pa. It has been studied most exhaustively in Herrenschmidt 1977. See also Bianchi 1988, Kellens 1989, Lincoln 2003a, and Herrenschmidt and Lincoln 2004.

Placement at the beginning. Almost all the later long inscriptions begin in one of two fashions: with the cosmogony (DNa, DNb, DPg, DSe, DSf, DSab, DZc, XPa, XPb, XPc, XPd, XPf, XPh, XPl, XV, A¹Pa, D²Ha, A²Hc, and A¹Pa) or with a list of royal titles (DH, DPe, DPf, DSj, DSz, DSaa, A²Sa, A²Sd), but titles always follow cosmogony in any inscription that contains both. Only one text differs from this pattern, beginning with a theological assertion, which is followed by a very partial account of creation (four of the usual five items omitted) and a reference to the rituals of royal investiture. Use of the verb ²*dā-* to describe the act of making Darius king is noteworthy and exceptional:

> The great Wise Lord is the greatest of the gods. He created Darius king. He bestowed the kingship/kingdom on him. By the Wise Lord's will, Darius is king.
>
> (DPd §1)

Xerxes' repetition and innovation. Every one of Xerxes' longer inscriptions begins with the cosmogonic narrative. In eight of nine instances (XPa, XPb, XPc, XPd, XPf, XPh, XE, XV), he follows the formula employed by Darius at DNa §1 and elsewhere; in the last case (XPl §1), he follows DNb §1. The sole innovation that he introduced is the identification of the Wise Lord as "greatest of the gods" at XE §1 and XV §1. One is tempted to relate this to the fact that the term translated "greatest" (Old Persian *maθišta*) can also be used as the title of the crown prince, i.e., the heir apparent and foremost of the king's sons. Xerxes proudly notes that he was given this title by Darius (XPf §4).

Cosmogonic consciousness. A classic body of literature has established the central importance of creation mythology in the history of religions, perhaps nowhere so much as in the ancient Near East. See, among others, Gunkel 1895, Langdon 1923, Hooke 1933, Engnell 1943, Heidel 1951, Eliade 1954, Brandon 1963, Long 1963, Loew 1967, Pettazzoni 1967, and Cross 1973. Of particular importance with reference to Iran is Molé 1963.

The most common account of creation. The passage quoted occurs, not only at DNa §1, but also, and in identical form, at DSf §1, DE §1, XPa §1, XPb §1, XPc §1, XPd §1, XPf §1, XPh §1, A¹Pa §1, D²Ha §1, and A¹Pa §1.

29 September 522. The date when Darius overthrew his predecessor and seized the kingship is given according to the Old Persian and Babylonian calendars at DB §13 and DB (Bab.) §12. The date of his ritual installation was some months later.

²dā- **and** *kar-.* Herrenschmidt 1984: 151–55, Bianchi 1988: 192–93, Kellens 1989.

Some unexpected event. If the Wise Lord was understood as omniscient, of course, then no event could really be unexpected. Zoroastrian texts address this issue by arguing that he anticipated the Assault of the Evil Spirit on the good creation and permitted, or even welcomed, it since this would let him lure his adversary onto a terrain of combat (i.e., time and space) where he could be defeated. See, e.g., *Selections of Zad Spram* 1.5–12 and 3.1–4, *Greater Bundahišn* 1.13–28 (TD² MS 6.9–12.7), and *Dadestan i Denig* 36.13.

II

Earth as including both earth and water. Herrenschmidt and Lincoln 2004. This is implicit in the Persian king's standard request that gifts of "earth and water" be given in token of submission, signifying that control over all territory (wet as well as dry) has, thereby, been relinquished. See further Kuhrt 1988.

Precedence of earth over sky. Only in DZc §1 does sky precede earth. Significantly, however, in the Babylonian version of DSab §1 sky once more takes first position, as it does in DPg, which exists only in Babylonian. Clearly, the Achaemenian scribes were aware of this alternative order, which they consciously rejected. Their reasons have been explicated in Herrenschmidt 1977: 43–45. On the near-universal classificatory practices that grant the high precedence over the low, see Schwartz 1981.

Cosmogony followed by royal titles. The two discourses are connected this way in seventeen inscriptions, which date from the later part of Darius's reign through that of Artaxerxes III: DNa §§1–2, DSe §§1–2, DSf §§1–2, DE §§1–2, DZc §§1–2, XPa §§1–2, XPb §§1–2, XPc §§1–2, XPd §§1–2, XPf §§1–2, XPh §§1–2, XE §§1–2, XV §§1–2, A¹Pa §§1–2, D²Ha §§1–2, A²Hc §§1–2, and A¹Pa §§1–2.

"Great" (Old Persian *vazṛka*). Benveniste 1969: 2:21–22.

The Evil Spirit. On the names and nature of the Wise Lord's great adversary, see Lommel 1930: 18 and 111–20, Christensen 1941, Widengren 1965: 76–78, Shaked 1967, Boyce 1975: 192–93 and 198–201, Hinz 1983, Schmidt 1996, and Stausberg 2002: 129–33.

The Assault of the Evil Spirit from below. Compare *Greater Bundahišn* 4.10 (TD² MS 41.10–42.3) and *Selections of Zad Spram* 1.31–33.

III

Original unity of the human species. As used in the cosmogonic account, Old Persian *martiya* ("man, mankind, humanity") denotes the totality of the human species, either as an undifferentiated mass or as having originally been encompassed in the body of the first-created individual. Darius's depiction of the rebellions that threatened the empire during his first year in power (DB §§10–55, DNa §4) implies his view of political fragmentation as a fall from the order and unity created by the Wise Lord, as Koch 1983: 293 recognized.

Human unity as thematized in Zoroastrian cosmogony. Zoroastrian texts describe one primordial exemplar of the species, named Gayomard, whose seed gave rise to all the differentiated nations and races only after his death. See *Yašt* 13.87, *Greater Bundahišn* 1.13 (TD² MS 21.11–22.1), 4.24–26 (TD² MS 44.15–45.5), 6F.9 (TD² MS 70.2–5), and 14.1–39 (TD² MS 100.3–107.13), *Denkard* 8.13.1–4, *Dadestan i Denig* 36.68, and *Menog i Xrad* 27.14–17. The classic treatment remains Christensen 1918: 7–101. Hartman 1953 is more useful for its collection of sources than its interpretation. Also useful are Widengren 1969, Lincoln 1981: 69–95 and 1997, and Shaked 1987 and 2005.

"Happiness" (*šiyāti*). Herrenschmidt 1991, Kellens 1995: 34–38, Piras 1994–95, Lincoln 2003c: lecture 1.

Three evils. Herrenschmidt 1991, Panaino 1986.

Truth and ritual speech. The crucial phrase in XPh §4d—"Worship the Wise Lord with ritual speech accompanied by truth"—has been discussed in, among others, Henning 1944, Kent 1945, Duchesne-Guillemin 1962a, Schmitt 1963: 442–45, Leroy 1967, Mawet 1978, Ito 1981, and Herrenschmidt 1993. The position of Henning, supported by Herrenschmidt, seems to me the most likely. With the exception of Skjærvø 1999: 46–47, comparable passages in Avestan have received less attention, but the following are important:

> Zarathustra asked the Wise Lord: "When a righteous man dies, where does his soul abide on the first night thereafter?" The Wise Lord said: "It stays close to his head, reciting prayers and sacred verses. On this night, the soul seeks as much happiness as all one seeks while still living."
>
> (*Hadoxt Nask* 2.2)

> May that man be happy—he who recites sacred formulas to one who is knowledgeable.
>
> (*Yasna* 51.8)

See also *Vispered* 7.3, *Yasna* 51.8 and 58.3, *Yašt* 8.59, 10.105, 17.6, and 19.34, and *Pursišniha* 23 and 34. Onomastic evidence also attests the importance of these concepts among the Achaemenians, on which see Benveniste 1966: 93, 98, and 119–21 and Mayrhofer 1973: 165–66, 231, and 234.

IV

Zoroastrian cosmogonies. The fullest accounts are those in Pahlavi that claim to reproduce material from a now-lost portion of the Sassanian Avesta titled the *Damdad Nask*. Those most frequently cited are *Greater Bundahišn* 1–6 and *Selections of Zad Spram* 1–3, but also useful are *Dadestan i Denig* 36, *Menog i Xrad* 8 (Andreas 1882), *Pahlavi Rivayat* accompanying *Dadestan i Denig* 46 (Williams 1990), and sections of *Denkard* 3. Beyond the *Damdad Nask,* one may perceive an older Avestan tradition, a tradition that finds expression in such passages as *Yasna* 37.1: "The Wise Lord, who established the cow, who established truth, who established water and plants, who established heaven and earth and all that is good." *Yasna* 44.3–6, 8.5–6, and 51.7 are also relevant. The relevant secondary literature includes Nyberg 1929 and 1931, Molé 1959, 1962, and 1963, Gnoli 1963, Shaked 1988 and 2005, and Jong 2005.

Six creations. Several variants, including *Greater Bundahišn* 3.8 (TD² MS 33.4–6) and *Selections of Zad Spram* 1.25, add fire as a seventh creation but give it a different status from the others and state that it is distributed through the other six. Both Zoroastrian and Achaemenian cosmogonies thus order creation as a series of $x + 1$ items, in which the last item (king or fire) stands apart from the others, with which it is intimately related.

Similarity of Pahlavi and Achaemenian cosmogonies. Herrenschmidt and Lincoln 2004.

Happiness, plants, and animals. Lincoln 2003c: lecture 1.

The Evil Spirit's miscreation. *Greater Bundahišn* 1.16–18 (TD² MS 4.9–5.1): "When the Foul Spirit saw the light of the Wise Lord, intangible and shining forth, owing to his envious nature and desire to smite he made an attack to destroy it. At that time, he saw bravery and triumph greater than his own, and he slunk back to the darkness. There, he fabricated many demons and destructive creatures that were needed for battle. When the Wise Lord saw the creatures of the Foul Spirit, those creatures seemed terrible, foul, vile, and evil, and they were not praised by him." Note that the verb "to create" (Pahlavi *dādan*) is never used of the Evil Spirit, being replaced by another verb (*kirrēnīdan*) that suggests an ugly process, one in which violence is mixed with creativity and disquieting products result. Compare *Greater Bundahišn* 1.47–49 (TD² MS 11.10–12.7), *Dadestan i Denig* 36.38–44, *Selections of Zad Spram* 2.11 and 2.19, and *Denkard* 3.162.

The Evil Spirit's stupidity. *Dadestan i Denig* 36.64: "Because of the ignorance of the Lie, however violently it struggles, the harm rebounds on the Lie itself." Compare *Greater Bundahišn* 1.3 and 1.15, *Dadestan i Denig* 36.4, and *Denkard* 3.108 and 3.173.

The Assault. *Greater Bundahišn* 22.1: "When the Evil Spirit rushed in, he mixed the poison of
vermin, the poison of sin, like that of the snake, the scorpion, the lizard, the ant, the fly,
the locust, and a great many others of this kind, with water, earth, and plants." For fuller
discussions, see *Selections of Zad Spram* 3, *Greater Bundahišn* 6A–6F (TD² MS 60.7–70.6),
Dadestan i Denig 36.4–18 and 36.31–37, and *Denkard* 3.123, 3.380, 3.399, and passim.

Mountains. *Greater Bundahišn* 6C.1 (TD² MS 65.12–14): "When the Evil One rushed in, the
earth quaked, and the substance of mountains was created in the earth." Compare *Selections of Zad Spram* 3.26–36 and *Dadestan i Denig* 70.2. For discussion of this motif, see Lincoln 1983 and Herrenschmidt and Lincoln 2004.

Creation as bait and the Wise Lord's plan. *Dadestan i Denig* 36.19–20: "He created the
middle third [i.e., the space between the above and the below], the material creation, as
the front line of the material and spiritual existences . . . and he made that third into a
battlefield for the combat of the two antithetical natures." Compare *Greater Bundahišn*
1.25–28 (TD² 6.3–7.6), *Selections of Zad Spram* 1.8–12, and *Dadestan i Denig* 36.10–20.

Nine thousand years. Virtually all the Pahlavi texts specify that the state of cosmic mixture
(*gumēzišnīg*) and combat between the good and the evil fractions of existence will last for
three periods of three thousand years, the number 9 and multiples thereof conveying a
sense of completion. Some variants add a fourth period that predates the conflict, thereby
creating a system of twelve millennia that is homologized to the months of the year and
the signs of the zodiac. The relation between these alternate systems has been discussed
in Lommel 1930: 130–43, Zaehner 1955: 96–100, Duchesne-Guillemin 1962b: 318–22, and
Boyce 1975: 285–93.

The Final Body, the Resurrection, the Renovation. *Selections of Zad Spram* 34–35, *Greater
Bundahišn* 34, *Pahlavi Rivayat* accompanying *Dadestan i Denig* 48. See esp. Molé 1963 and
Timus 2003.

V

Beneficent and noxious creatures. Herodotus 1.140 describes how the magi "waged a great
struggle" against animal species classified as evil, including ants, serpents, reptiles, and insects. This text and its resemblance to doctrines found in the Avesta (*Videvdad* 14.5–8,
16.12, 17.3, 18.2, 65, and 73) have been discussed in Benveniste 1929: 33–34, Zaehner
1961: 162, Widengren 1965: 113, Boyce 1975: 182–83 and 1979: 76, Jong 1997: 338–42,
and Herrenschmidt and Lincoln 2004.

Sweet and salt water. Note the Achaemenian kings' exaggerated concern to drink only
water from the Choaspes near Susa, understood to be sweetest, lightest, most healthful,
and most fully Persian. This water was boiled, placed in silver vessels, and carried with
the kings wherever they went. See Herodotus 1.188, Ctesias (preserved in Athenaeus,
Deipnosophistae 45b), and Aelian, *Varia historia* 12.40; cf. Athenaeus, *Deipnosophistae* 652b
(citing Deinon) and 515a. These materials have been studied most extensively in Briant
1994. Conversely, the Achaemenians' aversion to salt water is reflected in their classification of hostile lands and peoples as those "beyond the sea" (*paradraya*), their aversion to
naval warfare, and Xerxes' notorious attempt to punish the Hellespont—whose waters
he characterized as "bitter" and "salty"—for its resistance to him (Herodotus 7.35), on
which see Rocchi 1980 and Briquel and Desnier 1983. Darius's contrastive attitudes toward the salt water of the Pontus and the sweet, healing water of the Tearus is discussed
in Herrenschmidt and Lincoln 2004.

Mountains and plains. The term for "mountain" (Old Persian *kaufah*) appears three times in the Achaemenian corpus. One instance is unexceptionable (DSf §3g). The others make mountains the site where the most serious rebellions—those of Gaumata and Vahyazdata, which both occurred in Persia—began and ended (DB §§11 and 42). While far from conclusive, these texts associate mountains with violence, disorder, and the Lie. See further Herrenschmidt and Lincoln 2004. One might also consider Persian attitudes toward waterless desert land, as described in Herodotus 3.5–7 and 25.

Cambyses and Bardiya as full brothers. The same point is made in Herodotus 3.30 and Xenophon, *Anabasis* 3.1.17.

Cambyses chosen as Cyrus's heir. Thus Herodotus 1.208, Xenophon, *Cyropaedia* 8.7.9–11, and Ctesias, *Persica* 11 (preserved in Photius 72.8).

Marriage of Cambyses to his sisters and his childlessness. Herodotus 3.31–32. The narrative emphasizes the king's lack of heirs by relating that, in a fit of madness, he killed his younger wife when she was pregnant. Atossa, the elder, was taken first by Bardiya and then by Darius when they assumed the kingship, and she ultimately bore Xerxes, from whom the later Achaemenians descended. Darius also took Artystone, the youngest daughter of Cyrus, and Phaidyme, a daughter of Bardiya, thereby monopolizing all fertility in the line of Cyrus. The resultant relations are diagrammed as follows:

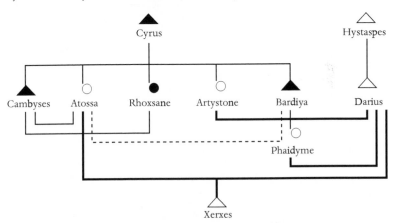

That Darius stood well outside the line of succession when Cambyses was alive is clear from the fact that he served as the latter's spear bearer in Egypt (Herodotus 3.139).

On the Achaemenian practice of marrying one's next of kin, see Herrenschmidt 1987b and 1994. The marriages of Atossa and Artystone to Bardiya and Darius are related at Herodotus 3.68 and 3.88, respectively.

Bardiya as heir apparent. On Cambyses' lack of progeny, see Herodotus 3.66. Ctesias, who on some points is better informed than Herodotus (see Dandamaev 1989: 84–85), states that Cyrus made Bardiya the governor of several eastern provinces, including Bactria and Parthia (Ctesias 9.8 [preserved in Photius]). Xenophon, *Cyropaedia* 8.7.11, has him as satrap of Media, Armenia, and the Cadusians.

Cambyses' purported murder of Bardiya. Variants on this story are found in Herodotus 3.30, Ctesias 12 (preserved in Photius), and Pompeius Trogus (preserved in Justinus 1.9.4–11). The facticity of this event has been much discussed, and most now regard it as a fabrication of Darius's propaganda. Within a large and constantly growing literature, see Bickerman and Tadmor 1978, Wiesehöfer 1978, Balcer 1987, Dandamaev 1989: 83–90, Zawadzki 1994, Briant 1996: 110–11, and Pongratz-Leisten 2002.

Events through December 520. The precise chronology of these events is difficult to establish from the Bisitun account, which may be deliberately distorted in order to cram the defeat of nine rebels (a ritually significant number) into the ritually significant period of one year, beginning with Darius's formal accession to the throne (December 522). For various attempts, see Poebel 1938, Hallock 1960, and Shahbazi 1972.

VI

Old Persian *fraša* **(wonder, marvel).** The fullest study is Lincoln 1996. Regarding the etymology and interpretation of this term and its Avestan cognate, see Lommel 1922, Bailey 1953 and 1956, Narten 1986: 199–203, Kellens and Pirart 1988–91: 2:270, and Hintze 1994: 107.

Zoroastrian usage of *fraša* **in cosmogonic discourse.** This is most evident in *Yašt* 19.10:

> We worship the royal charisma, created by the Wise One . . .
> Which belongs to the Wise Lord,
> Since the Wise Lord created the creations:
> Many and good, many and beautiful,
> Many and marvelous, many and *wondrous* [*fraša*],
> Many and splendid.

See also *Videvdad* 1.20, *Yasna* 50.11, and Hintze 1994: 107.

Zoroastrian usage of *fraša, frašō-kərəti,* **and** *frašgird* **in eschatological discourse.** See, e.g., *Denkard* 3.208:

> The Wise Lord, in his omniscient wisdom, desirous of judgment, by his action demarcates a limit to time, and in time a limit to action. The limit extends from what is first to what is last. When action is completed, it returns to the peace of the primordial era. When time is completed, its transitory nature returns to the limitlessness of the primordial era. This is the Renovation (or: "Wondermaking," *frašgird*): the destruction of the Lie, the Resurrection, the Final Body, the salvation of all creation, and eternal happiness.
> (Madan 1911: 228.3–8; Dresden 1966: 178.20–179.2)

It is perhaps noteworthy that the term used here to denote "happiness" (Pahlavi *šēdā*) usually refers to eschatological bliss and is cognate to Old Persian *šiyāti,* which names happiness as the fourth of the Wise Lord's original creations in Achaemenian accounts. Regarding the eschatological "Wondermaking," see also *Yasna* 24.5, 30.9, 34.15, 46.19, 55.6, and 62.3, *Yašt* 13.17, 13.58, 19.11, 19.22, and 19.89, *Selections of Zad Spram* 34–35, *Greater Bundahišn* 34 (TD² MS 220.15–228.5), *Pahlavi Rivayat* accompanying *Dadestan i Denig* 48, *Denkard* 3.114, 143, and 413, Lommel 1930: 224–26, Zaehner 1956: 139–50, Molé 1963: 412–18 and passim, Widengren 1965: 102–8, and Boyce 1975: 245–46.

Cosmogony and eschatology. Regarding the mirrored relation of the two, Molé 1963 remains fundamental.

5. MICROCOSMS, WONDERS, PARADISE

I

One plant, one animal, one human. Misleading translations notwithstanding, Pahlavi texts always use the singular when describing the first plant, as in *Selections of Zad Spram* 1.4, 1.25, 2.6–7, 2.18, etc., *Greater Bundahišn* 1.54 (TD² MS 15.3), 1A.4 (TD² MS 17.10), 1A.11 (TD² MS 20.8–11), 4.17 (TD² MS 43.7–8), etc., and *Pahlavi Rivayat* accompanying *Dadestan i Denig* 46.13. The first animal and first man are also always mentioned in the singular, and the former has a name that underscores this point: *Ewagdad* (Sole-created). I have discussed the plant in Lincoln 2003c, the animal and man in Lincoln 1981: 69–95. The best treatment of the first man (Gayomard, "Mortal life") remains Christensen 1918: 7–101, although Hartman 1953 is useful at points.

Original beings created in Iran, at the center of the earth. Thus, *Greater Bundahišn* 1A.11 (TD² MS 20.8), 1A.12 (TD² MS 20.15), and 1A.13 (TD² MS 21.7), *Pahlavi Rivayat* accompanying *Dadestan i Denig* 46.13 and 46.15, and *Selections of Zad Spram* 2.7 and 2.9. On the construction of Iran as the world's center, see chapter 2. See also Benveniste 1932–35, Christensen 1943, Gnoli 1989 and 1993, and Daryaee 2002.

Lack of omnipotence. Consider, e.g., *Menog i Xrad* 8.22–26:

> The Wise Lord always desires good and never accepts or seems evil. The Evil Spirit desires evil and never considers or accepts good. When he wishes, the Wise Lord has the power to work change on the Evil Spirit's creation, and, when the Evil Spirit wishes, he has the power to work change on the Wise Lord's creation, but his power to change is such that no harm comes to the Wise Lord in the making of the end, for the final victory is to the Wise Lord himself.

Final ordeal. Zoroastrian doctrine differs dramatically from Christian understandings of the Last Judgment. Briefly, it is thought that, since the Wise Lord is entirely benevolent, he could not imagine consigning any of his creatures to eternal punishment. The Renovation thus includes a fiery ordeal in which all those who have been resurrected are forced to wade through a river of molten metal, which burns off all impure accretions that have become a part of their being as a result of their moral failings. The pain endured thus varies according to ethical status. See *Greater Bundahišn* 34.19 (TD² MS 225.8–11), *Dadestan i Denig* 31.10 and 36.96, and *Pahlavi Rivayat* accompanying *Dadestan i Denig* 48.69–72.

Frašgird. Avestan sources include *Yasna* 30.7–9 and *Yašt* 19.10–11. Pahlavi sources provide more extended discussions, however. Thus *Greater Bundahišn* 34 (TD² MS 220.15–228.5), *Selections of Zad Spram* 34–35, and *Pahlavi Rivayat* accompanying *Dadestan i Denig* 48. Within an abundant secondary literature, see Lommel 1930: 224–25, Molé 1963: 172–75, Widengren 1965: 88, and Hintze 1994: 151–57.

Dialectical analysis of death and species immortality. Consider the following passages:

> Thus, the Creator of the world made the spiritual creation pure and undefiled. He made the material creation immortal, unaging, without hunger, without bondage, without sorrow, and without pain, until there erupted in the darkness the Lie of wickedness.
>
> (*Dadestan i Denig* 36.4)

> Now, the mortality and immortality of mortal bodies comes from the mixture of antithetical natures/substances produced by the Adversary's original Assault. The Creator does not preserve his creations as long as they are in the state of mixture produced by the Assault throughout the state of mixture. The reason [he lets] his progeny become mixed with mortality in the general course of things is so that the creations can participate in the Renovation, recovering that which they lost to the desire for death caused by the Adversary's Assault and putting an end to death itself and the Adversary.
>
> (*Denkard* 3.317)

> By a great mystery and total wonder, [the Wise Lord] gave long-standing immortality to living beings. More astonishing: The best, highest form is the immortality that derives from the Adversary. Because every living being always suffers pain from the Adversary, and the amazing power of those who obtain offspring is that they are ever young by virtue of offspring, family, and good generations that derive from the Adversary for the perpetuation of life.
>
> (*Dadestan i Denig* 36.29)

Differentiation of species and races. *Selections of Zad Spram* 3.37–76, *Greater Bundahišn* 3.13–14 (TD² MS 34.4–35.7), 4.17–18 (TD² MS 43.7–10), 4.26 (TD² MS 45.3–5), 6D.0–7 (TD² MS 67.1–15), 6E.0–6 (TD² MS 68.1–12), 6F.7–10 (TD² MS 69.13–70.6), 13.0–5 (TD² MS 93.8–94.9), and 14.0–11 (TD² MS 100.3–102.3). *Greater Bundahišn* 14 (TD² MS 100.3–107.14) gives an extremely complex narrative that derives twenty-five races from Gayomard, with the Iranians in first position and monkeys in last. *Denkard* 3.139 (Madan 1911: 143.5–19 and Dresden 1966: 108.17–109.6) has a much simpler account:

> In the era of mixture, the races of man are of three types: best, middle, and lowest. . . . The power advantage is in their belief, which makes good religion higher and evil religion lower. Thus, in general, by belief in the Good Religion the lowest races are elevated in their nature to the nature of the middle races. Similarly, by their desire, the middle races are elevated in their nature to the nature of the highest races. In time, the highest races become themselves like the gods. As regards those who are of an evil religion, in general the highest races descend in their nature to the nature of the lowest races. In time, the lowest races become like the demon, the Lie.

Eschatological reunion. Thus, *Greater Bundahišn* 34.20–21 (TD² MS 225.11–226.1):

> Then, with the greatest love, all people arrive together—fathers and sons, brothers, and all friends. They ask one another: "Where have you been these many years? And what was the judgment of your soul? Were you righteous or a follower of the Lie?". . . Then men all come together in collaboration, and they bear high praise to the Wise Lord and the beneficent immortals.

Compare *Denkard* 3.327, *Pahlavi Rivayat* accompanying *Dadestan i Denig* 48.102, and Plutarch, *Isis and Osiris* 47. *Selections of Zad Spram* 35 differs on this issue.

II

Rebellion. The Bisitun text deploys a rather nuanced vocabulary to treat different aspects of rebellion. Normally, a description begins by convicting a pretender of having lied about his name, lineage, and title (verb: *duruj-*, "to lie"). Then it accuses him of insubordination and overreaching (verb: *uda-pat-*, "to rise up"). There follow popular disorder (verb phrase: *hamiçiya bav-*, "to become rebellious"), military defection (verb: *šiyav-*, "to go over to"), and usurpation (verb phrase: *xšaçam grab-*, "to seize the kingship/kingdom"). See further Lincoln 2005.

Fourteen provinces. Significantly, it is the core of the empire that was most affected by these uprisings. Persia (DB §§11, 21, 40) and Media (§§11, 21, 24) each suffered three insurrections, Babylon (§§15, 49), Elam (§§15, 21), and Parthia (§§21, 35) two. Others that experienced rebellion were Assyria (§21), Egypt (§21), Armenia (§26), Scythia (§21), Sattagydia (§21), Arachosia (§45), Margiana (§§21, 38), Sagartia (§33), and Hyrcania (§35). DB §39 implies that Bactria also turned rebellious, but this is less than certain. Mention of unnamed "others" in DB §11 raises the possibility of still further disorder.

Attempts to seize control of the empire. These were the rebellions of Gaumata and Vahyazdata, both of whom—if Darius is to be believed—sought to pass themselves off as Bardiya, son of Cyrus (DB §§10–14 and 40–48, respectively).

Nationalism. On the political character of these rebellions, see Dandamaev 1989: 114–32 and Briant 1996: 132–33. The classic work on nationalism in antiquity is Eddy 1961.

III

Xerxes' speech. This passage has been much discussed. See, among others, Evans 1961.

The Persians' ancestral custom. On ceaseless expansionism as the Persian *nomos*, see the discussion in Evans 1961.

Greek perspective. This surfaces even more powerfully in the continuation of the passage, where Xerxes is made to gloat that all those whom the Persians conquer "will have to bear our yoke of slavery" (Herodotus 7.8).

"Kingdom" (*xšaça*) **and "land/people"** (*dahyu*). On *xšaça*, the discussion in Herrenschmidt

1976: 44–45 and 1979b is preferable to that in Gnoli 1972 or Bucci 1985. On *dahyu,* see Lecoq 1990a.

Terminology for "empire." Herrenschmidt 1976, esp. 42–45.

Ancient Indo-Iranian usage. Mayrhofer 1956–76: 2:513, Bartholomae 1904/1961: 969. The two Old Persian occurrences that preserve the meaning "soil" both come from detailed descriptions of palace building (DSf §§3e, 3f).

Cosmogonic contexts. DNa §1, DSe §1, DSf §1, DSt §1, DE §1, XPa §1, XPb §1, XPc §1, XPd §1, XPf §1, XPh §1, XE §1, XV §1, A¹Pa §1, A²Hc §1, and A¹Pa §1 are identical. DSs represents a minor variation from this formula and DZc §1 a somewhat greater departure. The same usage is found in one of the oldest Avestan texts, *Yasna* 37.1: "The Wise Lord, who established the cow, who established truth, who established water and plants, who established heaven and earth [*būmīm*] and all that is good."

Royal title. The simple formula ("King in this empire") appears at DSd §1, DSf §2, DSf §3b, DSg, DSi §1, DSi §2, DSj §1, DSm §2, DSy, DZb, XPf §3, XPj §1, D²Sb §1, A²Sa, A²Sd §1, A²Sc §2, A²Ha §1, A²Hc §2, A¹Pa §2, Wb, Wc, and Wd. Two expanded forms are also attested: "King in all the empire" (DSb, DSf §3c) and "King in this great, far-reaching empire" (DNa §2, DSe §2, DZc §2, DE §2, XPa §2, XPb §2, XPc §2, XPd §2, XPf §2, XPh §2, XE §2, XV §2, A¹Pa §2, A²Hc §3). Most often, this title appears as the culminating member in a set of four, as is true in all of those just mentioned, save DSf §3b, DSf §3c, DSm §2, DSi §2, and A²Hc §3. See further the discussion in chapter 1. In one Avestan text, *būmi* also appears in the context of royal rule, *Yašt* 19.26: "He ruled over the seven-partite earth [*būmīm*]." This is said of Haošyangha Paradata, a fabulously successful mythic king of the golden age who conquered the Evil Spirit (on whom see Christensen 1918: 107–64).

Seething in rebellion. Most literally, the verb *yaud-* denotes a boiling turbulence. In the Old Persian inscriptions, its usage is restricted to situations of rebellion (cf. DSe §4 and XPh §4a). The Avestan cognate *yaoz-* is also used of rebellion at *Yašt* 13.95, as was noted already in Bartholomae 1901: 134.

"I set things in place." The object pronoun in this phrase is in the singular, with *būmi* as its antecedent. A more literal translation would, thus, read: "I set it [the earth/empire] in place."

Throne bearers. Schmidt 1953–70: 3:84–86, 108–11, frontispiece, and pls. 18–52, Calmeyer 1975, Root 1979: 72–76 and 147–53, Gall 1989.

Captions beneath the throne bearers. DNe, which is trilingual, identifies each figure: "This is the Persian. This is the Mede. This is the Elamite, etc." Although the text is damaged, eighteen of the thirty identifications are legible, and their order matches that in which the lands/provinces are listed in DNa §3.

IV

Susa. On Susa and its importance, see Hinz 1976: 177–82, Dandamaev and Lukonin 1989: 256–59, Boucharlat 1990, and Muscarella, Caubet, and Tallon 1992. Strabo 15.3.3 says that the Persians adorned Susa more highly than any of their other cities, using a verb (*kosmeô*) that also suggests it was most perfectly ordered. At 15.3.6, he adds that it was the most beautifully appointed.

Subject peoples do as they are told. Often, subjects' obedience to the king is explicitly connected to their payment of tribute but implicitly goes beyond this to include obedience to the law, military service, etc. Consider, e.g., DB §7:

> Proclaims Darius the King: These lands/peoples which came to me, by the Wise Lord's will they were subject [lit. bondsmen] to me. They bore me tribute. What was proclaimed to them by me, by day or by night, that was done.

Construction projects. The verb *kar-* appears in the following passages: DSd §2, DSf §3e, XPd §3, XPj §2, XSc §2, D²Sb §2, A²Sd §2 (palaces); DSe §5 (defensive walls); XPa §3 (colonnade); A²Ha, A²Sa (reception hall); DSg §2 (columns); and DB §70 (inscription).

Inscriptions celebrating the wonder at Susa. In addition to the passage cited, see DSa §2, DSf §4 (which has the verb *fra-mā-* "to plan," instead of *kar-*), DSj §3, and DSo.

"By the Wise Lord's will." For the fullest treatment of this highly significant phrase, see Lincoln 1996. Ahn 1992: 196–99 is also useful.

"Well-made" or "well-built." This compound adjective is constructed on the verb *kar-*. It appears at DSj §2, DSl, and DSf §3d, always with reference to the palace at Susa. There is only one other occurrence, in the context of a general benediction (DB §66).

Foundation charters. Vallat published DSz and DSaa in Vallat 1971, and he discussed their relation to DSf in Vallat 1972. See also Herrenschmidt 1983.

Lands/peoples appearing in the foundation charters. DSf and DSz list the same seventeen lands and peoples, and DSaa has twenty-three. Eleven lands appear in all the lists (Elam, Media, Babylon, Assyria, Lydia, Ionia, Bactria, Sogdiana, Egypt, Gandhara, and Arachosia), five are in DSf and DSz only (Lebanon, Caria, Carmania, Ethiopia, and India), and twelve are in DSaa only (Persia, Arabia, "the lands by the sea," Armenia, Cappadocia, Parthia, Drangiana, Aria, Chorasmia, Scythia, Sattagydia, and Maka). When it is understood that both the Ionians and the Scythians were subject to further subcategorization, these texts thus account for all but two of the lands/peoples who appear in the list that was contemporary with the construction of the palace at Susa (DSe §3). The two exceptions—the Thracians and the Libyans—were at the outermost northwest and southwest peripheries, respectively. Even so, it is conceivable that they were subsumed in DSaa's mention of "the lands by the sea."

Processes of extraction. Greek sources also discuss the Achaemenian habit of requiring different peoples to contribute their best products, and they described this as an innovation of Darius's. Thus Herodotus 3.89–96 and Strabo 15.3.21. Xenophon, *Cyropaedia* 8.6.6 and 8.6.23 attributes something similar to Cyrus. On tribute in general, see the essays in Briant and Herrenschmidt 1989.

V

Royal banquet. The most important primary sources for the king's table are Herodotus 1.133 and 9.82, Xenophon, *Agesilaus* 9, Athenaeus, *Deipnosophistae* 144a–146c, 529d, 539b, 545d, and 608a, Polyaenus 4.3.32 (above all), and Esther 1:5–7. See Lewis 1987 and Briant 1989b.

Athenian figs. The story was recorded in Deinon's lost *Persika* and is preserved in Athenaeus, *Deipnosophistae* 652b and Plutarch, *Sayings of Kings and Generals* 173c. It has been discussed in Briant 1989b: 36 and 1994: 47–49. The high valuation of these figs and the legal regulation of their export are discussed in Istros (preserved in Athenaeus, *Deipnosophistae* 74e).

Apadana reliefs. For more elaborate photographs of this site and discussion of its details, see Schmidt 1953–70: 3:143–60, Burnett 1957: 65–72, Walser 1966, Hinz 1969: 95–114, Root 1979: 86–95 and 227–84, Koch 1983, and Jamzadeh 1992.

Animals borne in tribute. Schmidt 1953–70: 3:156–57. On some of the more exotic animals, see Afshar 1974 and 1978.

VI

Paradise. The classic piece on this topic is Fauth 1979, but there have been a number of excellent studies recently, including Tuplin 1996, Bremmer 1999, Hultgård 2000, and Briant 2003. I have discussed it on two occasions: see Lincoln 2003a and 2003c: lectures 1 and 4. Archaeological excavations have revealed the details of one paradise garden only, that at Pasargadae, on which see Stronach 1989. Akkadian testimonies regarding the Achaemenian paradise have been studied in Dandamaev 1984, Elamite in Uchitel 1997. Works that discuss the Persian institution with reference to the longer tradition of royal gardens in the ancient Near East include Stronach 1990 and Besnier 1999.

Ideal (warm, moist) climate. The abundant waters of a *paradeisos* are mentioned in Xenophon, *Anabasis* 1.2.7 (a paradise in Celaenae), Plutarch, *Alcibiades* 24.5 (one owned by Tissaphernes in Sardis), Diodorus Siculus 5.19.2 (one in Atlantis) and 19.21.3 (one in Persepolis), Curtius Rufus 8.1.12 (one in eastern Iran), Septuagint Genesis 2.10–14 (Eden), Ecclesiastes 2.6 (an imaginary paradise), and Song of Solomon 4.12–15 (another imaginary paradise). Irrigation is specifically mentioned in Arrian, *Anabasis* 6.29.4 (a paradise in Pasargadae) and Diodorus Siculus 5.19.2 (one in Atlantis). The contrast with surrounding areas that are too hot and dry figures in Arrian, *Indica* 8.40.2–3 (a paradise in Persia) and Diodorus Siculus 19.21.2–3 (one in Persepolis), with surrounding areas that are too cold in Arrian, *Indica* 8.40.3–4 (one in Persia) and Plutarch, *Artaxerxes* 25.1 (one in Cadusia). On warmth and moisture as the ideal life-sustaining qualities of Iranian cosmology, see Shaki 1970: 295–96 and Lincoln 1991: 209–18, 2001a, and 2003c: lecture 3.

Loanwords from Persian *paridaida*. Compare Akkadian *pardēsu*, Hebrew *pardēs*, Armenian *partēz*, Elamite *partētaš*, Arabic *firdaus*, and Greek *paradeisos*. The Old Persian term appears in one inscription only, A²Sd §2: "Proclaims Artaxerxes the King: By the Wise Lord's will, while living I made/built this palace that is a paradise." There are some scribal and phonological difficulties in this text, difficulties that troubled Lecoq deeply (see Lecoq 1990b). These have, however, been resolved (see Schmitt 1999: 82–85).

European words for "paradise." Thus, among others, Latin *paradisus*, Italian *paradiso*, Spanish *paraiso*, French *paradis*, English *paradise,* and German *Paradies*. Motivating this transmission was the Septuagint's use of Greek *paradeisos* to translate Hebrew *gan* (garden) with reference to Eden. Bremmer 1999 has argued that Hellenistic ideology informed these developments much more than anything Persian. Lincoln 2003c reasserts the importance of the Achaemenian background.

Animals "of every species." The quotation is from Xenophon, *Cyropaedia* 1.3.14. See also Xenophon, *Anabasis* 1.2.7 (the paradise at Celaenae), *Hellenica* 4.1.15–16 (that at Dascyleium) and 4.1.33 (numerous sites belonging to Cyrus the Younger), Arrian, *Indica* 8.40.3–4 (a paradise in Persia), Diodorus Siculus 19.21.3 (one in Persepolis), Curtius Rufus 8.1.11 (one in eastern Iran), and Achilles Tatius 1.15 (an unspecified paradise).

Plants "of every species." In addition to the passages cited in the text, see Xenophon, *Hellenica* 4.1.33 and *Œconomicus* 4.14 (both describing paradises of Cyrus the Younger), Arrian, *Indica* 8.40.3–4 (a paradise in Persia), Arrian, *Anabasis* 6.29.4 (one in Pasargadae), Diodorus Siculus 14.79.2 (a paradise of Tissaphernes in Sardis) and 19.21.3 (one in Persepolis), Longus 4.2 (a fictive paradise), and Achilles Tatius 1.15 (an unspecified one).

Paradise garden of Atlantis. The text quoted is Diodorus Siculus 5.19.2. See also two passages of the Hebrew Bible treating gardens so magnificent that the ordinary terminology (Hebrew *gan*) is inadequate to describe them and, thus, the loanword *pardēs* is employed: Eccles. 2.5 and Song of Sol. 4.13. The latter is particularly vivid:

> Your shoots are a paradise of pomegranates
>> with all choicest fruits,
>> henna with nard,
> Nard and saffron, calamus and cinnamon,
>> with all trees of frankincense,
>> myrrh and aloes,
>>> with all chief spices—
>> A garden fountain, a well of living water,
>>> And flowing streams from Lebanon.

VII

Arda Wiraz Namag. For an edition, see Vahman 1986.

Heaven as garden. This image is well attested in Zoroastrian literature, as in *Hadoxt Nask* 2.7, *Selections of Zad Spram* 30.52 and 55, *Greater Bundahišn* 30.15 (TD² MS 201.6–12), and *Arda Wiraz Namag* 8.15–19. An eschatological garden is the culmination of the Renovation, as narrated in the *Pahlavi Rivayat* accompanying *Dadestan i Denig* 48.107.

Heaven and happiness. The two are often associated, as in the Pahlavi supplementary texts to the *Šayest ne Šayest* 15.8 (Kotwal 1969), *Menog i Xrad* 7.14, *Selections of Zad Spram* 35.45, and *Dadestan i Denig* 18.6 and 31.13. The phrase "all-bliss" (*harwisp xwārīh* or *hamāg xwārīh*) is found in *Denkard* 5.8.3, *Arda Wiraz Namag* 13.17, and *Greater Bundahišn* 30.15 (TD² MS 201.11), while "all-happiness" (*hamāg-šādīh*) recurs in *Denkard* 5.8.11, in an eschatological context:

> No creature remains in the state produced by the Adversary's original Assault. The Evil Spirit, as well as the other demons and lies, is conquered, killed, and destroyed. All stain and evil are carried away from good creatures. And all creatures like us, whose original substance is light, are established in a state of holiness, purity, freedom from blemish, absence of need, with one's desires accomplished, without misfortune, *and all-happiness*.

Paradise garden named "All-happiness." The name appears in nos. 49 and 59 of the Persepolis Treasury Tablets (Cameron 1948: 160 and 172). The significance of this name was first recognized in Benveniste 1958: 57–58. The interpretation there has since been confirmed and expanded in Skjærvø 1994.

Happiness after death. The sole Achaemenian passage treating this theme is XPh §4d:

> You who [come] hereafter, if you should think, "May I be happy [*šiyāta*] when living, and may I be righteous [*artavan*] when dead," conduct yourself according to that law that the Wise Lord set down. Worship the Wise Lord with ritual speech accompanied by truth. The man who conducts himself according to the law that the Wise Lord set down and who worships the Wise Lord with ritual speech accompanied by truth, he becomes happy when living and righteous when dead.

Mardonius. Mardonius was son of Gobryas, who was one of the six "noble Persians" who helped Darius to the throne (DB §68) and who served as Darius's spear bearer (DNc), a high-ranking Achaemenian noble, bound to Darius and Xerxes through a thick net of kinship:

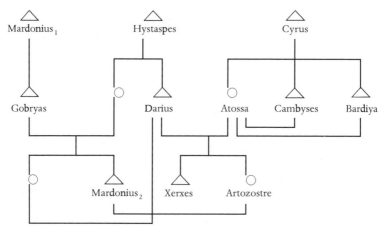

From 493 until his death at the battle of Plataea in 479, Mardonius directed Persian policy toward the Greeks. For a full collection of the evidence regarding his life, see Balcer 1993: 78–79. For a brief consideration of the channels through which Herodotus obtained his information regarding Mardonius, see Hegyi 1973: 85.

6. THE DARK SIDE OF PARADISE

I

Walls. Old Persian *paridaida* and its cognates are all compound terms, in which *daida* means "wall" and the first element is a preposition that signals its encircling nature (cf. Greek *peri*). The uncompounded term *didā* denotes defensive walls at DB §§13, 27, 28, 45, and 47.

Ecbatana. The walls of Ecbatana are mentioned at DB §32 and are described in Herodotus 1.98. Susa also had splendid wall decorations, as mentioned at DSf §§3i–3k and discussed in Muscarella, Caubet, and Tallon 1992: 223–41, with ample illustration.

Persepolis citadel. I follow the brilliant interpretation of the citadel facade advanced in Root 1990: 118–20.

The king's responsibility to restore the walls. This topos is well attested elsewhere in Mesopotamia and is asserted by the Achaemenians at CB §13 and DSe §5.

Zoroastrian enclosure. The passage describing the *pairidaēza* (*Videvdat* 3.15–21) occurs in the context of a chapter that contrasts the best and worst places in existence. The best places, like the Achaemenian paradise, are warm, moist spots where plant, animal, and human life abundantly flourishes (*Videvdat* 3.1–6, 12–14, and 22–34); the worst places are dry, subterranean (the abode of the Evil Spirit), corpse strewn, devoid of plant and animal life, and populated by demons (*Videvdat* 3.7–11). I discuss this text in Lincoln 1991: 110–11 and 2003c: lecture 4.

Death by old age and decrepitude. Literally, it is said that all the fluids of his body will dry out (*Videvdat* 3.19–20). Although Pahlavi translations of the text interpret this as a reference to sexual impotence, it is more broadly a description of the enclosure as cold and dry: Ahrimanian qualities antithetical to the flourishing of life.

II

Battle of Cunaxa. On the battle of Cunaxa and the struggle between Artaxerxes and Cyrus, see Rahe 1980, Bigwood 1983, Dandamaev 1989: 274–85, Wylie 1992, and Briant 1996: 274–85 and 634–53.

Variant accounts of Cyrus's death. The version most sympathetic to royal interests is that given in Deinon (preserved in Plutarch, *Artaxerxes* 10.1–3). Here, Cyrus attacked Artaxerxes and dismounted him twice but died at his brother's hand on the third assault. Deinon (Plutarch, *Artaxerxes* 10.3) also included a more critical variant, in which an unnamed Carian killed Cyrus, thereby winning the king's gratitude. Xenophon, *Anabasis* 1.8.26–27 cites Ctesias as his source and describes a sequence in which Cyrus wounded Artaxerxes, then was wounded below the eye by someone who remains unidentified. A melee between the immediate retinues of the two leaders followed; in it, Cyrus was killed, but no individual is credited with his death.

Ctesias as Plutarch's source regarding Cunaxa. This follows from citations embedded in the Plutarchan text (*Artaxerxes* 6.6, 9.1, 11.1, 2, and 6, 13.3, 14.1) and was recognized as early as Smith 1881.

Ctesias's narrative. Plutarch summarized Ctesias's version of Cyrus's death at *Artaxerxes* 11.1–6. A less elaborate version, also attributed to Ctesias, is given in Xenophon, *Anabasis* 1.8.26–27.

Artaxerxes arrogates credit for the death of Cyrus. Plutarch, *Artaxerxes* 14.3 and 16.1.

Xenophon, *Anabasis* 1.8.29 reports a similar state of confusion over whether Artaxerxes himself killed Artapates, Cyrus's most trusted retainer, or if he ordered others to do so.

Representation of the battle as a victory of truth over the Lie. This is the standard treatment of defeated rebels, as perfected by Darius at Bisitun. In effect, it constitutes the discursive consolidation of military victories. See further Lincoln 2005.

Gifts to Mithridates and the Carian. Plutarch, *Artaxerxes* 14.3, where the figure earlier identified as "Caunian" (11.5) now acquires stable identity as "Carian."

Reaction of the Carian. Plutarch, *Artaxerxes* 14.4. The text specifies that the man felt great outrage (*ēgenaktei*), bore formal witness (*marturomenos*), and shouted his testimony (*boōn*).

Parysatis. Half sister and wife to Darius II, mother of Artaxerxes II and Cyrus the Younger (the latter of whom she favored), Parysatis is a central figure in Ctesias's narrative and a classic expression of Greek stereotypes concerning all that was wrong with the Achaemenians. She thus manages to represent the disproportionate influence of women (and, thus, the effeminacy of Achaemenian rule), an excess of emotionality (especially the destructive emotions of resentment, jealousy, envy, hatred, and so forth), a shrewd, calculating, manipulative mentality (which she expressed in endless plotting, otherwise showing an absence of reason), a reliance on eunuchs (effeminacy, once more), and a capacity for appalling cruelty (the hallmark of barbarian tyranny). See further Sancisi-Weerdenburg 1983, Dandamaev 1989: 266, 274, and 288–91, and Briant 1996: 605–7 and 632–36.

Judicial ordeals by molten metal. The verse passage cited is *Yasna* 51.9, which comes from the oldest stratum of the Avesta, as do *Yasna* 30.7 and 32.7, which also speak of this ordeal. The prose passage comes from the Pahlavi supplementary texts to *Šayest ne Šayest* 15.15–17. See also *Selections of Zad Spram* 22.12, and *Denkard* 3.169 (Madan 1911: 182.13–19) and 5.22.4 (Madan 1911: 454.3–8). Such ordeals have been discussed in Lommel 1930: 109, 219–22, and 235, Widengren 1965: 32–33 and 87–88, Boyce 1975: 35–36 and 242–43, and Bucci 1975: 14–15.

The Last Judgment and molten metal. The text cited is *Greater Bundahišn* 34.19 (TD² MS 225.6–11). See also *Dadestan i Denig* 36.96 and *Pahlavi Rivayat* accompanying *Dadestan i Denig* 48.69–72. In their continuation of the eschatological account, these texts go on to describe how, after purifying all the dead, this molten metal flows off and seals the hole through which the Evil Spirit first entered the good creation, thereby ensuring that there will be no recurrence of the Assault. Thus *Greater Bundahišn* 34.31 (TD² MS 227.12–228.1) and *Pahlavi Rivayat* accompanying *Dadestan i Denig* 48.86.

Parysatis's name. This has been recognized since Justi 1895/1963: 244.

III

Mithridates and the troughs. The passage quoted is from Plutarch, *Artaxerxes* 16.2–4, summarizing information taken from Ctesias's lost *Persica*.

IV

Old Persian *fraθ-*. For discussion of the etymology, with comparison to Avestan *fras-* (to ask), Sanskrit *praśna-* (question), etc., see Brandenstein and Mayrhofer 1964: 119 and Mayrhofer 1956–76: 2:329. Only in Meillet and Benveniste 1931: 52, 67, and 115 is the term translated *interroger*, but not without reason.

Old Persian *pati-fraθ-*. This compound verb occurs with the sense "to read," i.e., to interrogate a text, at DB §§56, 58, 70.

Akkadian and Elamite translations of Old Persian *fraθ-*. For the Akkadian (DB [Bab.] §§8, 44, and 51), see Voigtlander 1978: 54, 60, and 61. For the Elamite (DB [Elam.] §§8, 44, and 51), see Grillot-Susini, Herrenschmidt, and Malbran-Labat 1993: 41 n. 103 and Hinz and Koch 1987: 619 and 941.

Needles through the tongue. Artaxerxes' use of this technique to punish less grievous lies is described in Plutarch, *Artaxerxes* 14.2. Liars receive similar punishment in hell, according to *Arda Wiraz Namag* 27.16–20 (vermin chew a slanderer's tongue), 29.2–7 (worms gnaw a liar's tongue), 41.3–8 (snakes gnaw the mouths of slanderers), 44.2–8 (seducers who deceive women have nails grow through their tongues), 50.11–16 (liars are stung by snakes, which then eat their tongues), and 53.5–10 (liars' tongues are cut out).

V

The king as the antithesis of the Lie. On the opposition truth/lie as a central structure of Indo-Iranian religion, see Lommel 1930: 40–52, Geiger 1934, Lüders 1959, Stausberg 2002: 91–95, and Skjærvø 2003. More specifically on the role of the Achaemenian king as the foremost antagonist of the Lie, see Bucci 1972 and 1983, Ahn 1992: 278–81 and 293–97, and Lincoln 2003c: lecture 2. Note that, although the Achaemenian inscriptions frequently depict the king in opposition to the Lie, they do not explicitly make him an active hero of truth. Indeed, the hope for truth in the fullest sense seems doubly deferred to the eschatological future since the relevant term occurs in only one inscription of Xerxes, where people living in the future are instructed how they may become "righteous [or: truthful (Old Persian *artavan*)] when dead" (XPh §4d).

Thought, word, and deed. On the importance of this triad, see Schlerath 1974. Note that Darius urged good interrogation/punishment for those guilty of falsehood at the same three levels: thought (DB §8), word (DB §§55, 64), and deed (DB §64).

Herodotus on the Persian reverence for truth. The crucial passages are Herodotus 1.136 and 1.138. At 7.61, the father of history also notes that, in antiquity, the Persians called themselves *Artaioi,* which means "the Truthful" (cf. Old Persian *arta,* Avestan *aša,* and Vedic *r̥tá,* all of which mean "truth, right, [cosmic] order"). See further Pirart 1995: 58–62.

Lying as a capital offense. For lists of such offenses, see *Denkard* 5.9.10, *Pahlavi Rivayat* accompanying *Dadestan i Denig* 41, and *Menog i Xrad* 36. Among the forms of lying that appear in these texts are delivering a false legal decision, teaching falsehood, perjury, Manichaean forms of heresy, other forms of heresy, breach of contract, slander, perjury, repudiation of true statements, and simply speaking falsehood or untruth. *Arda Wiraz Namag* 44.2–8 adds seduction to the forms of lying subject to terrible punishment. That lying had primacy among all crimes is asserted in the *Pahlavi Rivayat* accompanying *Dadestan i Denig* 3.1–2 in particularly interesting fashion:

> This too he asked of the Wise Lord: "If crime seizes every member of a man, which organ does the evil come to first?" The Wise Lord answered: "Because the tongue is more worthy than other limbs of the human body, it comes first to the tongue."

The end of hell at the end of history. The process through which this is accomplished is actually an extension of the eschatological ordeal:

> The molten metal flows into hell. The stench and filth that are on the earth where hell is, these burn in that molten metal, and hell becomes pure. The hole through which the Foul Spirit rushed in to attack the Good Creation, that is sealed off by the molten metal. Thus, hell is returned to the earth for the enlargement of the world, and the Renovation comes into being. As the Wise Lord desired, the world becomes immortal forever and ever.
>
> *(Greater Bundahišn* 34.31–32 [TD² MS 227.13–228.3])

Demons created by one's sins. Thus, e.g., *Dadestan i Denig* 31.4, which describes the soul of the liar as it is led off to hell, accompanied by

> spiritual demons, *which came into being from the evil he did* in many forms and places, and which resemble spoilers, harmers, killers, destroyers, scoundrels, evil bodies,

wrongdoers, those who are unseemly, most stingy, filthy, biting, and tearing vermin, stinking winds, dark, stinking, burning, thirsting, hungry, inexpiably sinful, and other most sin-causing and harm-causing demons, who become causes of pain for him [the liar] in the material as in the spiritual creation.

VI

Milk and honey. Milk is discussed at *Dadestan i Denig* 27.2 and 30.13, *Denkard* 3.374, *Selections of Zad Spram* 6.1, 10.11, 16.3, 30.58, and 34.40, *Greater Bundahišn* 14.17–19 and 34.1, and *Pahlavi Rivayat* accompanying *Dadestan i Denig* 23.17. A full discussion of milk's consistently positive significance would require a book unto itself. Honey is mentioned less frequently, the chief source being *Greater Bundahišn* 22.29 (TD² MS 146.13–15), which makes it an excellent product derived from an odious source by virtue of the Wise Lord's power: "In his omniscience, the Wise Lord turns many of these vermin back to the advantage of his creatures, like the bee that makes honey and the worm that makes silk."

Magi and vermin. Herodotus 1.140. Compare Plutarch, *On Envy and Hate* 537b, *Isis and Osiris* 370c, and *Quaestiones conviviales* 670d, Agathias, *Histories* 2.24, Widengren 1965: 113–14, and Jong 1997: 338–42.

"Vermin-killer." This is mentioned at *Videvdat* 14.8 and 18.2

Vermin. Lists of the species classified as verminous are found in *Videvdat* 14.5 and 18.65, *Sad Dar* 43.1–10 (West 1885: 306–7), and *Greater Bundahišn* 4.15 (TD² MS 43.2–6) and 22.1 (TD² MS 142.3–5). The fullest analytic description of verminous creatures is that of *Greater Bundahišn* 22.4–6 (TD² MS 142.13–143.5). The text is at pains to establish that, although vermin are overwhelmingly evil, even they possess some measure of good, as is true of all that exists in the mixed state of historical time:

> Their being, the light of their eyes, and the breath of their spirit are of the Wise Lord. . . . Their poison, sinfulness, and malevolence are of the Evil Spirit. This also is greatly advantageous: When people see them [by virtue of the light in their eyes, which makes them visible], they can kill them, or they avoid them. From this, too, it is revealed that they are not the creation of the Wise Lord, for their body and color are not at all like those of his good domestic and wild animals. The vermin's scurrying motion and the harm they do at night, for the sake of collaboration with darkness, are proof that they harm the good creatures through fear, injury, and smiting.

See further Lommel 1930: 97–98 and 114–16, Widengren 1965: 113–14, Bailey 1970: 25–28, and Boyce 1975: 90–91 and 298–300.

Creation of vermin. See *Selections of Zad Spram* 2.11 and *Greater Bundahišn* 1.47 (TD² MS 11.10–12), 4.15 (TD² MS 43.2–6), and 22.0–6 (TD² MS 142.2–143.5).

The Evil Spirit and "Corpse" take the form of a fly. *Greater Bundahišn* 4.10 states that Ahriman first assaulted the sky in the form of a snake (TD² MS 42.1–4), then the rest of creation in the form of a fly (TD² MS 42.9–10). The text cited from the Avesta that describes "Corpse" (*Nasu*) as a fly is *Videvdat* 7.2.

Digestion as a moral process. The passage cited is *Greater Bundahišn* 28.10 (TD² MS 192.6–12). Manichaean obsessions with the digestive process as a means for redeeming pure light trapped in dark matter (on which see Beduhn 2000 and 2001) are an elaboration of earlier Mazdaean constructs of the sort discussed in this passage. Yet another variation is found at *Denkard* 3.235 (Madan 1911: 260.12–15).

Blood and poison. Concerning the nature of blood, see *Selections of Zad Spram* 29.4 and 30.15. On poison, see *Greater Bundahišn* 22.1–3 (TD² MS 142.3–10), *Selections of Zad Spram* 3.14, *Dadestan i Denig* 36.31, and *Pahlavi Rivayat* accompanying *Dadestan i Denig* 8c4. *Selections of Zad Spram* 30.15 differentiates between two types of humors that it classifies as poisonous (*wiš*, translated as "bile" in this context, but elsewhere the generic term for "poison"): red and black. The latter is much more injurious, being cold and dry (instead of warm and dry), dark in color, and lowly in its bodily locus. For a fuller discussion, see Lincoln 1991: 209–18.

Excrement and filth. The passage cited, relating bodily filth to demonic presence, is *Denkard* 5.12.2 (Madan 1911: 444.22–445.4). See further *Denkard* 3.235 (Madan 1911: 260.11–19 and Dresden 1966: 195.17–196.4) and 5.24.19a–19b (Madan 1911: 463.7–22).

Demons. The best study of Iranian demons and demonology remains Christensen 1941. That this study was authored and published in Nazi-occupied Denmark strikes me as highly significant.

VII

Old Persian *gastā* and the olfactory code of evil. Regarding the interpretation of this term, see Kent 1953: 183, Meillet and Benveniste 1931: 120–21, and Mayrhofer 1956–76: 1:322. The cognate term in Avestan (*gainti*) occurs twice (*Videvdat* 7.56 and *Hadoxt Nask* 3.17), both in connection with the polluting stench of corpses. It is also worth noting that, in Pahlavi, the most common alternate name for the Evil Sprit (*Ahriman*) is "Foul Spirit" (*Gannāg Mēnōg*), although most translators render the two in identical fashion.

VIII

Ctesias. Most modern authorities have been inclined to treat this author with suspicion, given his penchant for lurid tales of palace intrigue, replete with the stereotypes of Orientalism: weak kings, sly eunuchs, conniving women, all in a milieu of luxury, decadence, and corruption. See further Momigliano 1969, Bigwood 1978, Sancisi-Weerdenburg 1983 and 1987, and Lenfant 1996. What survives of his work may be found in Auberger 1991, along with a useful introduction.

POSTSCRIPT

I

The imperial rhetoric of George W. Bush. I have written on this elsewhere. See Lincoln 2001b, 2003b: 19–32, 2004a, 2004b, 2004c, and forthcoming.

Implicit syllogism. To cite but one further example of this argument, Mr. Bush's third State of the Union address, delivered 28 January 2003, built to the following passage:

> Americans are a free people, who know that freedom is the right of every person and the future of every nation. The liberty we prize is not America's gift to the world, it is God's gift to humanity. We Americans have faith in ourselves—but not in ourselves alone. We do not claim to know all the ways of Providence, yet we can trust in them, placing our confidence in the loving God behind all of life, and all of history.
>
> (*We Will Prevail* 2003: 220–21)

See also my discussion of this and related texts in Lincoln 2004a.

Messianic claims. Like the Cyrus Oracle considered in chapter 3, Isa. 61:1 was written in the context of the Israelite captivity in Babylon and expresses the same hope of liberation through the agency of the Lord's "Anointed" (known in Hebrew as "the Messiah" and, later, in Greek as "the Christ"). The passage is set in the mouth of that savior figure, whose role Mr. Bush assumed when citing the text (see further Pitt 2003 and Lincoln 2004b).

Landing and speech on board the USS *Abraham Lincoln*. The full text of Mr. Bush's remarks is available at http://www.whitehouse.gov/news/releases/2003/05/20030501-15.html. The staged nature of this event has been much discussed. See, among others, Boje 2003, Bumiller 2003, Byrd 2003, Cochrane 2004, McLaren and Jaramillo 2004: 233–34, and Mral 2004: 60–62.

"Magic hour light." Bumiller 2003.

II

Iconoclasm in Firdos Square. For critical commentary, see Rampton and Stauber 2003, Rowe 2004: 575–76, Zucchino 2004, and Browne 2005.

Corporal Chin and the U.S. flag. The significance of this incident was immediately noted in Kaplan 2003.

Long shots of Firdos Square. The Reuters photographs were first made public in "A Tale of Two Photos" 2003 and "The Photographs Tell the Story . . ." 2003, after which they occasioned much discussion. A few journalists, notably Gilbert and Ryan 2003, were quick to voice skepticism about the credulous response of a media and a public hungry for a feel-good story.

III

"Spider hole." On the history and normal usage of the term, see Bowers 2003.

IV

Abu Ghraib photographs. These were first made public in Hersh 2004. Regarding the events at Abu Ghraib, see the official U.S. Army reports, Jones and Fay 2004 and Taguba 2004, as reported in Polk 2004. Commentary on the photographs and the events they document has been endless. Among others, Raimondo 2004, Sontag 2004, Baudrillard 2005, Davis 2005, and W. J. T. Mitchell 2005 are noteworthy. A number of useful links can be found at Lesage 2005.

"Just for fun." Private First Class England made this remark to Paul Arthur, the military investigator who first questioned her, as he reported at her court-martial, 3 August 2004 (see Polk 2004).

"Because they could." Special Agent Tyler Pieron gave his testimony at criminal proceedings in Baghdad, 1 May 2004, as reported in Higham, Stephens, and White 2004.

Unreleased photographs. In October 2003, the American Civil Liberties Union (ACLU) filed suit, pressing for the release of eighty-seven photographs and four videotapes from Abu Ghraib held by the Department of Defense. These photographs have been screened for members of Congress, who stated that they included scenes of rape, murder, and other atrocities. In its defense, the Pentagon maintained that the release of these materials would inflame anti-American sentiment and put military personnel at greater risk. On 29 September 2005, these arguments were rejected by U.S. District Judge Alvin K. Hellerstein, who ruled in favor of the ACLU. In April 2006, the Department of Defense released further photographs, for a total of seventy-three, along with three videotapes of prisoner abuse. At the same time, it announced that it was withholding an additional twenty-nine photographs and two videotapes. As I make my final revisions (October 2006), these materials are still being contested. See further Babington 2004 and G. Mitchell 2005a and 2005b.

V

Prisoner beaten to death. On the circumstances of Manadel al-Jamadi's capture, interrogation, and death, see Mayer 2005 and McChesney 2005.

Bibliography

Accame, Silvio. 1982. "La leggenda di Ciro in Erodoto e in Carone di Lampsaco." *Miscellanea Greca e Romana* 8:1–43.

Afshar, Ahmad. 1974. "Giraffes at Persepolis." *Archeology* 27:114–17.

———. 1978. "Camels at Persepolis." *Antiquity* 52:228–31.

Ahn, Gregor. 1992. *Religiöse Herrscherlegitimation im Achaemenidischen Iran: Die Voraussetzungen und die Struktur ihrer Argumentation.* Leiden: E. J. Brill.

———. 2002. "'Toleranz' und Reglement: Die Signifikanz achaimenidischer Religionspolitik für den jüdisch-persischen Kulturkontakt." In *Religion und Religionskontakte im Zeitalter der Achämeniden,* ed. Reinhard G. Kratz, 191–209. Gütersloh: Chr. Kaiser.

Aly, Wolf. 1921. *Volksmärchen, Sage und Novelle bei Herodot und seinen Zeitgenossen: Eine Untersuchung über die volkstümlichen Elemente der altgriechischen Prosaerzählung.* Göttingen: Vandenhoeck & Ruprecht.

Amiet, Pierre. 1979. "Alternance et dualité: Essai d'interprétation de l'histoire élamite." *Akkadica* 15:2–22.

Andreas, Friedrich-Carl, ed. 1882. *The Book of the Mainyo-i-Khard.* Kiel: Lipsius & Tischer.

———. 1904. "Über einige Fragen der ältesten Persischen Geschichte." In *Verhandlungen des XIII Internationalen Orientalisten-Congresses,* 93–99. Leiden: E. J. Brill.

Anklesaria, Behramgore Tehmuras, ed. and trans. 1956. *Zand-Akasih: Iranian or Greater Bundahišn.* Bombay: Rahnumae Mazdayasnan Sabha.

Anklesaria, Ervad Tahmuras Dinshaji, ed. 1908. *The Bundahišn: Being a Facsimile of the TD Manuscript No. 2 Brought from Persia by Dastur Tîrandâz and Now Preserved in the Late Ervad Tahmuras' Library.* Bombay: British India Press.

———, ed. n.d. *The Datistan-i Dinik: Pahlavi Text Containing 92 Questions, Asked by Mitr-Khurshit Atur-Mahan and Others, to Manush-Chihar Goshn-Jam, Leader of the Zoroastrians in Persia, about 881 A.D., and Their Answers.* Bombay: Fort Printing Press.

Armayor, O. Kimball. 1978. "Herodotus' Catalogues of the Persian Empire in Light of the Monuments and the Greek Literary Tradition." *Transactions of the American Philological Association* 108:1–9.

Asheri, David, and Silvio M. Medaglia, eds. Augusto Fraschetti, trans. 2000. *Erodoto, Le Storie: Libro III: La Persia.* 3rd ed. Florence: Arnaldo Mondadori.

Asmussen, Jes. 1960. *Historiske tekster fra Achæmenide tiden.* Copenhagen: Munksgaard.

———. 1968. "Iranica, A: The Death of Cambyses." *Acta Orientalia* 31:9–14.

Atkinson, K. M. T. 1956. "The Legitimacy of Cambyses and Darius as Kings of Egypt." *Journal of the American Oriental Society* 76:167–77.

Auberger, Janick, trans. 1991. *Ctésias: Histoires de l'Orient.* Paris: Les Belles Lettres.

Azarpay, Guitty. 1972. "Crowns and Some Royal Insignia in Early Iran." *Iranica Antiqua* 9:108–15.

Babington, Charles. 2004. "Lawmakers Are Stunned by New Images of Abuse." *Washington Post,* 13 May. Available at http://www.washingtonpost.com/wp-dyn/articles/A22464-2004May12.html.

Bailey, H. W. 1953. "Indo-Iranian Studies." *Transactions of the Philological Society,* 21–32.

———. 1956. "Armeno-Indoiranica." *Transactions of the Philological Society,* 100–104.

———. 1970. "A Range of Iranica." In *W. B. Henning Memorial Volume,* ed. Mary Boyce and Ilya Gershevitch, 20–36. London: Lund Humphries.

Balcer, Jack Martin. 1977. "The Athenian Episkopos and the Achaemenid 'King's Eye.'" *American Journal of Philology* 98:252–63.

———. 1984. *Sparda by the Bitter Sea: Imperial Interaction in Western Anatolia.* Chico, CA: Scholars'.

———. 1987. *Herodotus and Bisotun.* Wiesbaden: Franz Steiner.

———. 1993. *A Prosopographical Study of the Ancient Persians Royal and Noble, c. 550–450 B.C.* Lewiston, NY: Edwin Mellen.

Bartholomae, Christian. 1901. "Arica XIV." *Indogermanische Fragen* 12:92–150.

———. 1904/1961. *Altiranisches Wörterbuch.* Reprint. Berlin: Walter de Gruyter.

Baudrillard, Jean. 2005. "War Porn." Translated by Paul A. Taylor. *International Journal of Baudrillard Studies* 2, no. 1 (January). http://www.ubishops.ca/baudrillardstudies/vol2_1/taylor.htm.

Beaulieu, Paul-Alain. 1989. *The Reign of Nabonidus, King of Babylon, 556–539 B.C.* New Haven, CT: Yale University Press.

Beduhn, Jason. 2000. *The Manichaean Body: Its Discipline and Ritual.* Baltimore: Johns Hopkins University Press.

———. 2001. "The Metabolism of Salvation: Manichaean Concepts of Human Physiology." In *The Light and the Darkness: Studies in Manichaeism and Its World,* ed. Paul Mirecki and Jason Beduhn, 5–37. Leiden: E. J. Brill.

Belloni, Luigi. 1986. "I Persiani di Eschilo tra Oriente e Occidente." *Contributi dell' Istituto di Storia Antica dell' Università del Sacro Cuore* 12:68–83.

Benveniste, Émile. 1929. *The Persian Religion according to the Chief Greek Texts.* Paris: Librairie Orientaliste Paul Geuthner.

———. 1932–35. "L'Eran-vez et l'origine légendaire des Iraniens." *Bulletin of the School of Oriental Studies* 7:265–74.

———. 1938. "Traditions indo-iraniennes sur les classes sociales." *Journal Asiatique* 230:529–49.

———. 1945. "Études iraniennes." *Transactions of the Philological Society,* 39–78.

———. 1958. "Notes sur les tablettes élamites de Persépolis." *Journal Asiatique* 246:49–65.

———. 1966. *Titres et noms propres en iranien ancien.* Paris: C. Klincksieck.

———. 1969. *Le vocabulaire des institutions indo-européennes.* 2 vols. Paris: Minuit.

Benveniste, Émile, and Louis Renou. 1934. *Vṛtra et Vṛθraγna*. Paris: Imprimerie Nationale.

Besnier, Marie-Françoise. 1999. "La conception du jardin en Syro-Mésopotamie à partir des texts." *Ktema* 24:195–212.

Bianchi, Ugo. 1977. "L'inscription des daiva et le Zoroastrisme des Achéménides." *Revue de l'Histoire des Religions* 192:3–30.

———. 1988. "Dieu créateur et vision universaliste: Le cas de l'empire achéménide." In *La commémoration*, ed. Philippe Gignoux, 191–200. Louvain: Peeters.

Bichler, Reinhold. 1985. "Die 'Reichsträume' bei Herodot: Eine Studie zu Herodots schöpferischer Leistung und ihre quellenkritische Konsequenz." *Chiron* 15:125–47.

Bickerman, E. J., and H. Tadmor. 1978. "Darius I, Pseudo-Smerdis, and the Magi." *Athenaeum* 56:239–61.

Bidmead, Julye. 2002. *The Akîtu Festival: Religious Continuity and Royal Legitimation in Mesopotamia*. Piscataway, NJ: Gorgias.

Bigwood, Joan Mary. 1978. "Ctesias as Historian of the Persian Wars." *Phoenix* 32:19–41.

———. 1983. "The Ancient Accounts of the Battle of Cunaxa." *American Journal of Philology* 104:340–57.

Binder, Gerhard. 1964. *Die Aussetzung des Königskindes Kyros und Romulus*. Meisenheim am Glan: Anton Hain.

Black, J. A. 1981. "The New Year Ceremonies in Ancient Babylon: 'Taking Bel by the Hand' and a Cultic Picnic." *Religion* 11:39–59.

Boffo, Laura. 1983. "La conquista persiana delle città greche in Asia Minore." *Rendiconti dell' Accademia dei Lincei* 26:6–70.

Boje, David. 2003. "Bush as Top Gun: Deconstructing Visual Theatric Imagery." PeaceAware.com, 3 June. http://peaceaware.com/papers/Bush_Top_Gun.htm.

Bollweg, J. 1988. "Protoachämenidische Seegelbilder." *Archäologische Mitteilungen aus Iran* 21:53–61.

Boucharlat, Rémy. 1990. "Suse et la Susiane à l'époque achéménide: Données archéologiques." *Achaemenid History* 4:149–75.

Bowers, Andy. 2003. "What's a Spider Hole? And Since When Do Spiders Dig Holes, Anyway?" *Slate*, 15 December. http://www.slate.com/id/2092557.

Boyce, Mary. 1975. *A History of Zoroastrianism*. Vol. 1, *The Early Period*. Leiden: E. J. Brill.

———. 1979. *Zoroastrians: Their Religious Beliefs and Practices*. London: Routledge & Kegan Paul.

———. 1982. *A History of Zoroastrianism*. Vol. 2, *Under the Achaemenids*. Leiden: E. J. Brill.

———. 1988. "The Religion of Cyrus the Great." *Achaemenid History* 3:15–31.

Brandenstein, Wilhelm, and Manfred Mayrhofer. 1964. *Handbuch des Altpersischen*. Wiesbaden: Otto Harrassowitz.

Brandon, S. G. F. 1963. *Creation Legends of the Ancient Near East*. London: Hodder & Stoughton.

Bremmer, J. N. 1999. "Paradise: From Persia, via Greece, into the *Septuagint*." In *Paradise Interpreted: Representations of Biblical Paradise in Judaism and Christianity*, ed. Gerard P. Luttikhuizen, 1–20. Leiden: E. J. Brill.

Bresciani, Edda. 1981. "La morte di Cambise ovvero dell' empietà punita: A proposito della 'Cronaca Demotica,' Verso, col. C. 7–8." *Egitto e Vicino Oriente* 4:217–22.

———. 1985. "The Persian Occupation of Egypt." In *The Cambridge History of Iran*, vol. 2, *The Median and Achaemenian Periods*, ed. Ilya Gershevitch, 502–28. Cambridge: Cambridge University Press.

Briant, Pierre. 1982. "Sources grecques et histoire achéménide." In *Rois, tribut, et paysans: Études sur les formations tributaires du Moyen-Orient ancien,* 491–506. Paris: Les Belles Lettres.

———. 1986. "Polythéismes et empire unitaire." In *Les grands figures religieuses: Fonctionnement pratique et symbolique dans l'antiquité,* 425–43. Besançon: Université de Besançon, Centre de Recherches d'Histoire Ancienne.

———. 1987. "Pouvoir central et polycentrisme culturel dans l'empire achéménide (quelques réflexions et suggestions)." *Achaemenid History* 1:1–31.

———. 1988. "Ethno-classe dominante et populations soumises dans l'empire achéménide: Le cas de l'Égypte." *Achaemenid History* 3:137–73.

———. 1989a. "Histoire et idéologie: Les Grecs et la 'décadence perse.'" In *Mélanges Pierre Lévêque,* 2:33–47. Paris: Les Belles Lettres.

———. 1989b. "Table du roi, tribut et redistribution chez les Achéménides." In *Le tribut dans l'empire perse,* ed. Pierre Briant and Clarisse Herrenschmidt, 35–44. Paris: Peeters.

———. 1991. "Le roi est mort: Vive le roi! Remarques sur les rites et rituals de succession chez les Achéménides." In *La religion iranienne à l'époque achéménide,* ed. Jean Kellens, 13–21. Ghent: Iranica Antiqua.

———. 1992a. *Darius, les Perses et l'empire.* Paris: Gallimard.

———. 1992b. "La date des révoltes babyloniennes contre Xerxès." *Studia Iranica* 21:7–20.

———. 1994. "L'eau du grand roi." In *Drinking in Ancient Societies: History and Culture of Drinks in the Ancient Near East,* ed. Lucio Milano, 45–65. Padua: Sargon.

———. 1996. *Histoire de l'empire perse de Cyrus à Alexandre.* Paris: Arthème Fayard.

———. 2002. *From Cyrus to Alexander: A History of the Persian Empire.* Translated by Peter T. Daniels. Winona Lake, IN: Eisenbrauns.

———. 2003. "A propos du roi-jardinier: Remarques sur l'histoire d'un dossier documentaire." *Achaemenid History* 13:33–49.

Briant, Pierre, and Clarisse Herrenschmidt, eds. 1989. *Le tribut dans l'empire perse.* Paris: Peeters.

Briquel, Dominique, and Jean-Luc Desnier. 1983. "Le passage de l'Hellespont par Xerxès." *Bulletin de l'Association Guillaume Budé,* 22–30.

Brown, Stuart. 1988. "The *Medikos logos* of Herodotus and the Evolution of the Median State." *Achaemenid History* 3:71–86.

Brown, Truesdell S. 1982. "Herodotus' Portrait of Cambyses." *Historia* 31:387–403.

Browne, Harry. 2005. "An Anniversary Worth Remembering." LewRockwell.com, 11 April. http://www.lewrockwell.com/browne/browne48.html.

Bucci, Onorato. 1972. "Giustizia e Legge nel diritto persiano antico." *Apollinaris* 45:157–72.

———. 1975. "Elementi processuali nell antico diritto iranico." *Revue Internationale des Droits de l'Antiquité* 22:11–25.

———. 1983. "L'impero achemenide come ordinamento giuridico sovrannazionale e *arta* come principio ispiratore di uno 'jus commune Persarum' (*dāta-*)." In *Modes de contacts et processus de transformation dans les sociétés ancienne,* 89–122. Pisa: Scuola Normale Superiore.

———. 1985. "*Xšaça-* 'impero' / *xšāyaθiya xšāyaθiyānām-* 're dei re.'" *Annali della Scuola Normale di Pisa* 15:667–705.

Bumiller, Elisabeth. 2003. "Keepers of Bush Image Lift Stagecraft to New Heights." *New York Times,* 16 May. Available at http://www.nytimes.com/2003/05/16/politics/16IMAG.html.

Burn, Andrew Robert. 1962. *Persia and the Greeks: The Defense of the West, c. 546–478 B.C.* London: Edward Arnold.

Burnett, R. D. 1957. "Persepolis." *Iraq* 19:55–77.

Butler, S. A. L. 1998. *Mesopotamian Conceptions of Dreams and Dream Rituals.* Münster: Ugarit.

Byrd, Robert C. 2003. "A Troubling Speech." *Truthout*, 6 May. http://truthout.org/docs_03/050703B.shtml.

Calmeyer, Peter. 1975. "Zur Genese altiranischer Motive: III. Felsgräber." *Archäologische Mitteilungen aus Iran* 8:99–113.

———. 1977. "Stand der archäologischen Forschung zu den iranischen Kronen." *Archäologische Mitteilungen aus Iran* 10:168–90.

———. 1982. "Zur Genese altiranischer Motive: VIII. Die 'Statistische Landcharte des Perserreiches,'" pt. 1. *Archäologische Mitteilungen aus Iran* 15:105–87.

———. 1983a. "Zur Genese altiranischer Motive: VIII. Die 'Statistische Landcharte des Perserreiches,'" pt. 2. *Archäologische Mitteilungen aus Iran* 16:141–222.

———. 1983b. "Zur Rechtfertigung einiger grossköniglicher Inschriften und Darstellungen: Die Yauna." In *Kunst, Kultur und Geschichte der Achämenidenzeit und ihr Fortleben*, ed. Heidemarie Koch and D. N. MacKenzie, 153–67. Berlin: Dietrich Reimer.

———. 1987. "Zur Genese altiranischer Motive: VIII. Die 'Statistische Landcharte des Perserreiches': Nachträge und Korrekturen." *Archäologische Mitteilungen aus Iran* 20:129–46.

Cameron, George G. 1948. *Persepolis Treasury Tablets.* Chicago: University of Chicago Press.

Campbell, Joseph. 1949. *The Hero with a Thousand Faces.* New York: Pantheon.

Cantarella, Raffaele. 1965. "La Persia nella letteratura greca." In *Atti del convegno sul tema: La Persia e il mondo greco-romano*, 489–504. Rome: Accademia Nazionale dei Lincei.

Cartledge, Paul. 1990. "Herodotus and 'the Other': A Meditation on Empire." *Échos du Monde Classique* 34:27–40.

Charpentier, Jarl. 1911. *Kleine Beiträge zur indoiranischen Mythologie.* Uppsala: Akademische Buchdruckerei.

Choksy, Jamsheed K. 1990. "Gesture in Ancient Iran and Central Asia: I. The Raised Hand." *Acta Iranica* 30:30–37.

Christensen, Arthur. 1918. *Le premier homme et premier roi dans l'historie légendaire des iraniens: I. Gajōmard, Masjaγ et Masjānaγ, Hōšang et Taχmōruw.* Stockholm: Kunglige Boktryckeriet, P. A. Norstedt.

———. 1941. *Essai sur la démonologie iranienne.* Copenhagen: Det Kongelige Danske Videnskabernes Selskab.

———. 1943. *Le premier chapitre du Vendidad et l'histoire primitive des tribus iraniennes.* Copenhagen: Munksgaard.

Cizek, Alexander. 1975. "From the Historical Truth to the Literary Convention: The Life of Cyrus the Great Viewed by Herodotus, Ctesias, and Xenophon." *L'Antiquité Classique* 44:531–52.

Claessen, Henri J. M. 1989. "Tribute and Taxation; or, How to Finance Early States and Empires." In *Le tribut dans l'empire perse*, ed. Pierre Briant and Clarisse Herrenschmidt, 45–60. Paris: Peeters.

Clauss, Manfred. 1999. *Kaiser und Gott: Herrscherkult im römischen Reich.* Stuttgart: Teubner.

Clemen, Carl. 1920. *Fontes historiae religionis persicae.* Bonn: A. Marc & E. Weber.

Cochrane, Paul. 2004. "The Empiric Image—Imperialism, Propaganda, and the War on Iraq." Paper presented at the Third FEA Student Conference, Faculty of Engineering and Architecture, American University of Beirut, 27–28 May. Available at http://webfea.fea.aub .edu.lb/proceedings/2004/SRC-ArD-08.pdf.

Conrad, Geoffrey W., and Arthur A. Demarest. 1984. *Religion and Empire: The Dynamics of Aztec and Inca Expansionism*. Cambridge: Cambridge University Press.

Coreth, Anna. 2004. *Pietas austriaca*. West Lafayette, IN: Purdue University Press.

Cross, Frank Moore. 1973. *Canaanite Myth and Hebrew Epic: Essays in the History of the Religion of Israel*. Cambridge, MA: Harvard University Press.

D'Agostino, Franco. 1994. *Nabonedo, Adda Guppi, il deserto e il dio Luna: Storia, ideologia, e propaganda nella Babilonia del VI sec. A, C*. Pisa: Giardini.

Dalby, Andrew. 2000. "To Feed a King: Tyrants, Kings, and the Search for Quality in Agriculture and Food." *Pallas* 52:135–44.

Dandamaev, Muhammad A. 1972. "Politische und Wirtschaftliche Geschichte." In *Beiträge zur Achämenidengeschichte*, ed. Gerold Walser, 15–58. Wiesbaden: Franz Steiner.

———. 1975. "La politique religieuse des Achéménides." *Acta Iranica* 4:193–200.

———. 1976. *Persien unter den ersten Achämeniden*. Translated by Heinz-Dieter Pohl. Wiesbaden: Ludwig Reichert.

———. 1984. "Royal Paradeisoi in Babylonia." *Acta Iranica* 23:113–17.

———. 1985. "Herodotus' Information on Persia and the Latest Discoveries of Cuneiform Texts." *Storia della Storiografia* 9:92–100.

———. 1989. *A Political History of the Achaemenid Empire*. Translated by W. J. Vogelsang. Leiden: E. J. Brill.

Dandamaev, Muhammad A., and Vladimir G. Lukonin. 1989. *The Culture and Social Institutions of Ancient Iran*. Cambridge: Cambridge University Press.

Daryaee, Touraj. 2002. "The Changing 'Image of the World': Geography and Imperial Propaganda in Ancient Persia." *Electrum* 6:99–109.

Davis, Walter A. 2005. "Passion of the Christ in Abu Ghraib: Toward a New Theory of Ideology." *Socialism and Democracy* 19:67–93.

Depuydt, Leo. 1995. "Murder in Memphis: The Story of Cambyses's Mortal Wounding of the Apis Bull (ca. 523 B.C.E.)." *Journal of Near Eastern Studies* 54:119–26.

Descat, Raymond. 1985. "Mnésimachos, Hérodote et le système tributaire achéménide." *Revue des Études Anciennes* 87:97–112.

———. 1989. "Notes sur la politique tributaire de Darius Ier." In *Le tribut dans l'empire perse*, ed. Pierre Briant and Clarisse Herrenschmidt, 77–94. Paris: Peeters.

Doermann, Ralph W. 1987. "Cyrus, Conqueror of Babylon: Anointed (by the Lord) or Appointed (by Marduk)? A Reexamination of Conflicting Perspectives." *Proceedings of the Eastern Great Lakes and Midwest Bible Societies* 7:3–16.

Dougherty, Raymond Philip. 1923. *Archives from Erech: Time of Nebuchadnezzar and Nabonidus*. New Haven, CT: Yale University Press.

———. 1929. *Nabonidus and Belshazzar: A Study of the Closing Events of the Neo-Babylonian Empire*. New Haven, CT: Yale University Press.

Dresden, M. J., ed. 1966. *Dēnkart: A Pahlavi Text: Facsimile Edition of the Manuscript B of the K. R. Cama Oriental Institute, Bombay*. Wiesbaden: Otto Harrassowitz.

Drews, Robert. 1973. *The Greek Accounts of Eastern History*. Washington, DC: Center for Hellenic Studies.

———. 1974. "Sargon, Cyrus, and Mesopotamian Folk History." *Journal of Near Eastern Studies* 33:387–93.

Duchesne-Guillemin, Jacques. 1961. "Rituel et eschatology dans le Mazdéisme: Structure et evolution." *Numen* 8:46–50.

———. 1962a. "Old Persian *artācā brazmaniy.*" *Bulletin of the School of Oriental and African Studies* 25:336–37.

———. 1962b. *La religion de l'Iran ancien.* Paris: Presses Universitaires de France.

———. 1963. "Le *xvarenah.*" *Annali del Istituto Orientale di Napoli: Sezione Linguistica* 5:19–31.

———. 1966. Review of Marijan Molé, *Mythe, culte, et cosmologie dans l'Iran ancien. Revue de l'Histoire des Religions* 169:69–71.

———. 1966–67. Review of Marijan Molé, *Mythe, culte, et cosmologie dans l'Iran ancien. Oriens* 18–19:472–73.

———. 1967. "Religion et politique, de Cyrus à Xerxès." *Persica* 3:1–9.

———. 1972. "La religion des Achéménides." In *Beiträge zur Achämenidengeschichte*, ed. Gerold Walser, 59–82. Wiesbaden: Franz Steiner.

———. 1974. "Le dieu de Cyrus." *Acta Iranica* 3:11–21.

———. 1979. "La royauté iranienne et le *xvarenah.*" In *Iranica*, ed. Gherardo Gnoli, 375–86. Naples: Istituto per lo Studio del Medio ed Estremo Oriente.

Duleba, Wladyslaw. 1977. "Was Darius a Zoroastrian?" *Folia Orientalia* 18:205–9.

Dumézil, Georges. 1948. *Mitra-Varuna.* Paris: Gallimard.

———. 1958. *L'idéologie tripartite des Indo-Européens.* Brussels: Collection Latomus.

———. 1961. "Les 'trois fonctions' dans le Rg Veda et les dieux indiens de Mitani." *Bulletin de l'Académie Royale de Belgique* 47:265–98.

Dusinberre, Elspeth Rogers McIntosh. 1997. "Imperial Style and Constructed Identity: A 'Graeco-Persian' Cylinder Seal from Sardis." *Ars Orientalis* 27:99–129.

Eddy, Samuel K. 1961. *The King Is Dead: Studies in the Near Eastern Resistance to Hellenism, 334–31 B.C.* Lincoln: University of Nebraska Press.

Eilers, Wilhelm. 1964. "Kyros, eine namenkundliche Studie." *Beiträge zur Namenforschung* 15:180–236.

———. 1974. "The Name of Cyrus." *Acta Iranica* 3:3–9.

Eliade, Mircea. 1954. *The Myth of the Eternal Return: Archetypes and Repetition.* Princeton, NJ: Princeton University Press.

Engnell, Ivan. 1943. *Studies in Divine Kingship in the Ancient Near East.* Oxford: Alden.

Evans, J. A. S. 1961. "The Dream of Xerxes and the Nomoi of the Persians." *Classical Journal* 57:109–11.

Farina, G. 1929. "La politica religiosa di Cambise in Egitto." *Bilychnis* 18:449–57.

Fauth, Wolfgang. 1979. "Der königliche Gärtner und Jäger im Paradeisos: Beobachtungen zur Rolle des Herrschers in der vorderasiatischen Hortikultur." *Persica* 8:1–53.

Filippani-Ronconi, Pio. 1974. "La conception sacrée de la royauté iranienne." *Acta Iranica* 1:90–101.

Firpo, G. 1986. "Impero universale e politica religiosa: Ancora sulle distruzioni dei templi greci ad opera dei persiani." *Annali della Scuola Normale di Pisa* 16:331–93.

Flusin, Margaret. 1999. "Comment les Mèdes ont raconté leur histoire: L'épopée d'Arbacès et le *Médikos logos* d'Hérodote." *Ktema* 24:135–45.

Fornara, Charles. 1971. *Herodotus: An Interpretative Essay.* Oxford: Clarendon.

Francfort, Henri-Paul. 1985. "Note sur la mort de Cyrus et les Dardes." In *Orientalia Iosephi Tucci memoriae dicata*, ed. G. Gnoli and L. Lancioti, 395–400. Rome: Istituto Italiano per il Medio ed Estremo Oriente.

Frei, Peter, and Klaus Koch. 1984. *Reichsidee und Reichsorganisation im Perserreich.* Göttingen: Vandenhoeck & Ruprecht.

Fried, Lisbeth S. 2002. "Cyrus the Messiah? The Historical Background of Isaiah 45:1." *Harvard Theological Review* 95:373–93.

———. 2004. *The Priest and the Great King: Temple-Palace Relations in the Persian Empire.* Winona Lake, IN: Eisenbrauns.

Frye, Richard N. 1964. "The Charisma of Kingship in Ancient Iran." *Iranica Antiqua* 4:36–54.

———. 2003. "Cyrus Was No Achaemenid." In *Religious Themes and Texts of Pre-Islamic Iran and Central Asia: Studies in Honour of Professor Gherardo Gholi,* ed. C. Cereti et al., 111–14. Wiesbaden: Reichert.

Gall, Hubertus von. 1974. "Die Kopfbedeckung des persischen Ornats bei den Achämeniden." *Archäologische Mitteilungen aus Iran* 7:145–61.

———. 1989. "Das achämenidische Königsgrab: Neue Überlegungen und Beobachtungen." in *Archaeologica Iranica et Orientalis,* ed. L. de Meyer, 503–23. Ghent: Peeters.

Gammie, John G. 1986. "Herodotus on Kings and Tyrants: Objective Historiography or Conventional Portraiture?" *Journal of Near Eastern Studies* 45:171–95.

Garrison, Mark B. 2000. "Achaemenid Iconography as Evidenced by Glyptic Art: Subject Matter, Social Function, Audience, and Diffusion." In *Images as Media: Sources for the Cultural History of the Near East and Eastern Mediterranean,* ed. Christoph Uehlinger, 115–63. Fribourg: Fribourg University Press.

Garrison, Mark B., and Margaret Cool Root. 2001. *Seals on the Persepolis Fortification Tablets.* Vol. 1, *Images of Heroic Encounter.* Chicago: Oriental Institute.

Gärtner, H. A. 1983. "Les rêves de Xerxès et d'Artaban chez Hérodote." *Ktema* 8:11–18.

Geiger, Bernhard. 1934. "*Ṛta* und Verwandtes." *Wiener Zeitschrift für die Kunde des Morgenlandes* 41:107–26.

Georges, Pericles. 1994. *Barbarian Asia and the Greek Experience.* Baltimore: Johns Hopkins University Press.

———. 2000. "Persian Ionia under Darius: The Revolt Reconsidered." *Historia* 49:1–39.

Gershevitch, Ilya. 1959. *The Avestan Hymn to Mithra.* Cambridge: Cambridge University Press.

———. 1979. "The False Smerdis." *Acta Antiqua Academiae Scientiarum Hungaricae* 27:337–52.

———, ed. 1985. *The Cambridge History of Iran.* Vol. 2, *The Median and Achaemenian Periods.* Cambridge: Cambridge University Press.

Gignoux, Ph., and A. Tafazzoli, eds. and trans. 1993. *Anthologie de Zādspram.* Paris: Association pour l'Avancement des Études Iraniennes.

Gilbert, Matthew, and Suzanne C. Ryan. 2003. "Snap Judgments: Did Iconic Images from Baghdad Reveal More about the Media Than Iraq?" *Boston Globe,* 10 April. Available at http://www.boston.com/news/packages/iraq/globe_stories/041003_snap_judgements.htm.

Gnoli, Gherardo. 1963. "Osservazioni sulla dottrina mazdaica della creazione." *Annali del Istituto Orientale di Napoli: Sezione Linguistica* 12:95–125.

———. 1964. "Considerazioni sulla religione degli Achemenidi alla luce di una recente teoria [di M. Molé]." *Studi e Materiali della Storia delle Religioni* 35:239–50.

———. 1965. Review of Marijan Molé, *Culte, mythe et cosmologie dans l'Iran ancien. Rivista degli Studi Orientali* 40:334–43.

———. 1972. "Note su xšāyaθiya e xšaça." In *Ex orbe religionum: Studia Geo Widengren oblata,* 2:88–97. Leiden: E. J. Brill.

———. 1974. "Politique religieuse et conception de la royauté sous les Achéménides." *Acta Iranica* 2:117–90.

————. 1983. "Le dieu des Arya." *Studia Iranica* 12:7–22.

————. 1984. "Note sullo *xvarenah.*" *Acta Iranica* 23:207–18.

————. 1985. *De Zoroastre à Mani: Quatre leçons au Collège de France.* Paris: Travaux de l'Institut d'Études Iraniennes de l'Université de la Sorbonne Nouvelle.

————. 1988. "Cyrus et Zoroastre: Une hypothèse." In *La commémoration,* ed. Philippe Gignoux, 201–10. Louvain: Peeters.

————. 1989. *The Idea of Iran: An Essay on Its Origin.* Rome: Serie Orientale.

————. 1993. *Iran als religiöser Begriff im Mazdaismus.* Opladen: Westdeutscher.

Goldman, Bernard. 1974. "Political Realia on Persepolitan Sculpture." *Orientalia Lovaniensia* 5:31–45.

Goukowsky, Paul. 1978. *Essai sur l'origine du mythe d'Alexandre.* Nancy: Annales de l'Est.

Grabbe, Lester L. 1988. "The Belshazzar of Daniel and the Belshazzar of History." *Andrews University Seminary Studies* 26:59–66.

Gradel, Ittai. 2002. *Emperor Worship and Roman Religion.* Oxford: Oxford University Press.

Graf, David. 1984. "Medism: The Origin and Significance of the Term." *Journal of Hellenic Studies* 104:15–30.

Grayson, A. K. 1975. *Assyrian and Babylonian Chronicles.* Locust Valley, NY: J. J. Augustin.

Graziani, Simonetta. 1991. *Testi editi ed inediti datati al regno di Bardiya.* Naples: Istituto Universitario Orientale.

Greenfield, Jonas C., and Bezalel Porten, eds. and trans. 1982. *The Bisitun Inscription of Darius the Great: Aramaic Version.* London: Corpus Inscriptionum Iranicarum.

Grillot-Susini, Françoise, Clarisse Herrenschmidt, and Florence Malbran-Labat. 1993. "La version élamite de la trilingue de Behistun: Une nouvelle lecture." *Journal Asiatique* 281:19–59.

Gschnitzer, Fritz. 1977. *Die sieben Perser und das Königtum des Dareios: Ein Beitrag zur Achaimenidengeschichte und zur Herodotanalyse.* Heidelberg: Carl Winter Universitätsverlag.

————. 1988. "Zur Stellung des persischen Stammlandes im Achaimenidenreich." In *Ad bene et fideliter seminandum: Festgabe für Karlheinz Deller,* ed. Gerlinde Mauer and Ursula Magen, 87–122. Neukirchen-Vluyn: Butzon & Bercker Kevelaer.

Gunkel, Hermann. 1895. *Schöpfung und Chaos in Urzeit und Endzeit.* Göttingen: Vandenhoeck & Ruprecht.

Güntert, Hermann. 1914. *Über die ahurischen und daêvischen Ausdrücke im Awesta: Eine semasiologische Studie.* Sitzungsberichte der Heidelberger Akademie der Wissenschaften. Heidelberg: Carl Winter Universitätsverlag.

Hachmann, Rolf. 1995. "Die Völkerschaften auf den Bildwerken von Persepolis." In *Beiträge zur Kulturgeschichte Vorderasiens: Festschrift für Michael Boehmer,* U. Finkbeiner, R. Dittmann, and H. Hauptmann, 195–223. Mainz: Philipp von Zabern.

Haerinck, E. 1997. "Babylonia under Achaemenian Rule." In *Mesopotamia and Iran in the Persian Period,* ed. J. Curtis, 26–34. London: British Museum Press.

Hahn, Peter L., and Mary Ann Heiss, eds. 2001. *Empire and Revolution: The United States and the Third World since 1945.* Columbus: Ohio State University Press, 2001.

Hall, Edith. 1989. *Inventing the Barbarian: Greek Self-Definition through Tragedy.* Oxford: Clarendon.

Hallock, R. T. 1960. "The 'One Year' of Darius I." *Journal of Near Eastern Studies* 19:36–39.

Hansman, John. 1972. "Elamites, Achaemenians, and Anshan." *Iran* 10:101–25.

————. 1985. "Anshan in the Median and Achaemenian Periods." In *The Cambridge History of Iran,* vol. 2, *The Median and Achaemenian Periods,* ed. Ilya Gershevitch, 25–35. Cambridge: Cambridge University Press.

Harmatta, J. 1971a. "The Literary Patterns of the Babylonian Edict of Cyrus." *Acta Antiqua Academiae Scientiarum Hungaricae* 19:217–31.

———. 1971b. "The Rise of the Old Persian Empire: Cyrus the Great." *Acta Antiqua Academiae Scientiarum Hungaricae* 19:3–15.

———. 1976. "Darius' Expedition against the Sakā Tigraxaudā." *Acta Antiqua Academiae Scientiarum Hungaricae* 24:15–24.

Hartman, Sven. 1953. *Gayōmart: Étude de syncretisme dans l'ancien Iran.* Uppsala: Almqvist & Wiksells.

Hasel, G. F. 1981. "The Book of Daniel: Evidences Relating to Persons and Chronology." *Andrews University Seminary Studies* 19:37–49.

Hasenfratz, Hans-Peter. 1983. "Iran: Antagonismus als Universalprinzip." *Saeculum* 34:235–47.

Hegyi, Dolores. 1966. "The Historical Background of the Ionian Revolt." *Acta Antiqua Academiae Scientiarum Hungaricae* 14:285–302.

———. 1973. "Historical Authenticity of Herodotus in the Persian Logoi." *Acta Antiqua Academiae Scientiarum Hungaricae* 21:73–87.

Heidel, Alexander, ed. and trans. 1951. *The Babylonian Genesis.* Chicago: University of Chicago Press.

Helm, Peyton R. 1983. "Herodotus' *Mêdikos logos* and Median History." *Iran* 19:85–90.

Hempton, David. 1996. *Religion and Political Culture in Britain and Ireland: From the Glorious Revolution to the Decline of Empire.* Cambridge: Cambridge University Press.

Henning, W. B. 1944. "Brahman." *Transactions of the Philological Society,* 108–18.

Herrenschmidt, Clarisse. 1976. "Désignation de l'empire et concepts politiques de Darius Ier d'après ses inscriptions en Vieux Perse." *Studia Iranica* 5:33–65.

———. 1977. "Les créations d'Ahuramazda." *Studia Iranica* 6:17–58.

———. 1979a. "La Perse, rien que la Perse: Essai sur la royauté d'Ariyaramnès et d'Arsamès." In *Pad Nām i Yazdān,* 5–21. Paris: Institut d'Études Iraniennes.

———. 1979b. "La première royauté de Darius avant l'invention de la notion de l'empire." In *Pad Nām i Yazdān,* 23–33. Paris: Institut d'Études Iraniennes.

———. 1980. "La religion des Achéménides: État de la question." *Studia Iranica* 9:325–39.

———. 1982. "Les historiens de l'empire achéménide et l'inscription de Bisotun." *Annales ESC* 37:813–23.

———. 1983. "Sur la charte de fondation DSaa." *Revue d'Assyriologie* 2:177–79.

———. 1984. "Deux remarques sur les inscriptions royales achéménides." *Studia Iranica* 13:151–56.

———. 1987a. "Aspects universalistes de la religion et de l'idéologie de Darius Ier." In *Orientalia Iosephi Tucci memoriae dicata,* ed. G. Gnoli and L. Lancioti, 617–25. Rome: Istituto Italiano per il Medio ed Estremo Oriente.

———. 1987b. "Notes sur la parenté chez les Perses au début de l'empire achéménide." *Achaemenid History* 2:53–67.

———. 1989a. "Le paragraphe 70 de l'inscription de Bisotun." *Studia Iranica* 7:193–208.

———. 1989b. "Le tribut dans les inscriptions en Vieux-Perse et dans les tablettes élamites." In *Le tribut dans l'empire perse,* ed. Pierre Briant and Clarisse Herrenschmidt, 107–20. Paris: Peeters.

———. 1990. "Manipulations religieuses de Darius Ier." In *Mélanges Pierre Lévêque,* 4:195–207. Paris: Les Belles Lettres.

———. 1991. "Vieux-Perse *šiyāti.*" In *La religion iranienne à l'époque achéménide,* ed. Jean Kellens, 13–21. Ghent: Iranica Antiqua.

———. 1993. "Notes de Vieux Perse III." *Indo-Iranian Journal* 36:45–50.

———. 1994. "Le *xwētōdas*, ou marriages 'incestueux' en Iran ancien." In *Épouser au plus proche: Inceste, prohibitions et strategies matrimoniales autour de la Méditerranée*, ed. P. Bonte, 113–25. Paris: Editions de l'Ecole des Hautes Études en Sciences Sociales.

Herrenschmidt, Clarisse, and Bruce Lincoln. 2004. "Healing and Salt Waters: The Bifurcated Cosmos of Mazdaean Religion." *History of Religions* 43:269–83.

Herrmann, Gottfried. 1978. "Zu altpersisch *uv'mršiyuš 'mriyt'.*" *Zeitschrift der deutschen Morgenländischen Gesellschaft* 128:98–99.

Hersh, Seymour M. 2004. "Torture at Abu Ghraib: American Soldiers Brutalized Iraqis; How Far Up Does the Responsibility Go?" *New Yorker*, 10 May. Available at http://www.newyorker.com/fact/content/?040510fa_fact.

Higham, Scott, Joe Stephens, and Josh White. 2004. "Dates on Prison Photos Show Two Phases of Abuse." *Washington Post*, 1 June. Available at http://www.washingtonpost.com/wp-dyn/articles/A4810-2004May31.html?nav=rss_world.

Hintze, Almut. 1994. *Der Zamyād-Yašt*. Wiesbaden: Ludwig Reichert.

Hinz, Walther. 1969. *Altiranische Funde und Forschungen*. Berlin: Walter de Gruyter.

———. 1976. *Darius und die Perser: Eine Kulturgeschichte der Achämeniden*. Baden-Baden: Holle.

———. 1983. "Ahura Mazda und Ahriman: Der Dualismus von Licht und Finsternis im Zoroastrismus." In *"Und es ward Licht": Zur Kulturgeschichte des Lichts*, ed. Maja Svilar, 11–31. Bern: Franke.

Hinz, Walther, and Heidemarie Koch. 1987. *Elamisches Wörterbuch*. Berlin: Dietrich Reimer.

Hirsch, Steven W. 1985. *The Friendship of the Barbarians: Xenophon and the Persian Empire*. Hanover, NH: University Press of New England.

Hofmann, Inge, and Anton Vorbichler. 1980. "Der Kambysesbild bei Herodot." *Archiv für Orientforschung* 27:86–105.

Holloway, Steven W. 2002. *Aššur Is King! Aššur Is King! Religion in the Exercise of Power in the Neo-Assyrian Empire*. Leiden: E. J. Brill.

Hommel, H. 1899. "Assyriological Notes." *Proceedings of the Society for Biblical Archaeology* 21:115–39.

Hooke, S. H., ed. 1933. *Myth and Ritual: Essays on the Myth and Ritual of the Hebrews in Relation to the Cultural Pattern of the Ancient East*. Oxford: Oxford University Press.

Horsley, G. H. R. 1986. "Kleisthenes and the Abortive Athenian Embassy to Sardis." *Museum Philologum Londiniense* 7:99–107.

Howe, Stephen. 2002. *Empire: A Very Short Introduction*. New York: Oxford University Press.

Hultgård, Anders. 2000. "Das Paradies: Vom Park des Perserkönigs zum Ort der Seligen." In *La cité de Dieu/Die Stadt Gottes*, ed. Martin Hengel et al., 1–43. Tübingen: J. C. B. Mohr.

Humbach, Helmut, Josef Elfenbein, and Prods O. Skjærvø. 1991. *The Gāthās of Zarathushtra and the Other Old Avestan Texts*. 2 vols. Heidelberg: Carl Winter Universitätsverlag.

Husser, Jean-Marie. 1999. *Dreams and Dream Narratives in the Biblical World*. Translated by Jill Munro. Sheffield: Sheffield Academic.

Insler, Stanley. 1975. *The Gathas of Zarathustra*. Leiden: E. J. Brill.

Ito, Gikyo. 1981. "On Old Persian *'RT'C' BRZMNIY*." *Studia Iranica* 10:323–24.

Jaafari-Dehaghi, Mahmoud, ed. and trans. 1998. *Dādestān ī Dēnīg: Part One*. Paris: Association pour l'Avancement des Études Iraniennes.

Jacobs, Bruno. 1996. "Kyros der Grosse als Geisel am Medischen Königshof." *Iranica Antiqua* 31:83–100.

———. 1997. "Eine Planänderung an den Apadāna- Treppen und ihre Konsequenzen für die

Datierung der Planungs- und Bebauungsphasen von Persepolis." *Archäologische Mitteilungen aus Iran und Turan* 29:281–87.

———. 2003. "Die altpersischen Länder-Listen und Herodots sogenannte Satrapienliste (Historien III 89–94): Eine Gegenüberstellung und ein Überblick über die jüngere Forschung." In *Altertumswissenschaften im Dialog: Festschrift für Wolfram Nagel,* ed. Reinhard Dittmann, Christian Eder, and Bruno Jacobs, 301–43. Münster: Ugarit.

Jamzadeh, Parivash. 1992. "The Apadana Reliefs and the Metaphor of Conquest." *Iranica Antiqua* 27:125–47.

———. 1993. "A Few Remarks on the Significance of the Idea of Four Corners to the Achaemenids." *Iranica Antiqua* 28:137–40.

Johnson, Chalmers. 2004. *The Sorrows of Empire: Militarism, Secrecy, and the End of the Republic.* New York: Metropolitan.

Jones, Lieutenant General Anthony R., and Major General George R. Fay. 2004. *Investigation of Intelligence Activities at Abu Ghraib.* Available at www.defenselink.mil/news/Aug2004/d20040825fay.pdf.

Jong, Albert de. 1997. *Traditions of the Magi: Zoroastrianism in Greek and Latin Literature.* Leiden: E. J. Brill.

———. 2005. "The First Sin: Zoroastrian Ideas about Time before Zarathustra." In *Genesis and Regeneration: Essays on Conceptions of Origins,* ed. Shaul Shaked, 192–209. Jerusalem: Israel Academy of Sciences and Humanities.

Jouanna, Jacques. 1981. "Les causes de la défaite des barbares chez Eschyle, Hérodote et Hippocrate." *Ktema* 6:3–15.

Joxe, Alain. 2002. *Empire of Disorder.* Los Angeles: Semiotext(e).

Justi, Ferdinand. 1895/1963. *Iranisches Namenbuch.* Reprint. Hildesheim: Georg Olms.

Kaplan, Fred. 2003. "Toppled: National Styles of Pulling Down Statues." *Slate,* 9 April. http://www.slate.com/id/2081309.

Kaptan, Deniz, ed. 2002. *The Daskyleion Bullae: Seal Images from the Western Achaemenid Empire* (Achaemenid History, 12). 2 vols. Leiden: Nederlands Instituut voor het Nabije Oosten.

Kellens, Jean. 1969. "Sur un parallèle inverse à l'inscription des 'daiva.'" *Studi e Materiali di Storia delle Religioni* 40:209–13.

———. 1974. "Saošiiant." *Studia Iranica* 3:187–209.

———. 1976. "Trois réflexions sur la religion des Achéménides." *Studien zur Indologie und Iranistik* 2:113–32.

———. 1983. "Die Religion der Achämeniden." *Altorientalische Forschungen* 10:107–23.

———. 1987. "DB V: Un témoignage sur l'évolution de l'idéologie achéménide." In *Orientalia Iosephi Tucci memoriae dicata,* ed. G. Gnoli and L. Lancioti, 677–82. Rome: Istituto Italiano per il Medio ed Estremo Oriente.

———. 1989. "Ahura Mazdā n'est pas un dieu créateur." In *Études irano-aryennes offertes à Gilbert Lazard,* ed. C.-H. de Fouchécour and Ph. Gignoux, 217–28. Paris: Association pour l'Avancement des Études Iraniennes.

———, ed. 1991. *La religion iranienne à l'époque achéménide.* Ghent: Iranica Antiqua.

———. 1995. "L'âme entre le cadavre et le paradis." *Journal Asiatique* 283:19–56.

———. 1997. "Les Achéménides dans le contexte indo-iranien." *Topoi,* suppl. 1:287–97.

———. 2002. "L'idéologie religieuse des inscriptions achéménides." *Journal Asiatique* 290:417–64.

Kellens, Jean, and Eric Pirart. 1988–91. *Les textes Vieil-Avestiques.* 3 vols. Wiesbaden: Ludwig Reichert.

Kent, Roland G. 1933. "The Name Ahuramazda." In *Oriental Studies in Honour of Cursetji Erachji Pavry*, ed. J. D. C. Pavry, 200–208. London: Oxford University Press.

———. 1945. "Old Persian *artācā brazmaniya.*" *Language* 21:223–30.

———. 1953. *Old Persian: Grammar, Texts, Lexicon.* 2nd ed. New Haven, CT: American Oriental Society.

Khalidi, Rashid. 2004. *Resurrecting Empire: Western Footprints and America's Perilous Path in the Middle East.* Boston: Beacon.

Kienast, Burkhart. 1979. "Zur Herkunft der Achämenidischen Königstitulatur." In *Die Islamische Welt zwischen Mittelalter und Neuzeit: Festschrift für Hans Robert Roemer zum 65. Geburtstag*, ed. Ulrich Haarmann and Peter Bachmann, 351–59. Beirut: Franz Steiner.

———. 1999. "The So-Called 'Median Empire.'" *Bulletin of the Canadian Society for Mesopotamian Studies* 34:59–67.

Klinkott, Hilmar. 2001. "Yauna—die Griechen aus Persischer Sicht?" In *Anatolien im Lichte kultureller Wechselwirkungen*, ed. Hilmar Klinkott, 107–48. Tübingen: Attempto.

Koch, Heidemarie. 1977. *Die religiöse Verhältnisse der Dareioszeit.* Wiesbaden: Ludwig Reichert.

———. 1991. "Zu Religion und Kulten im achämenidischen Kernland." In *La religion iranienne à l'époque achéménide*, ed. Jean Kellens, 87–110. Ghent: Iranica Antiqua.

———. 1992. *Es Kündet Dareios der König . . . : Vom Leben im persischen Großreich.* Mainz: Philipp von Zabern.

Koch, Klaus. 1972. "Die Stellung des Kyros im Geschichtsbild Deuterojesajas und ihre überlieferungsgeschichtliche Verankerung." *Zeitschrift für die alttestamentliche Wissenschaft* 84:352–56.

———. 1983. "Die Völkerrepresentänten auf den Reliefs von Persepolis und den achaimenidischen Gräbern." *Zeitschrift der deutschen morgenlandischen Gesellschaft*, suppl. 5:290–300.

Köhnken, Adolf. 1988. "Der dritte Traum des Xerxes bei Herodot." *Hermes* 116:24–40.

Komoroczy, Géza. 1977. "Umman-Manda." *Acta Antiqua Academiae Scientiarum Hungaricae* 25:43–67.

König, Friedrich Wilhelm. 1965. *Die elamischen Königsinschriften.* Graz: E. Weidner.

Konstan, David. 1987. "Persians, Greeks, and Empire." *Arethusa* 20:59–74.

Kotwal, Firoze M. P., ed. and trans. 1969. *The Supplementary Texts to the Šayest ne Šayest.* Copenhagen: Munksgaard.

Kratz, Reinhard. 1991. *Kyros im Deuterojesaja-Buch.* Tübingen: J. C. B. Mohr.

———. 2002. "From Nabonidus to Cyrus." In *Ideologies as Intercultural Phenomena*, ed. A. Panaino and G. Pettinato, 143–56. Milan: University of Bologna.

Kuhrt, Amélie. 1983. "The Cyrus Cylinder and Achaemenid Imperial Policy." *Journal for the Study of the Old Testament* 25:83–97.

———. 1984. "The Achaemenid Concept of Kingship." *Iran* 22:156–60.

———. 1987a. "Survey of Written Sources Available for the History of Babylonia under the Later Achaemenids." *Achaemenid History* 1:147–58.

———. 1987b. "Usurpation, Conquest, and Ceremonial: From Babylonia to Persia." In *Rituals of Royalty: Power and Ceremonial in Traditional Societies*, ed. David Carradine and Sally Price, 20–55. Cambridge: Cambridge University Press.

———. 1988. "Earth and Water." *Achaemenid History* 3:87–99.

———. 1990a. "Achaemenid Babylonia: Sources and Problems." *Achaemenid History* 3:171–94.

———. 1990b. "Nabonidus and the Babylonian Priesthood." In *Pagan Priests: Religion and Power in the Ancient World*, ed. Mary Beard and John North, 119–55. Ithaca, NY: Cornell University Press.

————. 2002. *"Greeks" and "Greece" in Mesopotamian and Persian Perspectives*. Oxford: Leopard's Head.

————. 2003. "Making History: Sargon of Agade and Cyrus the Great of Persia." *Achaemenid History* 13:347–61.

Kuhrt, Amélie, and Susan Sherwin-White. 1987. "Xerxes' Destruction of Babylonian Temples." *Achaemenid History* 2:69–78.

Laato, Antti. 1992. *The Servant of YHWH and Cyrus: A Reinterpretation of the Exilic Messianic Programme in Isaiah 40–55*. Stockholm: Almqvist & Wiksell.

La Bua, V. 1977. "Gli Ioni e il conflitto lidio-persiano." *Miscellanea Greca e Romana* 5:1–64.

————. 1980. "La prima conquista persiana della Ionia." In *Philias kharin: Miscellanea di studi classici in onore di Eugenio Manni*, ed. M. J. Fontana et al., 4:1265–92. Rome: G. Brettschneider.

Lal, Vinay. 2002. *Empire of Knowledge: Culture and Plurality in the Global Economy*. London: Pluto.

Lambert, Wilfred G. 1972. "Nabonidus in Arabia." In *Proceedings of the Fifth Seminar for Arabian Studies*, 53–64. London: Seminar for Arabian Studies.

Lamberterie, Charles de. 1989. "Arménien *ari* et *anari*." In *Études irano-aryennes offertes à Gilbert Lazard*, ed. C.-H. de Fouchécour and Ph. Gignoux, 237–46. Paris: Association pour l'Avancement des Études Iraniennes.

Lang, Mabel. 1988. "Herodotus and the Ionian Revolt." *Historia* 17:24–36.

Langdon, Stephen. 1923. *The Epic of Creation*. Oxford: Clarendon.

Lateiner, Donald. 1982. "The Failure of the Ionian Revolt." *Historia* 31:129–60.

Lecoq, Pierre. 1974a. "La langue des inscriptions achéménides." *Acta Iranica* 3:55–62.

————. 1974b. "Le probléme de l'écriture Vieux Perse." *Acta Iranica* 3:25–107.

————. 1984. "Un problème de religion achéménide: Ahura Mazdā ou Xvarenah?" *Acta Iranica* 23:301–26.

————. 1990a. "Observations sur le sens du mot *dahyu* dans les inscriptions achéménides." *Transeuphratène* 3:131–40.

————. 1990b. "Paradis en Vieux Perse?" In *Contribution à l'histoire de l'Iran: Mélanges offerts à Jean Perrot*, ed. François Vallat, 209–12. Paris: Recherches sur les civilisations.

————. 1997. *Les inscriptions de la Perse achéménide*. Paris: Gallimard.

Lenfant, Dominique. 1996. "Ctésias et Hérodote, ou les réécritures de l'histoire dans la Perse achéménide." *Revue des Études Grecques* 109:348–80.

Leroy, Maurice. 1967. "Arta l'exaltée: À propos de l'inscription des daivas." *Studi e Materiali di Storia delle Religioni* 38:293–301.

Lesage, Julia. 2005. "Abu Ghraib and Images of Abuse and Torture." *Jump Cut* 47. Available at http://www.ejumpcut.org/archive/jc47.2005/links.html.

Lewis, Brian. 1980. *The Sargon Legend: A Study of the Akkadian Text and the Tale of the Hero Who Was Exposed at Birth*. Cambridge, MA: American Schools of Oriental Research.

Lewis, David M. 1977. *Sparta and Persia*. Leiden: E. J. Brill.

————. 1985. "Persians in Herodotus." In *The Greek Historians: Literature and History: Papers Presented to A. E. Raubitschek*, 101–17. Stanford, CA: Department of Classics, Stanford University.

————. 1987. "The King's Dinner (Polyaenus IV.3.32)." *Achaemenid History* 2:79–87.

Liagre-Böhl, Franz M. Th. De. 1962. "Die babylonischen Prätendenten zur Zeit des Xerxes." *Bibliotheca Orientalis* 19:110–14.

————. 1968. "Die babylonischen Prätendenten zur Anfangszeit des Darius." *Bibliotheca Orientalis* 25:150–53.

Lieshout, R. G. A. von. 1970. "A Dream on a Kairos of History: An Analysis of Herodotus, Hist. VII.12–19." *Mnemosyne* 23:225–49.

Lincoln, Bruce. 1981. *Priests, Warriors, and Cattle: A Study in the Ecology of Religions*. Berkeley and Los Angeles: University of California Press.

———. 1983. "The Earth Becomes Flat: A Study of Apocalyptic Imagery." *Comparative Studies in Society and History* 25:136–53.

———. 1991. *Death, War, and Sacrifice: Studies in Ideology and Practice*. Chicago: University of Chicago Press.

———. 1996. "Old Persian *Fraša* and *Vašna:* Two Terms at the Intersection of Religious and Imperial Discourse." *Indogermanische Forschungen* 101:147–67.

———. 1997. "Pahlavi *Kirrēnīdan* and Traces of Iranian Creation Mythology." *Journal of the American Oriental Society* 117:681–85.

———. 2001a. "The Center of the World and the Origins of Life." *History of Religions* 40:311–26.

———. 2001b. "The New Crusade: New Rounds in an Endless String of Reprisals." Tom Paine.com, 28 September. http://tompaine.com/Archive/scontent/4567.html.

———. 2003a. "À la recherche du paradis perdu." *History of Religions* 43:139–54.

———. 2003b. *Holy Terrors: Thinking about Religion after September 11*. Chicago: University of Chicago Press.

———. 2003c. *La politique du paradis perse*. Lecture series given at the Collège de France, Paris, May.

———. 2004a. "Bush's God Talk: Analyzing the President's Theology." *Christian Century*, 5 October, 22–29.

———. 2004b. "The Cyrus Cylinder, the Book of Virtues, and the 'Liberation' of Iraq: On Political Theology and Messianic Pretentions." In *Religionen in Konflikt: Vom Bürgerkrieg über Ökogewalt bis zur Gewalterinnerung im Ritual*, ed. Vasilios Makrides and Jörg Rüpke, 248–64. Münster: Aschendorf.

———. 2004c. "Words Matter: How Bush Speaks in Religious Code." *Boston Globe*, 12 September, D4. Available at http://www.boston.com/news/globe/editorial_opinion/oped/articles/2004/09/12/words_matter.

———. 2005. "Rebellion and Treatment of Rebels in the Achaemenid Empire." *Archiv für Religionsgeschichte* 7:167–79.

———. forthcoming. "On Political Theology, Imperial Ambitions, and Messianic Pretensions: Some Ancient and Modern Continuities." In *Religion and Violence across Time and Tradition*, ed. James Wellman. New York: Rowman & Littlefield.

Lloyd, Alan. 1988. "Herodotus on Cambyses: Some Thoughts on Recent Work." *Achaemenid History* 3:55–66.

Loew, Cornelius. 1967. *Myth, Sacred History, and Philosophy: The Pre-Christian Religious Heritage of the West*. New York: Harcourt, Brace & World.

Lommel, Herman. 1922. "Awestische Einzelstudien." *Zeitschrift für Indologie und Iranistik* 1:29–32.

———. 1930. *Die Religion Zarathustras nach dem Awesta dargestellt*. Tübingen: J. C. B. Mohr.

———. 1931. "Der medische Name Mazdaka." *Zeitschrift für vergleichende Sprachforschung* 58:140–42.

———. 1939. *Der arische Kriegsgott*. Frankfurt: V. Klostermann.

———. 1953. "Die Späher des Varuna und Mitra und das Auge des Königs." *Oriens* 6:323–33.

———. 1970. "Die Elemente im Verhältnis zu den Ameša Spentas." In *Zarathustra*, ed. Bernfried Schlerath, 377–96. Darmstadt: Wissenschaftliche Buchgesellschaft.

Long, Charles H. 1963. *Alpha: The Myths of Creation*. New York: George Braziller.

Lucrezi, Francesco. 1996. *Messianismo regalità impero: Idee religiose e idea imperiale nel mondo romano*. Firenze: Giuntina.

Lüders, Heinrich. 1959. *Varuṇa: II. Varuṇa und das Ṛta*. Göttingen: Vandenhoeck & Ruprecht.

Luraghi, Nino. 2001. "Local Knowledge in Herodotus' Histories." In *The Historian's Craft in the Age of Herodotus*, ed. Nino Luraghi, 138–60. New York: Oxford University Press.

Luschby, Heinz. 1968. "Studien zu dem Darius-Relief von Bisitun." *Archäologische Mitteilungen aus Iran* 1:63–94.

Madan, Dhanjishah Meherjibhai, ed. 1911. *The Complete Text of the Pahlavi Dinkard*. Bombay: Society for the Promotion of Researches into the Zoroastrian Religion.

Magstadt, Thomas M. 2004. *An Empire If You Can Keep It: Power and Principle in American Foreign Policy*. Washington, DC: CQ.

Mallowan, Max. 1985. "Cyrus the Great (558–529 B.C.)." In *The Cambridge History of Iran*, vol. 2, *The Median and Achaemenian Periods*, ed. Ilya Gershevitch, 392–419. Cambridge: Cambridge University Press.

Mawet, Francine. 1978. "Vieux-Perse *brazmaniy(a)*- et les nouvelles données de l'onomastique élamite." *Studia Iranica* 7:7–22.

Mayer, Jane. 2005. "A Deadly Interrogation: Can the C.I.A. Legally Kill a Prisoner?" *New Yorker*, 14 November. Available at http://www.newyorker.com/fact/content/articles/051114fa_fact.

Mayrhofer, Manfred. 1956–76. *Kurzgefasstes etymologisches Wörterbuch des Altindisches*. 3 vols. Heidelberg: Carl Winter Universitätsverlag.

———. 1973. *Onomastica Persepolitana: Das altiranische Namengut der Persepolis-Täfelchen*. Vienna: Österreichischen Akademie der Wissenschaften.

———. 1977. *Zum Namengut des Avesta*. Vienna: Österreichischen Akademie der Wissenschaften.

———. 1979. *Iranisches Personennamenbuch*. Vol. 1, *Die altiranischen Namen*. Vienna: Verlag der Österreichischen Akademie der Wissenschaften.

———. 1989. "Über die Verschriftung des Altpersischen." *Zeitschrift für vergleichende Sprachforschung* 102:174–86.

McChesney, John. 2005. "The Death of an Iraqi Prisoner." NPR, 27 October. Available at http://www.npr.org/templates/story/story.php?storyId=4977986.

Mclaren, Peter, and Nathalia E. Jaramillo. 2004. "A Moveable Fascism: Fear and Loathing in the Empire of Sand." *Cultural Studies—Cultural Methodologies* 4:223–36.

Meier, Mischa, Barbara Patzek, Uwe Walter, and Josef Wiesehöfer. 2004. *Deiokes, König der Meder: Eine Herodot-Episode in ihren Kontexten*. Wiesbaden: Franz Steiner.

Meillet, Antoine. 1907. "Le dieu indo-iranien Mitra." *Journal Asiatique* 10:143–59.

Meillet, A., and É. Benveniste. 1931. *Grammaire du Vieux Perse*. Paris: Honoré Champion.

Menasce, Jean de. 1940. "Observations sur l'inscription de Xerxès à Persepolis." *Vivre et penser* 49:124–32.

Miller, Peter N. 1994. *Defining the Common Good: Empire, Religion, and Philosophy in Eighteenth-Century Britain*. Cambridge: Cambridge University Press.

Miroschedji, P. de. 1985. "La fin du royaume d'Anšan et la naissance de l'empire perse." *Zeitschruft für Assyriologie* 75:265–306.

———. 1990. "La fin de l'Élam: Essai d'analyse et d'interpretation." *Iranica Antiqua* 25:47–95.

Mitchell, Greg. 2005a. "Judge Orders Release of Abu Ghraib Photos." *Editor and Publisher*, 29 October. Available at http://www.editorandpublisher.com/eandp/news/article_display.jsp?vnu_content_id=1001218842.

————. 2005b. "Pentagon Blocks Release of Abu Ghraib Images: Here's Why." *Propaganda Matrix*, 26 July. http://www.propagandamatrix.com/articles/july2005/260705pentagonblocks.htm.

Mitchell, W. J. T. 2005. "The Unspeakable and the Unimaginable: Word and Image in a Time of Terror." *English Literary History* 72:291–308.

Molé, Marijan. 1959. "La naissance du monde dan l'Iran préislamique." In *La naissance du monde*. Paris: Maison-Neuve.

————. 1960. "Rituel et eschatology." *Numen* 7:148–60.

————. 1961. "Réponse à M. Duchesne-Guillemin." *Numen* 8:51–63.

————. 1962. "Yasna 45 et la cosmogonie mazdéenne." *Zeitschrift der deutschen morgenlandischen Gesellschaft* 37:345–52.

————. 1963. *Culte, mythe, et cosmologie dans l'Iran ancien: Le problème zoroastrien et la tradition mazdéenne*. Paris: Presses Universitaires de France.

Momigliano, Arnaldo. 1969. "Tradizione e invenzione in Ctesia." In *Quarto contributo alla storia degli studi classici e del mondo antico*, 181–212. Rome: Edizioni di storia e letteratura.

Mowinckel, Sigmund. 1956. *He That Cometh: The Messiah Concept in the Old Testament and Later Judaism*. Translated by G. W. Anderson. New York: Abingdon.

Mral, Brigitte. 2004. *"We're a Peaceful Nation": War Rhetoric after September 11*. Västerås: SEMA.

Murray, Oswyn. 1987. "Herodotus and Oral History." *Achaemenid History* 2:97–115.

————. 1988. "The Ionian Revolt." In *The Cambridge Ancient History* (2nd ed.), vol. 4, *Persia, Greece, and the Western Mediterranean, c. 525 to 479 B.C.*, ed. John Boardman et al., 461–90. Cambridge: Cambridge University Press.

————. 2001. "Herodotus and Oral History Reconsidered." In *The Historian's Craft in the Age of Herodotus*, ed. Nino Luraghi, 314–25. New York: Oxford University Press.

Muscarella, Oscar, Annie Caubet, and Françoise Tallon. 1992. "Susa in the Achaemenid Period." In *The Royal City of Susa: Ancient Near Eastern Treasures in the Louvre*, ed. Prudence O. Harper, Joan Aruz, and Françoise Tallon, 215–52. New York: Metropolitan Museum of Art.

Nagy, Gregory. 1987. "Herodotus the *Logios*." *Arethusa* 20:175–84.

Narten, Johanna. 1986. *Der Yasna Haptaṅhāiti*. Wiesbaden: Ludwig Reichert.

Negri, Antonio, and Michael Hardt. 2000. *Empire*. Cambridge, MA: Harvard University Press.

Netzer, Amnon. 1974. "Some Notes on the Characterization of Cyrus the Great in Jewish and Judeo-Persian Writings." *Acta Iranica* 2:35–52.

Nyberg, Henrik Samuel. 1929. "Questions de cosmologie et de cosmogonie mazdéennes." *Journal Asiatique* 214:193–310.

————. 1931. "Questions de cosmologie et de cosmogonie mazdéennes." *Journal Asiatique* 219:1–134, 193–244.

Nylander, Carl. 1967. "Who Wrote the Inscriptions at Pasargadae?" *Orientalia Suecana* 16:135–80.

O'Hara, Daniel T. 2003. *Empire Burlesque: The Fate of Critical Culture in Global America*. Durham, NC: Duke University Press.

Olmstead, A. T. 1948. *History of the Persian Empire*. Chicago: University of Chicago Press.

————. 1968. "The Eyes of the Lord." *Journal of the American Oriental Society* 88:173–80.

Orlin, Louis L. 1976. "Athens and Persia ca. 507 B.C.: A Neglected Perspective." In *Michigan Oriental Studies in Honor of George G. Cameron*, ed. Louis L. Orlin, 255–66. Ann Arbor: Department of Near Eastern Studies, University of Michigan.

Pallis, Svend Aage. 1926. *The Babylonian Akitu Festival*. Copenhagen: A. F. Host.

Palomar, Natalia. 1987. "El logos de Deyoces, Heródoto 1.95–102." *Itaca* 3:23–25.

Panaino, Antonio. 1986. *"Hainā-, dušiyāra-, drauga-:* Un confronto antico-persiano avestico." *Socalizio glottologico Milanese* 27:95–102.

———. 2000. "The Mesopotamian Heritage of Achaemenian Kingship." In *The Heirs of Assyria*, ed. Sanna Aro and R. M. Whiting, 35–49. Helsinki: Neo-Assyrian Text Corpus Project.

———. 2003. "Herodotus I.96–101: Deioces' Conquest of Power and the Foundation of Sacred Royalty." In *Continuity of Empire (?): Assyria, Media, Persia*, ed. Giovanni B. Lanfranchi, Michael Roaf, and Robert Rollinger, 327–38. Padua: Sargon Editrice.

Passavant, Paul A., and Jodi Dean, eds. 2004. *Empire's New Clothes: Reading Hardt and Negri*. New York: Routledge.

Peat, Jerome A. 1989. "Cyrus 'King of Lands' and Cambyses 'King of Babylon': The Disputed Co-Regency." *Journal of Cuneiform Studies* 41:199–216.

Pelling, Christopher. 1996. "The Urine and the Vine: Astyages' Dream at Herodotus 1.107–8." *Classical Quarterly* 46:68–77.

Petschow, Herbert. 1988. "Das Unterkönigtum des Cambyses als 'König von Babylon.'" *Revue Assyriologique* 82:78–82.

Pettazzoni, Raffaele. 1967. *Essays in the History of Religions*. Translated H. J. Rose. Leiden: E. J. Brill.

"The Photographs Tell the Story . . . : Is This Media Manipulation on a Grand Scale?" 2003. Information Clearing House.com, 13 April. http://www.informationclearinghouse.info/article2842.htm.

Pirart, Eric. 1995. "Les noms des Perses." *Journal Asiatique* 283:57–68.

———. 1996. "Le sacrifice humain dans l'Avesta." *Journal Asiatique* 284:1–36.

———. 2002. "Le Mazdéisme politique de Darius Ier." *Indo-Iranian Journal* 45:121–51.

Piras, Andrea. 1994–95. "A proposito di antico-persiano *šiyāti*." *Studi Orientali e Linguistici* 5:91–97.

Pitt, William Rivers. 2003. "George W. Christ?" *Truthout*, 5 May. http://www.truthout.org/docs_03/050503A.shtml.

Poebel, Arno. 1938. "Chronology of Darius' First Year of Reign." *American Journal of Semitic Languages and Literatures* 55:142–65, 285–314.

Polk, James. 2004. "Testimony: Abu Ghraib Photos 'Just for Fun.'" CNN, 4 August. http://www.cnn.com/2004/LAW/08/03/england.hearing.

Pongratz-Leisten, Beate. 2002. "'Lying King' and 'False Prophet': The Intercultural Transfer of a Rhetorical Device within Ancient Near Eastern Ideologies." In *Ideologies as Intercultural Phenomena*, ed. A. Panaino and G. Pettinato, 215–43. Milan: University of Bologna.

Posener, Georges. 1936. *La première domination perse en Egypte: Recueil d'inscriptions hiéroglyphiques*. Cairo: Institut Français d'Archéologie Orientale.

Potts, D. T. 2005. "Cyrus the Great and the Kingdom of Anshan." In *Birth of the Persian Empire*, ed. V. S. Curtis and S. Stewart, 7–28. London: I. B. Tauris.

Pritchard, James B. 1969. *Ancient Near Eastern Texts Relating to the Old Testament*. 3rd ed. Princeton, NJ: Princeton University Press.

Rabassa, Carles, and Ruth Stepper, eds. 2002. *Imperios sacros, monarquías divinas: Primer Coloquio Internacional del Grupo Europeo de Investigación Histórica "Religión, Poder y Monarquía"* (= *Heilige Herrscher, göttliche Monarchien: erstes Internationales Kolloquium der Europäischen Forschungsgruppe "Religion, Macht, Monarchie"*). Castelló de la Plana: Universitat Jaume I.

Raglan, FitzRoy Richard Somerset, Baron. 1937. *The Hero: A Study in Tradition, Myth, and Drama*. New York: Oxford University Press.

Rahe, Paul. 1980. "The Military Situation in Western Asia on the Eve of Cunaxa." *American Journal of Philology* 101:79–96.

Raimondo, Justin. 2004. "Abu Ghraib and the Pornography of Power: A 'Few Bad Apples'— or a Part of the Game Plan?" Antiwar.com, 14 May. http://www.antiwar.com/justin/?articleid=2574.

Rampton, Sheldon, and John Stauber. 2003. "How to Sell a War: The Rendon Group Deploys 'Perception Management' in the War on Iraq." *In These Times*, 4 August. http://www.inthesetimes.com/site/main/article/how_to_sell_a_war/P40.

Rank, Otto. 1922. *Der Mythus von der Geburt des Helden: Versuch einer psychologischen Mythendeutung.* Leipzig: F. Deuticke.

Raubitschek, A. E. 1964. "The Treaties between Persia and Athens." *Greek, Roman, and Byzantine Studies* 5:151–59.

Roaf, Michael. 1974. "The Subject Peoples on the Base of the Statue of Darius." *Cahiers de la Délégation Archéologique Française en Iran* 4:73–160.

———. 1990. "Sculptors and Designers at Persepolis." In *Investigating Artistic Environments in the Ancient Near East*, ed. Ann C. Gunter, 105–14. Washington, DC: Arthur M. Sackler Gallery, Smithsonian Institution.

Rocchi, Maria. 1980. "Serse e l'acqua amara dell' Elloesponto (Hdt. 7.35)." In *Perennitas: Studi in onore di Angelo Brelich*, ed. Giulia Piccaluga, 417–29. Rome: Edizioni dell' Ateneo.

Rollinger, Robert. 1998. "Der Stammbaum des achaimenidischen Königshauses oder die Frage der Legitimität der Herrschaft des Dareios." *Archäologische Mitteilungen aus Iran und Turan* 30:155–209.

———. 1999a. "Xerxes und Babylon." *NABU* 8:9–12.

———. 1999b. "Zur Lokalisation von Parsu(m)a(š) in der Fars und zu einigen Fragen der frühen persischen Geschichte." *Zeitschrift für Assyriologie* 89:115–39.

———. 2000. "Herodotus and the Intellectual Heritage of the Ancient Near East." In *The Heirs of Assyria*, ed. Sanna Aro and R. M. Whiting, 65–83. Helsinki: Neo-Assyrian Text Corpus Project.

Root, Margaret Cool. 1979. *The King and Kingship in Achaemenid Art: Essays on the Creation of an Iconography of Empire.* Leiden: E. J. Brill.

———. 1990. "Circles of Artistic Programming: Strategies for Studying Creative Processes at Persepolis." In *Investigating Artistic Environments in the Ancient Near East*, ed. Ann C. Gunter, 115–39. Washington: Smithsonian Institution.

———. 2003. "Hero and Worshipper at Seleucia: Reinventions of Babylonia on a Banded Agate Cylinder Seal of the Achaemenian Empire." In *Culture through Objects: Ancient Near Eastern Studies in Honour of P. R. S. Moorey*, ed. Timothy Potts et al., 249–83. Oxford: Griffith Institute.

Rostworowski de Diez Canseco, María. 1983. *Estructuras andinas del poder: Ideología religiosa y política.* Lima: Instituto de Estudios Peruanos.

Rowe, John Carlos. 2004. "Culture, US Imperialism, and Globalization." *American Literary History* 16:575–95.

Sack, Ronald H. 1997. "Nabonidus of Babylon." In *Crossing Boundaries and Linking Horizons: Studies in Honor of Michael C. Astour on His 80th Birthday*, ed. Gordon D. Young et al., 455–73. Bethesda, MD: CDL.

Sancisi-Weerdenburg, Heleen W. A. M. 1980. *Yaunā en Persai: Grieken en Persen in een ander Perspectief.* Groningen: Druckerij Dijkstra Niemeyer.

———. 1981. "Legitimatie in het Achaemenidenrijk." In *Legitimiteit of leugen, achtergronden van macht en gezag in de vroege Staat*, ed. R. Hagesteijn and Ch. L. van der Vliet, 147–81. Leiden: Institute of Cultural and Social Studies.

———. 1982. "Medes and Persians: To What Extent Was Cyrus the Heir of Astyages and the Median Empire? Some Remarks." *Persica* 10:278.

———. 1983. "Exit Atossa: Images of Women in Greek Historiography on Persia." In *Images of Women in Antiquity*, ed. Averil Cameron and Amélie Kuhrt, 21–33. London: Croom Helm.

———. 1985. "The Death of Cyrus: Xenophon's *Cyropaedia* as a Source for Iranian History." In *Papers in Honour of Mary Boyce*, 2:459–71. Leiden: E. J. Brill.

———. 1987. "Decadence in the Empire or Decadence in the Sources? From Source to Synthesis: Ctesias." *Achaemenid History* 1:33–45.

———. 1988. "Was There Ever a Median Empire?" *Achaemenid History* 3:197–212.

———. 1989. "Gifts in the Persian Empire." In *Le tribut dans l'empire perse*, ed. Pierre Briant and Clarisse Herrenschmidt, 129–46. Paris: Peeters.

———. 1994. "The Orality of Herodotus' *Medikos logos;* or, The Median Empire Revisited." *Achaemenid History* 8:39–55.

———. 1995. "Persian Food: Stereotypes and Political Identity." In *Food in Antiquity*, ed. John Wilkins, David Harvey, and Mike Dobson, 286–302. Exeter: University of Exeter Press.

———. 1998. "*Bāji.*" *Achaemenid History* 11:23–34.

———. 2001a. "The Problem of the Yauna." In *Achaemenid Anatolia*, ed. T. Bakir, 1–11. Leiden: Nederlands Historisch-Archaeologisch Instituut te Istanbul.

———. 2001b. "Yaunā by the Sea and across the Sea." In *Ancient Perceptions of Greek Ethnicity*, ed. Irad Marlkin, 323–46. Washington, DC: Center for Hellenic Studies.

Sancisi-Weerdenburg, Heleen, and Amélie Kuhrt, eds. 1987. *The Greek Sources* (Achaemenid History, 2). Leiden: Nederlands Instituut voor het Nabije Oosten.

Saporetti, Claudio. 1996. *Come sognavano gli antichi: Sogni della Mesopotamia e dei popoli vicini.* Milano: Rusconi.

Schaeder, H. H. 1934. *Iranica: 1. Das Auge des Königs; 2. Fu-lin.* Göttingen: Gesellschaft der Wissenschaften zu Göttingen, phil.-hist. Klasse.

———. 1946. "Des eigenen Todes sterben." In *Nachrichten der Akademie der Wissenschaften, Göttingen, phil.-hist. Klasse*, 24–36. Göttingen: Gesellschaft der Wissenschaften zu Göttingen, phil.-hist. Klasse.

Schaudig, Hanspeter, ed. and trans. 2001. *Die Inschriften Nabonids von Babylon und Kyros' des Großen samt den in ihrem Umfeld entstanden Tendenzschriften.* Münster: Ugarit.

Schlerath, Bernfried. 1974. "Gedanke, Wort und Werk im Veda und im Awesta." In *Antiquitates Indogermanicae: Studien zur indogermanischen Altertumskunde und zur Sprach- und Kulturgeschichte der indogermanischen Völker: Gedenkschrift für Hermann Güntert*, ed. Manfred Mayrhofer et al., 201–21. Innsbruck: Innsbrucker Beiträge zur Sprachwissenschaft.

Schmidt, Erich. 1953–70. *Persepolis.* 3 vols. Chicago: University of Chicago Press.

Schmidt, Hanns-Peter. 1978. "Indo-Iranian Mitra Studies: The State of the Central Problem." In *Études mithriaques: Actes du 2e Congrès International, Téhéran, du 1er au 8 septembre 1975*, 345–93. Leiden: E. J. Brill.

———. 1996. "The Non-Existence of Ahreman and the Mixture (*Gumēzišn*) of Good and Evil." In *K. R. Cama Oriental Institute, Second International Congress Proceedings*, 79–95. Bombay: K. R. Cama Oriental Institute.

Schmitt, Rüdiger. 1963. "Ein altpersisches *ghostword* und das sog. 'inverse ca.'" *Orientalia* 32:437–48.

———. 1977. "Königtum im alten Iran." *Saeculum* 28:384–95.

———. 1990. "The Name of Darius." *Acta Iranica* 30:194–99.

———, ed. and trans. 1991a. *The Bisitun Inscriptions of Darius the Great: Old Persian Text.* London: Corpus Inscriptionum Iranicarum.

———. 1991b. "Zu dem 'arischen Ahuramazdā.'" *Studia Iranica* 20:189–92.

———. 1997. "Onomastica Iranica symmicta." In *Scríbthair a ainm n-ogaim: Scritti in memoria di Enrico Campanile,* ed. Riccardo Ambrosini et al., 921–27. Pisa: Pacini.

———. 1999. *Beiträge zu altpersischen Inschriften.* Wiesbaden: Ludwig Reichert.

———. 2000. *The Old Persian Inscriptions of Naqsh-i Rustam and Persepolis.* London: Corpus Inscriptionum Iranicarum.

Schreiber, Stefan. 2000. *Gesalbter und Konig: Titel und Konzeptionen der koniglichen Gesalbtenerwartung in fruhjudischen und urchristlichen Schriftgen.* Berlin: Walter de Gruyter.

Schulze, W. 1912. "Der Tod des Kambyses." In *Sitzungsberichte der preussischen Akademie der Wissenschaft zu Berlin, hist.-phil. Klasse,* 685–703. Berlin: Preussischen Akademie der Wissenschaften.

Schwartz, Barry. 1981. *Vertical Classification: A Study in Structuralism and the Sociology of Knowledge.* Chicago: University of Chicago Press.

Schwartz, Martin. 1985. "The Religion of Achaemenian Iran." In *The Cambridge History of Iran,* vol. 2, *The Median and Achaemenian Periods,* ed. Ilya Gershevitch, 664–97. Cambridge: Cambridge University Press.

Scott, James C. 1990. *Domination and the Arts of Resistance: Hidden Transcripts.* New Haven, CT: Yale University Press.

Scurlock, J. A. 1990. "Herodotos' Median Chronology Again?!" *Iranica Antiqua* 25:149–63.

Shahbazi, A. S. 1972. "The 'One Year' of Darius Re-Examined." *Bulletin of the School of Oriental and African Studies* 35:609–14.

———. 1974. "An Achaemenid Symbol: I. A Farewell to 'Fravahr' and 'Ahuramazda.'" *Archäologische Mitteilungen aus Iran* 7:136–44.

———. 1980. "An Achaemenid Symbol: III. Farnah '(God Given) Fortune' Symbolised." *Archäologische Mitteilungen aus Iran* 13:119–47.

———. 1983. "Darius' 'Haft Kishvar.'" In *Kunst, Kultur und Geschichte der Achämenidenzeit und ihr Fortleben,* ed. Heidemarie Koch and D. N. MacKenzie, 239–46. Berlin: Dietrich Reimer.

Shaked, Shaul. 1967. "Some Notes on Ahreman, the Evil Spirit, and His Creation." In *Studies in Mysticism and Religion Presented to Gershom G. Scholem,* ed. E. E. Urbach et al., 227–34. Jerusalem: Magnes.

———. 1987. "First Man, First King: Notes on Semitic-Iranian Syncretism and Iranian Mythological Transformations." In *Gilgul: Essays on Transformation, Revolution, and Permanence in the History of Religions Dedicated to R. J. Zwi Werblowsky,* ed. S. Shaked et al., 238–56. Leiden: E. J. Brill.

———. 1988. "Mythes d'origine comme actes de commemoration et de différenciation en Iran sassanide." In *La commémoration,* ed. Philippe Gignoux, 211–18. Louvain: Peeters.

———. 2005. "Cosmic Origins and Human Origins in the Iranian Cultural Milieu." In *Genesis and Regeneration: Essays on Conceptions of Origins,* ed. Shaul Shaked, 210–22. Jerusalem: Israel Academy of Sciences and Humanities.

Shaki, Mansour. 1970. "Some Basic Tenets of the Eclectic Metaphysics of the Dēnkart." *Archiv Orientální* 38:272–312.

Shea, William H. 1982. "Nabonidus, Belshazar, and the Book of Daniel: An Update." *Andrews University Seminary Studies* 20:133–49.

Skalmowski, Wojciech. 1988. "Old Persian *Vazraka.*" In *A Green Leaf: Papers in Honour of Professor Jes P. Asmussen,* 39–42. Leiden: E. J. Brill.

Skjærvø, Prods Oktor. 1994. "Achaemenid **Vispašiyātiš-,* Sasanian *Wispšād.*" *Studia Iranica* 23:79–80

———. 1999. "Avestan Quotations in Old Persian? Literary Sources of the Old Persian Inscriptions." *Irano-Judaica* 4:3–64.

———. 2003. "Truth and Deception in Ancient Iran." In *Ataš-e Dorun: The Fire Within: Jamshid Soroush Sorouschian Commemorative Volume,* ed. Carlo G. Cereti and Farrokh Vajifdar, 383–434. N.p.: Mehrborzin Soroushian.

———. 2005. "The Achaemenids and the Avesta." In *Birth of the Persian Empire,* ed. V. S. Curtis and S. Stewart, 52–84. London: I. B. Tauris.

Smith, Charles Foster. 1881. *A Study of Plutarch's Life of Artaxerxes, with Especial Reference to the Sources.* Leipzig: Metzger & Wittig.

Smith, Jonathan Z. 1982. "A Pearl of Great Price and a Cargo of Yams." In *Imagining Religion: From Babylon to Jonestown,* 90–101. Chicago: University of Chicago Press.

Smith, Morton. 1963. "II Isaiah and the Persians." *Journal of the American Oriental Society* 83:415–21.

Smith, Sidney. 1944. *Isaiah, Chapters XL–LV.* London: Oxford University Press.

Solmsen, Lieselotte. 1943. "The Speeches in Herodotus' Account of the Ionic Revolt." *American Journal of Philology* 64:194–202.

Sontag, Susan. 2004. "Regarding the Torture of Others." *New York Times,* 23 May. Available at http://donswaim.com/nytimes.sontag.html.

Stausberg, Michael. 2002. *Die Religion Zarathustras.* Vol. 1, *Geschichte—Gegenwart—Rituale.* Stuttgart: W. Kohlhammer.

Strohm, Paul. 1998. *England's Empty Throne: Usurpation and the Language of Legitimation, 1399–1422.* New Haven, CT: Yale University Press.

Stronach, David, ed. 1978. *Pasargadae.* Oxford: British Institute of Persian Studies.

———. 1985a. "The Apadana: A Signature of the Line of Darius." In *De l'Indus aux Balkans: Recueil à la mémoire de Jean Deshayes,* ed. J.-L. Huot et al., 433–45. Paris: Recherche sur les Civilizations.

———. 1985b. "Pasargadae." In *The Cambridge History of Iran,* vol. 2, *The Median and Achaemenian Periods,* ed. Ilya Gershevitch, 838–55. Cambridge: Cambridge University Press.

———. 1989. "The Royal Garden at Pasargadae: Evolution and Legacy." In *Archeologia iranica et orientalis: Miscellanea in honorem Louis van den Berghe,* ed. L. de Meyer and E. Haerinck, 1:475–502. Ghent: Peeters.

———. 1990. "The Garden as a Political Statement: Some Case Studies from the Near East in the First Millennium B.C." *Bulletin of the Asia Institute* 4:171–80.

———. 1997. "On the Interpretation of the Pasargadae Inscriptions." In *Ultra terminum vagari: Scritti in onore di Carl Nylander,* ed. Börje Magnusson et al., 323–39. Rome: Quasar.

———. 2000. "Of Cyrus, Darius, and Alexander: A New Look at the 'Epitaphs' of Cyrus the Great." In *Variatio Delectat: Iran und der Westen: Gedenkschrift für Peter Calmeyer,* ed. Reinhard Dittmann et al., 681–702. Münster: Ugarit.

Szemerenyi, Oswald. 1975. "Iranica V." *Acta Iranica* 5:313–94.

Szpakowska, Kasia Maria. 2003. *Behind Closed Eyes: Dreams and Nightmares in Ancient Egypt.* Swansea: Classical Press of Wales.

Tadmor, Hayim. 1965. "The Inscriptions of Nabonaid: Historical Arrangement." In *Studies in*

Honor of Benno Landsberger on His Seventy-fifth Birthday, 351–63. Chicago: University of Chicago Press.

Taeger, Fritz. 1957–60. *Charisma: Studien zur Geschichte des antiken Herrscherkultes.* Stuttgart: W. Kohlhammer.

Taguba, Antonio M. 2004. "Article 15-6 Investigation of the 800th Military Police Brigade." Prepared for Lieutenant General Ricardo Sanchez, Commander of Joint Task Force-7. Available at http://www.thememoryhole.org/war/iraqis_tortured/taguba_report.htm.

"A Tale of Two Photos." 2003. Information Clearing House.com, 9 April. http://www.informationclearinghouse.info/article2838.htm.

Tanner, Marie. 1993. *The Last Descendant of Aeneas: The Hapsburgs and the Mythic Image of the Emperor.* New Haven, CT: Yale University Press.

Tatum, James. 1989. *Xenophon's Imperial Fiction: On the Education of Cyrus.* Princeton, NJ: Princeton University Press.

Thieme, Paul. 1957. *Mitra and Aryaman.* New Haven, CT: Yale University Press.

———. 1975. "The Concept of Mitra in Aryan Belief." In *Mithraic Studies,* ed. John Hinnells, 21–39. Manchester: Manchester University Press.

Thomas, Rosalind. 2000. *Herodotus in Context: Ethnography, Science, and the Art of Persuasion.* Cambridge: Cambridge University Press.

Tichy, Eva. 1983. "Vedisch *dvitā* und altpersisch *duvitāparanam.*" *Münchener Studien zur Sprachwissenschaft* 42:207–41.

Timus, Mihaela. 2003. "Le 'corps eschatologique' *(tan ī pasēn)* d'après la théologie zoroastrienne." *Studia Asiatica* 4:779–808.

Tourraix, Alexandre. 1995. "Hérodote et la légende royale iranienne." *Ktema* 20:117–24.

Tozzi, Pierluigi. 1977. "Per la storia della politica religiosa degli Achemenidi: Distruzioni persiane di templi greci agli inizi del V secolo." *Rivista Storica Italiana* 89:18–32.

———. 1978. *La rivolta ionica.* Pisa: Giardini.

Tuplin, Christopher. 1990. "Persian Decor in the *Cyropaedia:* Some Observations." *Achaemenid History* 5:17–29.

———. 1994. "Persians as Medes." *Achaemenid History* 8:235–56.

———. 1996. "The Parks and Gardens of the Achaemenid Empire." In *Achaemenid Studies,* 80–131. Stuttgart: Franz Steiner.

———. 2003. "Xenophon in Media." In *Continuity of Empire (?): Assyria, Media, Persia,* ed. Giovanni B. Lanfranchi, Michael Roaf, and Robert Rollinger, 351–89. Padua: Sargon Editrice.

Uchitel, Alexander. 1997. "Persian Paradise: Agricultural Texts in the Fortification Archive." *Iranica Antiqua* 32:137–44.

Vahman, Fereydun, ed. and trans. 1986. *Arda Wiraz Namag: The Iranian "Divina Commedia."* London: Curzon.

Vallat, François. 1971. "Deux nouvelles chartes de fondation d'un palais de Darius Ier à Suse." *Syria* 48:53–59.

———. 1972. "Deux inscriptions élamites de Darius Ier (DSf et DSz)." *Studia Iranica* 1:3–13.

———. 1997. "Cyrus l'usurpateur." *Topoi,* suppl. 1:423–34.

van der Veer, Peter. 2001. *Imperial Encounters: Religion and Modernity in India and Britain.* Princeton, NJ: Princeton University Press.

Vaux, Roland de. 1971. "Le roi d'Israël, vassal de Yahvé." In *The Bible and the Ancient Near East,* ed. Roland de Vaux, 152–80. Garden City, NY: Doubleday.

Vidal, Gore. 2004. *Imperial America: Reflections on the United States of Amnesia.* New York: Nation.

Vogelsang, Willem. 1992. *The Rise and Organisation of the Achaemenian Empire: The Eastern Iranian Evidence*. Leiden: E. J. Brill.

Voigtlander, Elizabeth N. von, ed. and trans. 1978. *The Bisitun Inscription of Darius the Great: Babylonian Version*. London: Corpus Inscriptionum Iranicarum.

von Soden, Wolfram. 1983. "Kyros und Nabonid: Propaganda und Gegenpropaganda." In *Kunst, Kultur und Geschichte der Achämenidenzeit und ihr Fortleben*, ed. Heidemarie Koch and D. N. MacKenzie, 61–68. Berlin: Dietrich Reimer.

Vorbichler, Anton. 1981. "Kambyses in Ägypten." *Studien zur altägyptischen Kultur* 9:179–99.

Wackernagel, Jacob. 1932. "Indoiranica." *Zeitschrift für vergleichende Sprachwissenschaft* 59:19–30.

Wallinga, H. T. 1984. "The Ionian Revolt." *Mnemosyne* 37:401–37.

Walser, Gerold. 1966. *Die Völkerschaften auf den Reliefs von Persepolis: Historische Studien über den sogennanten Tributzug an der Apadanatreppe*. Berlin: Deutsche archäologisches Institut.

———. 1983. "Der Tod des Kambyses." In *Althistorische Studien Hermann Bengtson zum 70. Geburtstag darbebracht von Kollegen und Schülern*, ed. Heinz Heinen, 8–18. Wiesbaden: Franz Steiner.

———. 1984. *Hellas und Iran*. Darmstadt: Wissenschaftliche Buchgesellschaft.

Waschke, Ernst-Joachim. 2001. *Der Gesalbte: Studien zur alttestamentlichen Theologie*. Berlin: Walter de Gruyter.

Waters, Matthew W. 1996. "Darius and the Achaemenid Line." *Ancient History Bulletin* 10:11–18.

———. 1999. "The Earliest Persians in Southwestern Iran: The Textual Evidence." *Iranian Studies* 32:99–107.

———. 2004. "Cyrus and the Achaemenids." *Iran* 42:91–102.

Weber, Ursula, and Josef Wiesehöfer. 1996. *Das Reich der Achaimeniden: Eine Bibliographie*. Berlin: Dietrich Reimer.

Wechsler, Howard J. 1985. *Offerings of Jade and Silk: Ritual and Symbol in the Legitimation of the T'ang Dynasty*. New Haven, CT: Yale University Press.

Weisberg, David B. 1997. "Polytheism and Politics: Some Comments on Nabonidus' Foreign Policy." In *Crossing Boundaries and Linking Horizons: Studies in Honor of Michael C. Astour on His 80th Birthday*, ed. Gordon D. Young et al., 547–56. Bethesda, MD: CDL.

Wells, J. 1907. "The Persian Friends of Herodotus." *Journal of Hellenic Studies* 27:37–47.

West, E. W. 1885. *Pahlavi Texts*. Pt. 3, *Dina-i Mainög i Khirad, Sikand-Gümanik Vigar, Sad Dar*. Oxford: Clarendon.

We Will Prevail: President George Bush on War, Terrorism, and Freedom. 2003. With a foreword by Peggy Noonan and an introduction by Jay Nordlinger. New York: Continuum.

Westenholz, Joan. 2000. "The King, the Emperor, and the Empire: Continuity and Discontinuity of Royal Representation in Text and Image." In *The Heirs of Assyria*, ed. Sanna Aro and R. M. Whiting, 99–125. Helsinki: Neo-Assyrian Text Corpus Project.

Widengren, Geo. 1959. "The Sacral Kingship of Iran." In *La regalità sacra: Contributi al tema dell' VIII Congresso Internazionale di Storia delle Religioni*, 242–57. Leiden: E. J. Brill.

———. 1965. *Die Religionen Irans*. Stuttgart: W. Kohlhammer.

———. 1969. "The Death of Gayōmart." In *Myths and Symbols: Studies in Honor of Mircea Eliade*, ed. Joseph M. Kitagawa and Charles H. Long, 179–94. Chicago: University of Chicago Press.

———. 1974. "La royauté de l'Iran antique." *Acta Iranica* 1:84–89.

Wiesehöfer, Josef. 1978. *Der Aufstand Gaumatas und die Anfänge Dareios I*. Bonn: Rudolf Habelt.

———. 1987. "Kyros und die unterworfenen Völker: Ein Beitrag zur Entstehung von Geschichtsbewußtsein." *Quaderni di Storia* 26:107–26.

———. 1988. "Das Bild der Achaimeniden in der Zeit des Nationalsozialismus." *Achaemenid History* 3:1–14.

———. 1989. "*Tauta gar en atelea*: Beobachtungen zur Abgabenfreiheit im Achaimenidenreich." In *Le tribut dans l'empire perse*, ed. Pierre Briant and Clarisse Herrenschmidt, 183–92. Paris: Peeters.

———. 1990. "Zur Geschichte der Begriffe 'Arier' und 'Arisch' in der Deutschen Sprachwissenschaft und Althistorie des 19. und der ersten Hälfte des 20. Jahrhunderts." *Achaemenid History* 5:149–65.

———. 1996. *Ancient Persia from 550 B.C. to 650 A.D.* Translated by Azizeh Azodi. London: I. B. Tauris.

———. 2002. "Kontinuität oder Zäsur? Babylonien unter den Achämeniden." In *Religion und Religionskontakte im Zeitalter der Achämeniden*, ed. Reinhard G. Kratz, 29–48. Gütersloh: Chr. Kaiser.

Williams, A. V., ed. and trans. 1990. *The Pahlavi Rivayat Accompanying the Dadestan i Denig*. Copenhagen: Munksgaard.

Williams, G. M. E. 1982. "Athenian Politics 508/7-480: A Reappraisal." *Athenaeum* 60:521–44.

Wills, Garry. 2001. *Venice, Lion City: The Religion of Empire*. New York: Simon & Schuster.

Wylie, G. 1992. "Cunaxa and Xenophon." *L'Antiquité Classique* 61:119–31.

Yamauchi, Edwin M. 1996. *Persia and the Bible*. Grand Rapids, MI: Baker.

Zaehner, R. C. 1955. *Zurvan: A Zoroastrian Dilemma*. Oxford: Oxford University Press.

———. 1956. *The Teachings of the Magi: A Compendium of Zoroastrian Beliefs*. London: Allen & Unwin.

———. 1961. *The Dawn and Twilight of Zoroastrianism*. New York: Putnam's.

Zawadzki, Stefan. 1988. "Umman-Manda: Bedeutung des terminus und Gründe seiner Anwendung in der Chronik von Nabopolassar." In *Šulmu: Papers on the Ancient Near East Presented at International Conference of Socialist Countries*, ed. Petr Vavroŝek and Vladimir Souiek, 379–87. Prague: Charles University.

———. 1994. "Bardiya, Darius, and Babylonian Usurpers in the Light of the Bisitun Inscription and Babylonian Sources." *Archäologische Mitteilungen aus Iran* 27:127–45.

Zucchino, David. 2004. "Army Stage-Managed Fall of Hussein Statue." *Los Angeles Times*, 3 July. Available at http://www.commondreams.org/headlines04/0703-02.htm.

Index

Note: The letter *f* following a page number denotes a figure; the letter *t* denotes a table.

Abu Ghraib prison complex, 2, 101–7
Achaemenes, 3–4
Achaemenian Empire
    ahistorical portrayal in inscriptions, 12–13,
      61–62
    aversion to salt water in, 128n
    Cambyses' conquests, 7–8
    capital offenses in, 139n
    center and periphery in, 11, 17–32, 43, 60,
      70, 75–76, 95, 132n
    Cyrus's conquests, 5–6, 36–40
    Darius's conquests, 72–73
    fear and tribute in, 25–26, 27*t*, 76, 77*f*, 78,
      134n
    foreign historical sources on, 14–15
    founding of, 3
    global ambitions of, 69–70, 80–81
    Greeks and, 13, 14, 26, 28–32, 69–70, 76, 80–81
    ideology of, 70–72, 74–75, 76, 81, 89, 95
    limits of, 116n
    menaces to, 11–12, 12*t*, 32, 69, 79, 80*t*
    microcosmic representations of, 14, 72–81
    moral contradictions in, 95–96
    obedience to law in, 26, 31, 56, 74, 133n
    paradise gardens as models for, 1, 15, 78–80
    perception of "others" in, 26, 28–29, 95
    post-Darius historical events, 14–15
    rebellions against Darius, 8–9, 40, 69, 126n,
      130n, 132n
    religious tolerance in, 43–44
    subjugated lands and peoples listed at Susa,
      134n

    term *"būmi"* used for, 13
    terminology for evil, 93–94
Achaemenian kings and kingship. *See also*
    specific rulers
    as antithesis of the Lie, 11–12, 48–49, 139n
    charisma of, 22, 33, 42, 45–46
    creative actions of, 74
    enumeration of lands and peoples ruled,
      23–25
    as God's chosen rulers, 9, 11–12, 15, 17, 22,
      25, 33–49, 71, 89, 95
    legitimation of, xiv–xv, 2, 3–5, 9, 33, 43–44,
      46–48, 89–90
    myths about, 6, 34–35
    opportunistic theology of, 43–44
    perceived threats to, 1–2, 8, 85, 88–89
    ritual investiture of, 46, 47*t*
    royal banquet table, 14, 76
Achaemenian religion. *See also* cosmogony,
    Achaemenian; cosmology, Achaemen-
    ian; eschatology, Achaemenian; soteri-
    ology, Achaemenian; Zoroastrianism
    core principles of, xiii–xiv
    dualism concept in, 9, 11, 15, 17–18, 20, 41–
      42, 95
    imperialism and, 2, 13, 16, 45–46, 70, 75
    luxury and generosity in, 14, 76
    ritual practices and symbolism, 14–16, 31, 46
    spatial contrast in, 17–18, 20–22, 53–54
    studies on, xii–xiv
    torture and, 96
    Zoroastrianism compared with, 15–16, 115n

Made in the USA
San Bernardino, CA
13 January 2016